WHEN LEADERSHIP FAILS

OBSERVATIONS IN EDUCATION

Ray C. Rist, series editor

Matters of education remain an enduring debate in American society. Whether the debates focus on underlying philosophical assumptions, policy decisions, or the consequences of programs, education is one area where opinions abound and where there is little hesitance to express them. The books in this series, individually and collectively, assume the challenge of careful reflection about this most controversial of social issues. To observe American education—be it philosophical, empirical, or policy-oriented observation—is the contribution of this series. Each book probes a particular aspect of education, clarifies the questions, and works through the implications of the answers.

WHEN LEADERSHIP FAILS

Desegregation and Demoralization in the San Francisco Schools

DORIS R. FINE

Transaction Books
New Brunswick (U.S.A.) and Oxford (U.K.)

**To the Memory
of My Father**

Library of Congress Catalog Number: 86-4336
ISBN: 0-88738-079-4
Printed in the United States of America

Library of Congress Cataloging-in-Publication Data

Fine, Doris R.
    When leadership fails.

    Includes index.
    1. School integration—California—San Francisco.
2. Education and state—California—San Francisco.
3. School management and organization—California—San
Francisco. 4. Leadership. I. Title.
LC214.23.S23F56 1986   370.19'342   86-4336
ISBN 0-88738-079-4

Preface

It was June 1969, the last month of my first year as a teacher. My fourth graders and I at the John Muir School, a mostly black elementary school in the inner-city of San Francisco, were reviewing the events of the school year, and I remember that we were feeling rather satisfied with our accomplishments. But one morning, without any explanation, a few children arrived late, and seemed sad and somewhat sullen. The reason they were upset, I later learned, was that something had happened to Melissa (not her real name), a friend and former classmate, something they could not bring themselves to tell me. Melissa was an intelligent and precocious child, but lately she had taken to hanging around after school with older women on street corners. After talking with her mother, a social worker had arranged to have Melissa transferred to another school in a nearby middle-class neighborhood. This involved a short public bus ride every day, but Melissa was so street-wise, no one gave it a second thought. I had received encouraging reports about her from her new teacher, and so I was totally unprepared for the shocking news I read in the paper that day over lunch. Melissa was dead. She had been accidentally killed, run over by a bus as, unseen by the driver, she tried to board just as he was pulling away from the curb. Her friends knew but would not tell me, because I, a white teacher, had conspired in the plan that resulted in her untimely death.

The following school year I joined a teachers' task force to help plan for school desegregation. I wanted children like Melissa to be bused safely to integrated schools where they could have opportunities to develop into educated and capable citizens. I later volunteered to teach in one of the pilot desegregation programs I had helped plan.

There I saw the educational and social benefits of an interracial context, but I also realized how vital it was to have adequate resources and administrative support. When the elementary division was desegregated under court order in 1971, I saw little evidence of institutional commitment to the desegregation plan. On the contrary, not only was the community divided on the issue of busing, but it was obvious that school leaders did not understand what was at stake. For lack of leadership, the opportunity to help children like Melissa was being wasted; worse, the public schools were rapidly deteriorating, and desegregation was being perceived as an educational disaster.

Frustrated and disillusioned, hundreds of students and teachers began leaving the San Francisco schools. In 1975, I also resigned to continue graduate work at the University of California, Berkeley. There I found opportunities to undertake research for this study, first as assistant to David Kirp of the Graduate School of Public Policy, and later with Philippe Nonet at the Center for the Study of Law and Society. I am grateful to them and to the National Institute of Education for a grant which helped support the gathering of materials for portions of this study.

Minutes of school board meetings, newspaper articles, school district documents, and legal materials were primary sources of data. I also conducted over 100 interviews with school officials, teachers, and community leaders. As a former teacher, I was fortunate to have access to persons who talked freely to me, and from whom I learned a great deal about the inner workings of the school system. Later, in my capacity as staff director of a school-community agency, the San Francisco Center for Public Education, I attended meetings of the blue-ribbon commission appointed by the state superintendent of schools to conduct an inquiry into the San Francisco schools. Staff members and commission consultants were very helpful, and kindly shared their data and results with me. While I cannot acknowledge everyone who assisted me, I would like them to know how much I appreciated their insights and valued the time they gave me.

I should also like to mention several members of the school administration who were a source of inspiration to me and many others in the school community: Isadore Pivnick, a gifted principal and program director, communicated in word and deed his belief that every pupil—black, white, rich, or poor—was deserving of care, attention, and quality teaching; George Karonsky and Carlos Cornejo devoted years to building special programs, planning desegregation, and serving as principals in difficult and challenging schools; Betty de La Sada, until 1982 the district's public relations officer, helped countless pupils and parents cope with an otherwise difficult and confusing system. Without these individuals and others like them, teaching would have been even more crushing and disheartening. They lent tremendous talent and energy to the sustenance of the San Francisco schools during the demoralized and difficult times described in this account.

I should also like to acknowledge some of the people who helped me complete this study. I owe thanks to Guy Benveniste, Ray Rist, Guy Swanson, David Tyack, and Harold Wilensky for their advice and encouragement. My colleagues Joyce Bird, Carol Silverman, and Laurie Wermuth were constant companions and critics. To my husband, Philip Selznick, I owe a special debt for the line-by-line attention he gave to an early draft of the manuscript, and more generally, for the enrichment of his ideas on leadership and institutions. My work also greatly benefited from the many relaxing hours we enjoyed together away from our desks.

Doris R. Fine

Contents

1

Introduction: Social Policy and the Demoralization of Institutions

> The problem is not whether the schools should participate in the pro-
> duction of a future society (since they do so anyway), but whether
> they should do it blindly and irresponsibly, or with the maximum
> possible of courageous intelligence and responsibility.[1]

There is a widespread belief that desegregation in the public
schools has been a failed and costly policy. Standards suffer and
public support declines, it is said, when the schools are used as
agencies of social reform. But public education is an integral part
of society and government. It cannot escape the winds of change.
Therefore the question must be put another way: Are the schools'
difficulties due to the policy of desegregation or, instead, to
deficiencies of leadership and organization? This study suggests
that failure of leadership must bear a large burden of responsibility.

My conclusion is based on a study of desegregation in the San
Francisco public schools. The experience of the San Francisco
schools from 1960-80 affords the opportunity for an analysis of the
dynamics and outcomes of institutional change. What happens
when new policies are imposed without adequate attention to the
way schools are organized and to the everyday realities of teaching?
To find out what occurs when new policies are adopted and implemented, I take a close look at organizational capacities, such as
leadership, and their effects on reform. My main concern is *institutional integrity* and the *demoralization* that develops when integrity
is undermined. Part I traces the origins, and Part II the dynamics
of demoralization. Part III highlights outcomes—the consequences
of demoralization on the mission and competence of the schools.

---

[1] John Dewey, *Intelligence in the Modern World* (New York: Modern Library, 1939),
p. 692.

1

Among the questions addressed are these:

- How did San Francisco's public schools become a central arena for community conflict over issues of civil rights and equality?
- What options of response did school leaders have?
- What were some of the values at stake?
- What role did school leadership play?
- How did the dispute become a legal question?
- What happens when a political and educational controversy is resolved in federal court?
- Under what conditions do court orders help or hinder institutional reform?
- What adjustments in the leadership and internal dynamics of public schools are necessary for change to be effective?

The politics of desegregation is the subject of Chapter 2. The story begins with an analysis of school structure and organization, and an examination of the official school stance regarding social issues, such as civil rights and racial equality. Then the reform movement is characterized, and various events and turning points in the struggle to alter administrative priorities and practices are reviewed.

Interwoven with this political analysis is an assessment of the strengths and weaknesses of the San Francisco schools as an institution. In Chapter 3, I argue that demoralization had its origins in a definite structural weakness: the political incapacity of the school system. This vulnerability undermined the autonomy and leadership of the school administration, and gave rise to a *withdrawal of energies*, the earliest manifestation of demoralization. This finding leads me to conclude that institutional dynamics, not the policy of desegregation, is the key to explaining demoralization.

Reorganization of the schools under desegregation is the subject of Chapter 4. The implementation of the court-ordered plan is described, including its impact on pupils and teachers in the elementary schools and its ramifications for the secondary schools and the administration. In Chapter 5, competing community issues and conflicting administrative agendas are discussed, and their effects on desegregation are assessed. The role of leadership remains a major theme. I argue that during the administration of the desegregation plan, the school district suffered from fragmentation of purpose and organization, and that leadership, yielding to opportunism, allowed the schools to drift and educational programs to founder. Disorder and loss of institutional coherence characterize the second phase of demoralization.

In a social process as complex as demoralization, there are no clear-cut beginnings or endings. The withdrawal of energies continued under conditions of fragmentation, and divisions within the school community aggravated the loss of participation. In addition, there was a marked loss of confidence in the schools' mission. As the effects of disorganization began to take tangible form in declining achievement scores, teachers' strikes, truancy, and vandalism, the competence of school management was placed in question. A third process was at work—an erosion of legitimacy.

Chapters 6 and 7 follow the schools into court to assess the impact of judicial review on institutional reform. Given that courts can clarify and strengthen values, and that the legal system has the power to remedy flagrant abuses and deficiencies, one might suppose that some of the thorny problems besetting the schools could be resolved in court. However, I will argue that the federal district court lacked sufficient resources to rehabilitate the ailing schools. As we shall see, court-ordered desegregation accelerated the erosion of legitimacy.

In Part III, I look at some outcomes of the schools' demoralization. Chapter 8 analyzes the attempt by local citizens and school officials to restore order to the San Francisco schools. The recommendations of a blue-ribbon commission, I suggest, amounted to a "last hurrah" for public participation and local leadership. A disheartened school community and its mood of disenchantment and apathy are described in Chapter 9. Although public education in San Francisco has not collapsed, its quality and authority have undergone serious setbacks. As a consequence of demoralization, the schools currently suffer from poverty of vision and resources, and are mainly preoccupied with retrenchment.

At one level, as this overview suggests, this is a self-contained study of school desegregation in San Francisco. At another level, however, I have tried to provide an interpretation that relates the specific experiences of the San Francisco schools to general issues of organization and governance in public education. In the remainder of this chapter, I introduce the concepts that have been helpful to me in achieving a broader perspective: (1) institutional dynamics, such as autonomy and organizational responsiveness; (2) the responsibility of leadership for policy; and (3) democracy and the tension between institutional integrity and government by consent. An understanding of these themes, I believe, will add depth to my argument that failure of leadership, not desegregation, was responsible for demoralization of the schools. Readers primarily interested in the experience of the San Francisco schools may want to turn directly to Chapter 2.

Drawing some lessons from this story, a concluding chapter highlights the issue of local control, a key, I suggest, to understanding the failures of leadership. Local control in its present form effectively limits the capacity of school leadership to respond to difficult and sensitive policy issues. San Francisco's experience demonstrates some pitfalls of local control, in particular, its insufficiency as a safeguard for the protection of educational standards and institutional integrity.

Democracy and Integrity

Broadly conceived, this is a study of social policy and institutional dynamics. An important theme is the tension between democracy and integrity. While no institution is immune from the vicissitudes of changing circumstances or new expectations regarding its performance, democratic institutions face special dilemmas, because their integrity is peculiarly vulnerable. As embodiments of social values, all institutions are bound to undertake reforms when cultural transformations call for revision of conventional practices and acquisition of new competencies. Even a traditional institution, such as a church, must accommodate to new conditions. However, it can do so by modifying doctrine and justifying new rituals with arguments that preserve the sanctity of core values. Since its traditions provide its distinctive character, they are extended and enriched, not undermined, by such elaboration.

Institutions founded and maintained on nontraditional, democratic principles have more difficulty accommodating change while retaining integrity. The competence of democratic institutions is particularly threatened by change because the values at stake lack clarity and definition. Democratic aims are inherently subject to revision in the light of changing conditions and expectations. But when aims are in flux, goals diffuse and open-ended, institutions become vulnerable, and the soundness of their organization is more easily shaken. People outside, not bound by bonds of tradition, tend to lose confidence in the performance of a faltering institution; the people inside, the members, cease believing in the worth of what they do, work at their tasks half-heartedly, or abandon them. The mission of the institution loses its salience and fails to attract or engage creative energies.

Thus democratic institutions face a dilemma: They must be *both* open to criticism *and* self-regarding; ready and willing to adapt to changing needs and conditions, yet attached to a distinctive identity. Their legitimacy depends, on the one hand, on responsiveness to the polity whose purposes they serve and, on the other, on the preservation of internal commitments. Responsiveness requires the capacity to transform institutional conduct in accordance with the public will. Integrity, however, requires that adaptation take into account prior obligations and continuity of performance. The possession of sufficient structural capacity is essential; otherwise, pressures to restructure priorities risk compromising basic principles, undermining integrity. Institutional capacity to muster resources and embrace new commitments is variable, however, and rarely perfectly assured. Any one of a number of incapacities—incompetent staff, inadequate resources, weak leadership, poor management—may itself be the source of criticism and disaffection.

Public schools have special difficulty identifying their distinctive values and competence, and therefore their integrity is particularly vulnerable.[2] School practices and curriculum are an endless source of public debate and controversy. Moreover, whenever a social problem surfaces, there is a tendency to turn to the schools for a solution. From the socialization of immigrants, to the provision of day care and vocational training, schools have been expected to accommodate the changing needs of society.[3] Compared to what the polity asks and expects, however, it seldom provides sufficient resources and support.

School resources and capacities thus become strained, and prior commitments neglected. Having to satisfy society's ever-changing moods and demands, schools, in the defense of integrity, at times sidestep certain issues and give what amounts to lip-service to

[2] The dilemma of education in a democratic society is described by Hannah Arendt as follows: "The problem of education in the modern world lies in the fact that by its very nature it cannot forego either authority or tradition, and yet must proceed in a world that is neither structured by authority nor held together by tradition." Hannah Arendt, "The Crisis in Education," in *Between Past and Future* (Cleveland, Ohio: Meridian Books, 1963), p. 195.

[3] The current complaint is "mediocrity." Typically, the charges form the basis for policy recommendations that do not address questions of capacity and prior commitments. "A Nation at Risk," Report of the National Commission on Excellence in Education (Washington, D.C.: U.S. Government Printing Office, April, 1983.) For similar criticism of the report, see Paul Peterson, "Did the Education Commission Say Anything?" *The Brookings Review* (Winter 1983): 3-11.

others. A disposition to defensiveness, typical of institutions dependent on public approval but whose performance cannot bear close scrutiny, has thus become deeply ingrained. Defensiveness, however, is no guarantee of integrity. On the contrary, as we shall see, the demoralization of the public schools had its origins in the protection of vested interests, disguised as defense of integrity, at the expense of social responsiveness.

Another dilemma for democratic institutions is that their constituencies can exercise the privilege of rational choice and withdraw. In response to perceived failures, those who especially value the expected services may be among the first to withdraw, leaving behind others who care less or are constrained by circumstances to remain. Institutional suffering then increases, insofar as withdrawal of participation reduces financial resources, diminishes demand as well as productivity, and dampens public interest. Those who stay on out of loyalty to the institution are weakened by loss of support and, together with those forced to remain, are more likely to compromise prior commitments. Institutional integrity is thus further eroded.

The metaphors of voice and exit have been suggested to capture these dilemmas. Voice refers to the use of political channels for protest and criticism, and speaks to the issue of legitimacy; exit points to opportunities for withdrawal made available by a market economy. It has been argued that voice and exit are normal alternatives for restoring "proper functioning."[4] But what if neither is sufficient to improve performance or satisfy expectations? What if the institutional degeneration entailed by loss of integrity and public support is not only highly resistant to these counteragents, but irreversible?

When neither voice nor exit suffices to arrest the erosion of performance, the institution in question may be regarded as suffering from a kind of debilitating "disease." Symptoms of the malaise may go unnoticed at first; upon diagnosis, however, the institution's

---

[4] "Each society learns to live with a certain amount of dysfunctional or misbehavior; but lest the misbehavior feed on itself and lead to general decay, society must be able to marshal from within itself forces which will make as many of the faltering actors as possible revert to the behavior required for proper functioning." Albert Hirschman, *Exit, Voice & Loyalty: Responses to Decline in Firms, Organizations and States* (Cambridge, Mass.: Harvard University Press, 1970), p. 1. I think what I am dealing with satisfies Hirschman's notion of "mis-behavior that feeds on itself"; democratic institutions are more vulnerable to self-destructive responses, in effect, reacting with a "bad conscience" to criticism of their inadequacies.

impaired condition becomes obvious. The spirit of social participation will be noticeably weakened, and the vitality necessary to sustain and invigorate shared activities markedly diminished. The distinctive mission of the enterprise becomes enfeebled, and its values attenuated. Confusion and conflict accompany dissolution of purpose, resulting in loss of institutional coherence and the decline of competence. I use the term *demoralization* to denote both the process and the end-state that attends an erosion of institutional integrity, and this concept informs my analysis of desegregation in the San Francisco schools.

Institutional Autonomy and Responsiveness

A basic principle of the structure of many modern institutions, including the public schools, is autonomy. This principle, when well established, provides assurance that the interests of the institution will not be subject to the pressures and influence of external forces. The possession of autonomy guarantees independent authority and self-government. Autonomy protects the institution and enables it to fulfill its mission unhampered by the claims of special interests.

The autonomy of public education was the result of an historic "bargain" reached early in the century. Before then, like other agencies of government, schools had been organized on a decentralized ward basis and were closely tied to local politics. Contracts, appointments, and major budgetary decisions were made by political "bosses" responsive to local constituencies. Progressively, however, in conjunction with charges of corruption and the break-up of "machine politics," school governance shifted into the domain of nonpartisan, professional educators trained in scientific principles of management and administration. School boards, whether appointed or elected, relinquished major decision-making powers.

The political community, in effect, delegated to the school administration a limited authority that it could exercise free from political intrusion, on the condition that it remove itself from the struggle for political power and influence. Those were the terms of the schools' autonomy.[5] Autonomy—independent authority—was

---

[5] The separation of law and politics, and the rise of medicine as a sovereign profession depend on a similar "bargain." See Morton J. Horwitz, *The Transformation of American Law* (Cambridge, Mass.: Harvard University Press, 1977), pp. 255-66, and Paul Starr, *The Social Transformation of American Medicine* (N.Y.: Basic Books, 1982), pp. 78-144.

achieved when school professionals accepted restraints on the exercise of power. *This achievement depended on severing the ties between education and politics.* The judgments of educators, in accordance with this separation, were expected to rise above politics. Possession of a special educational competence was substituted as the source of their authority.

With regard to educational matters, the authority of school professionals thus became firmly established. Their distinctive sphere sheltered and protected educators from political struggles. Political influence was also considered suspect if exerted by members of the school board. Their responsibility became limited to hiring a competent chief executive, and keeping the schools insulated from local politics. All that was expected from the board was that it delegate authority to the school superintendent. As a corollary, the superintendent, in defending his authority, had to be sure that his justifications invoked educational, not political, considerations.

The emergence of professional standards of conduct, together with the development of a bureaucratic structure (a hierarchy of officials responsible to the chief executive), served to turn the schools away from earlier patterns of conflict politics. The principle of autonomy provided legitimacy, and the separation between the schools and local politics helped to establish professional autonomy as the foundation of policy and organization in public education.

This achievement was important to the development of a competent, smooth-running school system. However, there is an inherent danger in a too-rigid attachment to the principle of autonomy, namely, a loss of responsiveness to changing social needs. Accountability to rules and internal standards tends to foster self-protection at the expense of social responsibility. The maintenance of autonomy becomes an end in itself, and an obstacle to responsiveness. Challenges to the aims of the institution are perceived as political intrusions, i.e. as threats to autonomy. As such, they are fended off and resisted. But the autonomy of democratic institutions can be upheld and supported only when officials are able to meet and satisfy public challenges, and willing to alter priorities and practices, as necessary, to meet changing needs. If they cannot meet these tests, institutional integrity suffers. As we shall see, this was the experience of the San Francisco schools.

Desegregation Policy: A Challenge to Leadership

The civil rights movement of the sixties promised to put the schools more closely in touch with their civic purpose, to undo inequities, and to remedy injustices in the treatment of racial minorities. The struggle for civil rights is of interest, therefore, on two counts: (1) as an opportunity for the schools to reassert their civilizing mission and move closer to its realization; and (2) as a challenge to professional autonomy and leadership.

Civil Rights and Racial Justice

Under the Constitution, every person is entitled to equal treatment under the law. This is the legal basis for civil rights and equality of opportunity in the public schools. It is sometimes forgotten that schools were not always guided by this principle, and that at various times and places children were treated unequally, and even excluded altogether (e.g. the Chinese in San Francisco at the turn of the century). In the south, black children were only gradually and grudgingly admitted to *separate* public schools, and their education, like their citizenship, was generally inferior. After World War II, public consciousness of this injustice was markedly heightened and acts of racial discrimination, at least in public, were effectively suppressed (if not eliminated). This historic transformation, symbolized by the 1954 *Brown* decision, was the hard-won accomplishment of years of conflict, initially in the South.[6] But by 1960, the civil rights struggle had moved north as well, where racial discrimination was less obvious, but no less odious.

Under *Brown*, the desegregation of schools began simply enough with the requirement that state-imposed racial distinctions be eliminated. This meant dismantling the prevailing dual educational system in the South. It did not at first entail the assignment of pupils by race. The dispersion of black pupils among whites, however, soon became legally required practice because voluntary or "free choice" plans were revealed as blatant disguises for the perpetuation of racial separation. Southern intransigence was responsible for the elaboration of a legal doctrine in which desegregation quickly became synonymous with pupil assignment by race. By the late sixties, the establishment of desegregated school systems was

---

[6] *Brown* v *Board of Education*, 347 U.S. 483 (1954). For a history of this struggle, see Richard Kluger, *Simple Justice: The History of Black America's Struggle for Equality* (New York: Alfred A. Knopf, 1976).

expected to result in a random racial mixture, eliminating separate schools and guaranteeing "just schools."[7]

Meanwhile, predominantly black schools in northern city ghettos, typically overcrowded and staffed by less experienced teachers, also became suspect. The separation of the races in northern schools was not brought about by state policy (de jure); more commonly it was de facto, the unintentional result of racial prejudice and discrimination in housing. Northern school districts consequently did not recognize any special obligation to undo segregated schools. Instead, school administrators commonly defined the problem of black schools in terms of "racial imbalance."

Northern school systems, like San Francisco's, accepted an implicit definition of racial justice that held that so long as all children were offered a place in a unitary system, justice was satisfied. "Racial imbalance," provided it was not the product of deliberately maintained separate systems, was acceptable under this definition. Justice, blindfolded and unable to perceive distinctions of color or race, required only that access to the schools be free and open to all. Compared to outright exclusion or explicit racial separation, the standard of "color-blindness" constituted a principle of justice, but one that might be regarded as baseline, or entry-level justice. Equal access is only a starting point for equal treatment under law.

The presence of "racial imbalance" raised important new issues of equality that were not satisfied by the elementary principle of entry-level justice: What is the civic purpose of the public schools? How should schools be organized and pupils assigned to meet that purpose? Who should go to school with whom? If all that is expected from schools is the maintenance of prevailing social arrangements, with all their defects and inequities, then neighborhood schools are the obvious answer. There, social and family background and the wealth (or poverty) of the local district determine the quality and character of the schools. But if schools serve a public purpose, that is, if they are expected to mediate between family background and the community, then to achieve that purpose they must aim to prepare all children equally for effective membership. If there is any policy that serves the public interest in a democracy, it is education for citizenship; an educated citizenry is the foundation of democracy.

---

[7] "The School Board must . . . fashion steps which promise realistically to convert promptly to a system without a white school and a Negro school, but just schools." *Green* v *County School Board,* 392 U.S. 430 (1968).

The basic civil right is the personal right to equal respect. Schools are uncivil when this right is neglected, when children are stereotyped, classified arbitrarily, their behavior labeled, and their character and social habits maligned. All children, conceived as future citizens, have the same need to know, and are best served if they are all taught fundamental skills, as well as the lessons of a common culture. Teaching children to read is an egalitarian task; every citizen, regardless of family background, interest, or talent should be a reader. There is no privileged access to citizenship, no way of achieving it better or faster; all pupils need to achieve the same level of literacy. "The system of education in a state must . . . be one and the same for all, and the provision of this system must be a matter of public action."[8]

With the erosion of church and family, the privatization of neighborhood and community, and the separation between home and workplace, the school is the only institution available and capable of instilling the values and habits essential to a shared, public life. As Dewey argued, this is the distinctive competence of the public school.[9] As vehicles of public purpose, it becomes the schools' responsibility to formulate racially aware assignment policies. If the school is truly a *civic* institution, not bound to special interests, but responsive to the needs of the children and the larger community, it must have the authority to desegregate, that is, to assign children by race. Respect, courtesy, and moral sensitivity can be preached at home or in church, but they come to life in the school setting where children from various family, social, and religious backgrounds are grouped for shared instruction. Desegregation provides the opportunity for schools to ensure that certain common values, as well as common skills, are made available to all children equally, forming the basis for common citizenship and full participation in social and economic life.

More than the equal access afforded by entry-level justice is at stake. Equality has been enlarged to include the provision of equal respect. To treat children equally, i.e. with equal respect, involves acknowledging, not ignoring real differences of race and family background, but expecting that each child can and must learn the basic skills and disciplines required for full membership (political, social, and economic) in the community. The provision of equal respect requires establishing universal standards of competence, and

---

[8] Aristotle, *Politics* (London: Oxford University Press, 1948), Book VIII, pp. 332-33.
[9] John Dewey, *The Public and Its Problems* (Chicago: Swallow Press, 1927), p. 63.

then compensating for children's various entry-level abilities and talents so as to equalize their educational opportunities.

Desegregation—pupil assignment by race—is one means of carrying out the provision that all children be treated with equal respect. Desegregation does not eliminate racial discrimination, but by directing energies toward the realization of racial justice desegregation infuses the schools with moral purpose. This purpose is implicit in the expectation that public education will provide all children with a mastery of basic skills and disciplines both for their benefit and for the social good. A desegregation policy that requires children to attend school with classmates of different races and backgrounds, from different families and neighborhoods, similarly aims to benefit both the children and, by instilling a sense of common destiny, to strengthen social bonds and foster "public-spiritedness."[10]

The civil rights movement challenged school officials to reconsider their definition of justice. The policy of desegregation offered school leaders the opportunity to replace the principle of equal access with that of equal respect. Desegregation was an opportunity to decide how to assign pupils and revise educational arrangements, preserving the competence and integrity of the institution while responding to the public will. Desegregation, in short, was an opportunity for leadership.

It is a mistake to reify desegregation, to think of it as an active agent able to succeed or fail by itself. The policy of desegregation was not self-made, nor self-imposed; assignment plans and school reorganization schemes did not determine for themselves how they would be conceived and executed. School policy-makers made those decisions. The quality of school leadership, in particular its ability to resolve political and organizational problems and to align institutional conduct to new ends, was critical. An account of the success or failure of school desegregation, therefore, must look to the capacities and limitations of leadership.

The challenge for school leadership was twofold: (1) to develop a framework for understanding the issues at stake and their implications for institutional competence and integrity; and (2) to assess the resources and opportunities, both internal and external, for generating cooperation and support for new priorities and programs. Pupil assignment as a vehicle for achieving justice was new and

---

[10] This term is suggested by George Will. See his article, "Excellence in Education," *San Francisco Chronicle*, May 3, 1983.

untried; moreover, it was in potential conflict with old values of "color-blindness." Leadership would have to clarify and resolve this conflict of values while reaching beyond entry-level justice for a higher level of organizational commitment. To achieve this commitment, leadership would have to assess and strengthen the capacity of the schools to sustain educational standards. Leadership would have to design adaptations in organization and social structure, taking into account institutional identity and distinctive role. Leadership would have to assume responsibility for the development of doctrines and programs, and for the selection and training of individuals to carry them out. It would be up to leadership to realign forces; plan strategies, timing, and tactics; reconcile conflicts; and seek out opportunities for cooperation and the achievement of ends.[11]

These, needless to say, are ideal guidelines, dependent on place and circumstance for their realization. They serve a useful purpose, however, in assessing how leadership, as it was manifested in various settings—the school administration, the school board, the courts, and a blue-ribbon citizen commission—affected the fate of school desegregation in one community. In my concluding chapter, I will suggest that the challenge of desegregation was beyond the capacities of local leadership, that the issue of racial justice in the public schools warranted national commitment and national leadership. This outcome was precluded, however, by an unnecessary, yet pervasive attachment to the outmoded doctrine of "local control."

Disarray. One aspect of the challenge to leadership deserves special mention—disarray, the unruly companion of social change, an all-too-familiar and undesirable aspect of modern society. However, disarray can also be the prelude to an emergent and more just order. Without confusion, there might be less impetus for clarification and enlightenment. Despite its discomforts, therefore, disarray has potential benefits.

---

[11] The relationship between policy and administration, and the critical role of leadership are the themes of Philip Selznick's *Leadership in Administration* (New York: Harper & Row, 1957). In Selznick's words, "Leadership sets goals, but in doing so takes account of the conditions that have already determined what the organization can do and to some extent what it must do. Leadership creates and molds an organization embodying—in thought and feeling and habit—the value premises of policy. Leadership reconciles internal strivings and environmental pressures, paying close attention to the way adaptive behavior brings about changes in organizational character" (p.62).

During the sixties, disarray was the external manifestation of profound undercurrents of social and political unrest, expressing widespread dissatisfaction with prevailing patterns and relationships. Disarray was evident in dislocations of status and role, challenges to entrenched authority and redefinitions of personal identity. As part of a quest for personal freedom, disarray promised to bring new vitality to daily life, oust outmoded and stale practices, and, in the schools, liberate a repressed love of learning.

In the schools we shall study, however, precarious issues of *civil* rights tended to become entangled and confused with issues of *personal* rights. The provision of equal respect depends upon the creation of a school community whose members voluntarily accept self-restraint for the sake of a common good. In the absence of such a community, resistance to authority invites divisive and self-regarding assertions and claims. Moreover, under conditions of disarray, energies aimed at undoing the effects of racial discrimination and relieving educational inequities are more easily diverted to lesser causes and special interests. Schools can become *uncivil* when private needs and pressures overwhelm the quest for enlargement of civil purpose.

In San Francisco, a proliferation of claims to legitimacy and entitlement placed extraordinary demands on school leadership. Students, teachers, and parents seeking the power to affect curriculum, assignments, grades, principal selection, etc., distracted attention from the major effort required to overcome racial discrimination. Minority groups other than blacks sought their own ends, including equal treatment, but their claims clashed with the demands of desegregation. School officials and policy-makers, lacking guidelines for assessing the merits of various claims, could not distinguish legitimate rights from political preferences, and thus were unable to prevent the schools from opportunism and drift.

The resulting disarray invited a reaction that resulted in the restoration of order. Restraints imposed to restore calm gave short shrift to individual claims and demands, but also placed in jeopardy the precarious and still unrealized values of civil rights and racial justice. Acquiescence in the restoration of order, I shall argue, was the result of institutional exhaustion and demoralization.

PART I: ORIGINS

2

Politics and Educational Leadership

> To recognize a period of transformation when it comes, and to adapt
> themselves honestly and rationally to its laws, is perhaps the nearest
> approach to perfection of which men . . . are capable.[1]

"It will take a generation or more to repair the damage that's
been done to the schools," observed a leading liberal spokesman in
the mid-seventies, referring to the public schools of San Francisco.
"All my energies are consumed by efforts to bail out this sinking
ship," the president of the San Francisco school board told me
before relinquishing office in 1980. The frustration and despair
contained in these remarks were typical. The situation of the public schools appeared grim. What had happened to them, and why
was there such a drain of energies within the school community?
This and the following chapter explore the origins of demoralization in the San Francisco schools.

We begin by reviewing events of the sixties that led up to the
court-ordered desegregation of the elementary schools in 1971.
Since the first phase of demoralization within the school system
roughly coincides with the onset of school desegregation, it is logi-
cal to begin by examining the relationship between them. Did the
desegregation of the schools cause their demoralization? I shall
argue *not*. Rather, demoralization was the result of an institutional
weakness, namely, the inability of school leaders to adapt to
significant social change. Their rigidity and defensiveness
prevented an early accommodation with the forces of civil rights.
The school board, because of lack of experience and a weak sense
of its authority, proved unable to resolve the growing controversy.
Disarray in the schools and the community was followed by a gradual withdrawal of energies, the first phase of demoralization.

---

[1] Matthew Arnold, "Democracy," in *The Portable Matthew Arnold*, (N.Y.: Viking
Press, 1949), p. 468.

A key theme in the interplay between the politics of the civil rights movement and school leadership is the historic separation between education and politics. Our story begins with an analysis of this source of structural constraint.

Separating Education from Politics

For fifty years, from 1922 to 1972, the San Francisco board of Education consisted of seven citizens appointed by the Mayor.[2] By informal agreement, members of the board represented the three major religious faiths, as well as labor and business; in addition, since the late fifties, at least one member has been a woman, and one a person from the black community. The school board's composition, it was widely understood, thus reflected the business and social elite of this cosmopolitan city.

As trustees of the local community, board members took seriously their responsibility for ensuring a school system that was nonsectarian, apolitical, and free from social controversy. To maintain social order without disruption or political conflict was central to their mission. Committed to remaining "above politics," they ruled as a body and by consensus. The principle of equal access to the public schools more than satisfied their sense of civic obligation. As respectable property owners, they did not notice nor complain that the system, supported primarily by local taxes, was limited in its educational efforts. From their perspective, the public schools were satisfactory as long as they adequately served the interests of the upwardly mobile classes.

The term of office for board members was five years, but since their duties were not onerous, it was not uncommon for individuals to serve two or more terms. Independent of the city and county government of San Francisco, the school board set its own tax rate, and adopted a budget drawn up by its appointed executive, the school superintendent. Beyond these formal powers, the board had very little authority over the operation of the schools. Its most important duty was the selection of the superintendent; approval of the chief executive's actions was almost always automatic. But although its role was thus limited, the board nevertheless served a key function, namely the legitimation of administrative policies and

---

[2] Members of the board had been selected by appointment since 1898. Until 1922, however, the superintendent was an elected official with close ties to the city's "machine politics."

the protection of institutional autonomy.[3]

Legitimization might be, and commonly was, a mere formality; everyone understood that authority resided in the administration. But as boosters and public relations agents for the schools, board members helped to inhibit or divert public criticism. And as gate-keepers, they served to deflect those seeking entry to the schools for purposes extraneous to the aims of education as defined by the administration. However, the school board also had the power to open doors and offer legitimacy to new demands, if it so chose. Thus, the board could be the entry-point for the forces of social change.

The nonpartisan nature of San Francisco city politics did not require the organization or backing of a local party machine; its model was consensus politics. However, mayors of the late sixties, who happened to be Democrats, inherited a relatively conservative school board appointed by their Republican predecessors. Members included Reynold Colvin, a lawyer who later represented the school administrators' union in its suit against "deselection"; Mrs. Lawrence Draper, Jr., the wife of a prominent businessman; Edward Kemmitt, the representative of organized labor; Mrs. Ernest Lilienthal, since 1962 the chair of the board's Ad Hoc Committee on Civil Rights; Joseph A. Moore, Jr., a civic leader and member of the Board of Regents of the University of California; James Stratten, an active Republican and figure-head for the black community; and Adolfo de Urioste, member of an old San Francisco family.

The superintendent of schools in the early sixties was Dr. Harold Spears, a nationally recognized specialist on school curriculum, member of a UNESCO advisory committee, and president of the American Association of School Administrators. These exemplary credentials assured the board that Spears' professional management of the schools met the highest educational standards. Spears' competence was an important source of his authority and also a means for sustaining the separation between education and politics.

With board support, Spears "ran his own ship," as one member recalled. "The board relied completely on Spears for advice, and he had virtually total command over the operation of the schools,"

---

[3] San Francisco's school board was not unique in performing this role. Comparative studies of the period indicate that local school boards typically functioned to legitimize administrative decisions. See N.D. Kerr, "The School Board as an Agency of Legitimation," *Sociology of Education* 38 (1964): 33-59.

according to another observer. "He refused to let the schools become a political battlefield."

Defense against political intrusion was regarded as the *sine qua non* of professionalism. The removal of the schools from politics, an appropriate response to political corruption in the early part of the century, had become a standard, if stale, battlecry. Preoccupation with the elimination of political influences of any kind became a habit of thought and action so deeply ingrained that it tended toward mindlessness. Like the Spartans whose downfall resulted from a failure to adapt their military expertise to new social conditions, the school administration's rigid behavior interfered with its ability to recognize and address itself to new social forces. Nevertheless, commitment to maintaining a strict separation between education and politics could not safeguard the administration from the stresses and strains of the movement for civil rights that was in full force in the early sixties.

The vulnerability of the schools to this kind of external pressure, however, was hardly the perception of participants at the time. On the contrary, the schools then appeared as solid as a fortress, and also as impenetrable. This perspective was due to a constellation of features characteristic of the social organization of public schools in the early sixties. These included: (1) distance between the school board and the community, (2) the bureaucratic character of the administration, (3) the routinized quality of classroom life, (4) exclusion of controversial subject-matter from the school curriculum, and (5) limited participation on the part of parents.

Distance

The selection of school board members was removed from local politics and, as a consequence, a sense of distance developed between members of the board and the school community. The apolitical method of appointment resulted in a governing body that had no need to stay in touch with grass-roots public sentiment. What began as a strategy for protecting the schools from greed and self-interest became an obstacle to the responsiveness required for adaptation to new conditions.

Bureaucracy

The requirements of managing a large, complex system of schools and programs called for a specialized staff whose focus and interests were necessarily directed toward their immediate tasks. Teachers taught, and supervisors were devoted to upholding the standards of their disciplines. While this provided protection against potential lapses of duty, it also inhibited the capacity for innovation. The bureaucratic character of the system meant that a certain amount of conservatism and even inertia was built into its structure and operation. As a result, both in the classroom and at the administrative level, resources and talents required to revise goals and procedures in the light of new conditions were insufficiently developed.

Routines of Daily Life

The routines and schedules of classroom life persisted like clockwork, day after day, year after year. The socialization of teachers and students entailed adaptation to these routines. A standardized curriculum of basic educational and social skills reinforced the unchanging character of everyday life. Classroom routines were consistent with a bureaucratic mode of organization in which rules and regulations determined virtually every aspect of school activity. Routines were also a way of coping with a heterogeneous and lively pupil clientele. This aspect of the schools' structure was so pervasive that it tended to be taken for granted.

Exclusion of Controversy

Subjects likely to arouse a difference of opinion were either forbidden or transformed, disguising and mitigating any potential for stirring up conflict. Excluded were moral and religious topics, as well as any social or political ideas about which there might be arguments or criticism. The removal of controversy from the curriculum and the classroom served to isolate the schools from their social context, reinforcing the separation between education and politics.

Limited Parent Participation

Parents and the community in general were defined as outsiders. Their participation was limited by the school administration and staff to certain standard rituals, such as Parents' Nights. Both as a form of defense against unwarranted intrusion and as a means of promoting professional autonomy, the setting of limits to the interactions between the schools and the public effectively restricted the potential contribution ongoing parent participation might offer to the revision of educational goals and procedures.

Finally, to complete this portrait of the San Francisco schools, and also to introduce the controversy that served to challenge and eventually disrupt their apparently solid structure and smoothness of organization, we must mention another feature, the pupil population. Under statewide compulsory attendance laws, local schools were required to enroll all pupils regardless of sex, race, national origin, or social class. (A small private-school population, serving a largely religious-oriented clientele, coexisted alongside the public system, but had very little effect on its makeup or problems.) During the sixties, as a result of demographic shifts since World War II, San Francisco's schools began to enroll increasing numbers of black and other minority children. The assignment, discipline, and instruction of this new population comprised the schools' daily and increasingly challenging tasks, calling for adaptations that proved beyond the structural capacities of the schools.

Summary. In retrospect, these school arrangements look rather attractive. The community, by virtue of its acquiescence, appeared to acknowledge and even take pride in the schools' accomplishments. The board and the administration had no reason to doubt that their efforts were respected, even appreciated. There was apparent willingness to leave the policies and practices of the schools to the experts. The public seemed satisfied that what the professionals did, and how they did it was, after all, their business. Besides, everyone could take credit for upholding the appearance, if not the reality, of local control.

Nevertheless, for all its attractiveness and accomplishments, the school system did not have the skill or the capacity to cope with a major political challenge. This failing was the product of an administrative perspective that regarded all political issues as alike in that all were to be avoided, and deliberately *not* dealt with. The ability to distinguish between trivial or illegitimate items, on the one hand, and issues of major public significance, on the other, was totally undeveloped. In the rumblings of civil rights activists, therefore, school officials did not recognize the initial symptoms of a movement that would present serious and legitimate issues of social policy. Moreover, members of the school board, in their responses to early contacts with the movement, demonstrated naivety and lack of political experience.

One after the other, actions of the administration undertaken to defend its autonomy, and preserve the principle of separation from politics that once had bolstered the schools' authority, failed. The schools could not extricate themselves from the political controversy over civil rights. Moreover, their defensiveness served to antagonize the opposition, escalating the conflict. Because both vested interests and racial pride were at stake, the struggle became highly charged and emotional. Events reached a crisis in 1970 with the filing of an NAACP lawsuit whose outcome—court-ordered desegregation—transformed the schools and the community. The foundation, as well as the characteristic features of the school system, were fatefully altered by this upheaval.

Civil Rights: A Threat to School Autonomy

The process of change involving issues of civil rights began innocently enough with an administrative decision that was surprisingly repudiated by the school board. It was the fall of 1961, and the administration was arranging to move Lowell High—the city's academic high school—from its cramped, but centrally located, quarters to a new facility located on a large expanse of open space near the city's outskirts. The administration had decided that the new school should be designated a comprehensive high school, offering both academic and nonacademic courses, and drawing its population from the adjacent middle-class neighborhood. As a city-wide academic high school, the old Lowell was an anachronism in terms of prevailing educational theory and practice. Nevertheless, Lowell was a highly revered local institution. Its graduates, many of whom had gone on to the University of California, constituted a powerful alumni association, and the faculty also had a vested interest in perpetuating the school's special academic status.

Debate as to whether Lowell should be an academic versus a comprehensive high school was nothing new: the city's first professional school superintendent had tried unsuccessfully in the twenties to convert Lowell from its strictly academic outlook to a more modern orientation.[4] Tradition won, however, and the school survived. But now a new issue appeared—the racial makeup of the student body.

Racially defined schools and neighborhoods were recent phenomena in San Francisco. Until World War II, the proportion of nonwhites in the city and in the schools had been negligible. By

---

[4] Frank Dohrman, Jr., *Three Years on a Board* (San Francisco: privately published, 1924), a personal account of the experiences of a member of the board during the period of de-politicization of the schools.

1960, however, increases in both black and other ethnic minority groups were clearly evident.[5]

A slight decline in the city's population between 1950 and 1960, combined with real increases in the nonwhite population, almost doubled the percentage of nonwhites in the city from 10 percent to 18 percent. Moreover, certain residential areas within the city were acquiring distinctive racial identities.

In the case of Lowell, the old issue of academic status was thus joined with the problem of open enrollment. As a specialized school, Lowell was open to any student who met its academic standards, regardless of where the student resided. A neighborhood-based high school in the new location, however, would automatically exclude blacks and other minorities, since few resided within the proposed new district. Lowell alumni and faculty, in their arguments to preserve Lowell as an academic school, found themselves bolstered by representatives of various newly formed civil rights organizations who pressed the educational advantages for blacks of Lowell's open enrollment policy.

This policy was an exception to the district's general rule of pupil assignment by neighborhood. Despite the de facto segregation existing in many schools, the administration remained committed to neighborhood schools. Spears made a series of public statements to that effect in which he maintained, paradoxically, that the *neighborhood* school policy served as a safeguard against racial discrimination. "Integration is no problem here," Spears informed a reporter during the crisis over school integration in Little Rock, Arkansas. "Everyone living within a certain area, regardless of race, goes to the school in that area . . . . We have all races in our schools."[6] "We have not manipulated boundaries to segregate racial

---

[5] See the following table:

Population of San Francisco			
	1950	1960	1975
White	693,388	604,403	325,000
Nonwhite	81,469	135,913	315,000
Total	**774,857**	**740,316**	**640,000**

Sources: 1960 figures—San Francisco Chamber of Commerce; 1950 figures—Leonard Austin, *Around the World in San Francisco, A Guidebook to the Racial and Ethnic Minorities of the San Francisco-Oakland District,* (San Francisco: Abbey Press, 1955); 1975 figures—S.F. Public Health Department, "Weekly Bulletin," February, 1976. The city and county of San Francisco are coterminous.

[6] *San Francisco Call-Bulletin*, September 4, 1957.

groups in our schools,"Spears repeatedly insisted. "We treat everyone fairly."[7]

While Spears' views still carried the greatest weight, differences of opinion on this matter were beginning to emerge. The issue of open enrollment, not only on the basis of merit, as in the case of Lowell, but for purposes of relieving segregation, was being discussed locally among a growing group of civil rights advocates. Those opposed to the establishment of the new Lowell as a comprehensive neighborhood school began to wonder about the administration's real intentions, and to question the sincerity of Spears' views regarding race.

The unexpected effectiveness of public debate on this issue, culminating in the school board's rejection of the superintendent's recommendation, stimulated the development of a protest movement. Its aim was to challenge the district's racial policies. Civil rights advocates felt encouraged enough to concert their energies for an assault on these policies, and they succeeded in forcing the district to defend itself against a barrage of public criticism.

At first, the challenge was directed primarily at the superintendent, the spokesman and leader of the school district. Civil rights leaders understood that authority over school policy resided with him. In an attempt to discredit Spears' racial views, they reminded members of the school board of their responsibilities as representatives of the community to pay attention to public criticism. An appeal was made to their racial consciousness.

Members of the board in the sixties belonged to the generation of Americans who grew up during World War II. In their lifetime, civil rights and individual liberties had become important values, values for which they and their peers had fought and sacrificed. That government should treat people with equal respect and not discriminate against persons on the basis of race was a natural lesson and a strongly felt conclusion following America's encounter with Nazi Germany. The reform of government so as to advance the cause of civil rights was an ideal with compelling appeal. When prodded by civil rights advocates, members of the San Francisco school board, despite their conservative orientation, began to ask themselves: What was the schools' obligation toward its new clientele, migrants from the South constrained by backgrounds of poverty and neglect, and their children, innocent victims of prior practices of slavery and racial discrimination?

---

[7] *San Francisco Examiner*, March 16, 1961.

This was a novel question for school policymakers. Heretofore the plight of poor and minority group children had been regarded as society's responsibility, not the schools. But with civil rights advocates pressing the issue of equality of educational opportunity, the question became more urgent. Since Horace Mann, the public schools had been idealized as society's "great equalizer," offering the opportunity of upward mobility to the poor and downtrodden, extending to everyone, regardless of social origin, the benefits of a free education. That not everyone could take advantage of this opportunity was never considered a problem for the schools. Public schools were not expected to make special provisions for the welfare of the poor, not to provide additional resources for the educationally disadvantaged. Now, however, individual board members were unable to ignore criticisms that pointed to inequalities of conditions discriminating against black and poor pupils. On the contrary, such complaints provided the occasion for several board members to activate inner strivings for engagement with the significant ideals of their generation, and, by the late sixties, these members became a majority.

The gradual transformation of the consciousness of the school board began in the fall of 1961. At that time, the board listened sympathetically to minority spokesmen who asked that the existence of de facto segregation of black pupils be acknowledged and declared undesirable, and that actions be taken to eliminate policies and practices contributing to such segregated conditions.[8] The board not only listened, it responded by requesting Superintendent Spears to respond to the charges of racial discrimination.

Spears remained the district's official leader. That the board should refer controversial matters to him was a practice he expected and encouraged. A few years earlier, for example, there had been considerable public agitation, post-Sputnik, over the adequacy of the school curriculum. Spears defused the controversy by appointing a commission of university professors to review the matter and make recommendations. But by the time their study was concluded, as might be expected, public interest had waned, and the schools continued their usual curriculum practices.[9] This

[8] San Francisco Board of Education transcript, December 5, 1961, pp. 23-24.

[9] At the federal level, however, the National Defense Education Act of 1958, a billion dollar investment, subsequently helped support improvements of math and science teaching at the local level and provided loans to college students for training in those fields.

time, however, Spears took it upon himself personally to respond to the board's request for a full report, a reflection both of the sense of urgency communicated by the charges and of the greater threat posed by this issue to the autonomy of the school administration.

The superintendent responded with a 25-page report, to which was attached a 1960 census map with statistics on the percentages of nonwhite city residents under age 25.[10] (Note that this was not a census of the schools' racial distribution.) In formulating the report, Spears, accompanied by board president Claire Lilienthal, visited eight major city school districts across the country, and under the auspices of the U.S. Office of Education, conferred with representatives of the 15 largest city school districts. In addition to this national survey, Spears looked at all 135 San Francisco public schools, and attended over a dozen meetings in the community to gather data and opinions. Thus informed, he reported to the board:

> Providing the non-white child a proper education is a highly complicated educational matter . . . . It begins with the desire to do right by every pupil who enters the school, and it taxes the strength and ingenuity of every teacher and school administrator who battles such odds as disproportionate housing, indifferent parents, limited job opportunities for youth, and unresponsive pupils.[11]

New practices and programs were being developed to address these problems, Spears continued, noting some current innovations such as SCIP (School Community Improvement Plan, a Ford Foundation program), a precursor of the federally funded programs for disadvantaged pupils that began in the mid-sixties. Spears indicated that such programs, under staff guidance and direction, constituted the appropriate response to the problem of educating nonwhite pupils in San Francisco. He made it very clear that his administration would not accommodate any demands for altering the policy of neighborhood schools, nor would he permit the actual racial distribution of pupils in the schools to be made public.

> We are now faced with the movement to emphasize differences in the color and races of pupils. In some school systems, such records are now prepared annually. One asks for what purpose do we so label a child and in turn, post a sign on his school indicating the racial

---

10 Dr. Harold Spears, "The Proper Recognition of a Pupil's Racial Background," San Francisco Unified School District (hereafter referred to as SFUSD), June 19, 1962.
11 Ibid., p. 17.

make-up of the student body at the moment? If we are preparing to ship these children to various schools, in predetermined racial allotments, then such brands would serve the purpose they have been put to in handling livestock. But until somebody comes up with *an educationally sound plan* for such integration, then this racial accounting serves nothing but the dangers of putting it to ill use.[12]

Spears concluded his report with a statement of his views on the purpose of the public schools. He distinguished between education as enlightenment and education as a vehicle of social change, pointing out that

the school is actually an instrument of social change, but as such an instrument, the children are not to be used as the tools. Instead, through their education, and consequently their enlightenment, society is better assured of their adult adjustment as self-paying members of the economy, and as active participants in the civil and cultural affairs of the community.[13]

Observing that over the years more and more demands have been placed upon the schools "to correct the inadequacies of outside community conditions," Spears questioned whether this direction reflected the fundamental purpose of the public schools, which, according to the Educational Code, is "instruction in specific subjects, such as reading, writing, spelling, arithmetic, English, geography, history, civics and so on." In conclusion, Spears stated:

Returning to the specific case at hand, I have *no educationally sound* program to suggest to the board to eliminate the schools in which the children are predominantly of one race.[14]

Spears presented his report at a well-attended public meeting. He apparently expected his thoroughly researched conclusions to settle the matter, resolving any doubts board members may have had regarding the unfairness of the district's racial policies, because his delivery coincided with what should have been a routine administrative recommendation regarding the conversion of the old Lowell High School building to a needed junior high. The new junior high, to be called Central, was designed to serve youngsters from several inner city elementary schools and was expected to have a student body that would be about half white and half black.

---

12 Ibid., pp. 23-24, emphasis supplied.
13 Ibid.
14 Ibid., p. 25, emphasis supplied.

Because this issue was on the agenda, the audience that evening included parents and representatives of local chapters of the NAACP and CORE who had come to oppose the proposal. The new school, they pointed out, was likely to reach a "tipping point" very rapidly; opening it was tantamount to creating a segregated school. Their belligerence aroused, the protestors, hearing Spears' report on racial conditions and school policy and listening to him state publicly that he had "no educationally sound" program to offer, responded with a deep determination to challenge and discredit the report and the district's racial policy. Spears' public statement was, in effect, the flinging of a gauntlet.

The campaign began with an immediate and rapid mobilization of forces to resist the proposal for Central Junior High.[15] Public appeals were issued through the media. Support was sought from teachers' groups, the San Francisco Labor Council, and the mayor. The NAACP hastily filed a lawsuit charging that opening Central Junior High would constitute a deliberate act of racial discrimination, in violation of the constitutional rights of the black pupils affected.

An opposition group also sprang into action, the Citizen's Committee for Neighborhood Schools. Its aim was to deter the administration from reaching a compromise that would involve assigning additional white pupils to the new facility (so as to avoid the immediate establishment of a majority-black school). As both sides gathered their forces, the summer of 1962 offered no respite for the superintendent and his administration.

Over 1,200 people attended a meeting that fall at which a decision was to be announced. To everyone's surprise, Spears retreated. He informed the school board that he could no longer recommend opening Central Junior High. To subdue the rising community pressure and avoid further political controversy, Spears elected to abandon his proposal. The administration's capitulation was regarded as a stunning success by the groups that had opposed the plan. If it was intended as a cooling-off maneuver, Spears' concession thus backfired; rather than assuaging the civil rights movement, it served to encourage even more organized efforts to challenge and change the district's racial policy.

At that time, civil rights was primarily conceived in terms of the rights of blacks to be free from racially discriminatory practices

---

[15] For a description of the Central Junior High controversy, see Robert Crain, *The Politics of School Desegregation* (Chicago: Aldine Press, 1968), pp. 83-87.

inhibiting their full citizenship. The media, in following the vicissitudes of the civil rights movement, helped to make highly visible the historic plight of blacks and the nation's current efforts to eliminate racial barriers. In the South, despite local resistance, the desegregation of schools and other public facilities was well underway. However, not having to dismantle dual school systems, no major city outside the South had as yet undertaken the task of school desegregation. De facto segregation was the common and accepted practice among northern schools in black neighborhoods and, particularly in urban schools, commonly existed in conjunction with overcrowded classroom conditions and inexperienced teachers.

The education committee of the San Francisco NAACP, a small, racially mixed group of civil rights activists, concluded that desegregation—the assignment and distribution of pupils by race—as it was being implemented in the South, was also the best way to improve opportunities for black pupils in San Francisco. The committee based this conclusion on a study of pupil enrollment statistics, staff salaries, and the age and condition of school buildings used for elementary black pupils. Its findings included inequities in the distribution of resources, along with the concentration of black teachers and overcrowding in predominantly black schools. Although there was no evidence that desegregation would eliminate racial discrimination, there was no reason *not* to suppose that desegregation would, at least, achieve a fairer distribution of resources. From the NAACP committee's perspective, therefore, the administration's resistance to desegregation seemed unfounded and biased. Spears' insistence that he had "no educationally sound" plan to offer that would remedy segregation appeared to be based on racial prejudice. Whether or not Spears believed that black pupils were unlikely to benefit from improved opportunities, and/or that white pupils might suffer educational harm as a consequence of racial mixing, his statement could be interpreted as implying that black pupils were inferior.

The NAACP committee was small in numbers, but it had in hand a powerful moral weapon, the justice of equal opportunity for black children. Advocates of desegregation were not concerned with details of educational organization, nor were they intimidated by the administration's expertise. They had witnessed the administration's authority weaken and succumb under pressure. Sidestepping confrontation with civil rights leaders would not help the administration avoid further conflict. Neither the protagonists nor the issues were about to go away.

Conflict and Change

The school board, having delegated its authority to the administration, was politically ineffectual. The practice of consensus politics and the absence of party organization in San Francisco also weakened the board. It was not able to cope with controversial issues. The school boards most capable of accommodating civil rights issues during this period, according to Robert Crain, were the elite, appointed boards that had the backing of a local party machine and were therefore not afraid to take the risk of stirring up resistance.[16] San Francisco's board displayed no initiative, preferred to defer to the administration, and was accustomed to standing behind its chief executive's policies. It was not the school board, but the superintendent, who capitulated on the issue of Central Junior High.

Following this incident, board members persisted in upholding the powers and privileges of the administration. To minimize controversy and conflict, they accepted the superintendent's report without question, maintaining the board's traditional role as guardian of the orderly operation of the schools. Nevertheless, a willingness to listen and an inclination to sympathize with the cause of civil rights helped to reduce the distance between the schools and public opinion, and the forum provided by the board's public meetings had become an important political arena.

At first, the voices of protest assumed a moderate tone. Moderates and NAACP activists, including those responsible for the Lowell High School protest, formed an alliance with the understanding that legitimacy for the aims of the movement could best be obtained through a broad-based coalition.[17] Leaders, such as local black lawyer Terry Francois, articulated their concern for eliminating racial imbalance, but they also indicated that the black community would accept less than full racial integration.[18] To establish a basis for compromise, other considerations were mentioned, including black-studies courses to instill "racial pride and motivation in the black child,"[19] an increase in the number of black teachers,[20] and more involvement of black parents at the

---

[16] Ibid., pp. 81-94.
[17] Statements by the NAACP and the Council of Civic Unity, included in official transcripts of the school board meeting, September 5, 1962.
[18] Transcript of the school board meeting, September 18, 1962.
[19] Afro-American Association statement to the school board, transcript of the school board meeting, ibid.
[20] Phi Beta Sigma Fraternity, transcript of the school board meeting, ibid.

school sites.[21]

The critics of school racial policy attempted to establish a citizen's committee to advise the school board on matters of civil rights. The board balked at this suggestion, however, and instead reconstituted its own Ad Hoc Committee to conduct a series of public meetings. Angered by this rebuff, CORE staged a sit-in and threatened to take direct action, and the NAACP filed a lawsuit.[22] These gestures were intended to induce the board to act, and they succeeded. In 1963 the board issued a report that recommended that "wherever practicable and reasonable and consistent with the neighborhood school plan, *the factor of race* be included in the criteria used in establishing new attendance zones, and in redrawing existing boundaries."[23]

Despite an insistence that overt segregation had never been school policy, the Ad Hoc Committee's endorsement of the "factor of race" satisfied the protagonists. With acknowledgment of the racial "factor," the barrier of "color-blindness" had begun to break down. However, the committee's recommendations also proved convenient for the administration in that they bought time to consolidate tactics of resistance. Bureaucratic procedures proved quite useful for this purpose. For example, the administration created a new staff position to take on the responsibility for implementing the revised racial policy. A national search was conducted to find the best candidate to head this Human Relations Office (later called the Community Relations Office). The appointment a year later of a long-time district employee, Dr. William Cobb, revealed the delaying tactics. Cobb was the first black appointed to the central school administration. (Despite his advanced degree, he had served for years as an elementary school principal.) An increasingly impatient community dismissed him as an "Uncle Tom."

Despite the new policy that called for taking the factor of race into account, other considerations beyond Cobb's control always outweighed those of racial balance. Enmeshed in bureaucratic

---

[21] Percy Moore, representing the Hunters Point-Bayview Citizens Committee, statement in the transcript of the school board meeting, ibid.

[22] *Brock* v *The Board of Education* (N.D. Calif. October 2, 1962). The suit charged racial discrimination and demanded desegregation. Before the submission of evidence, however, the suit was dropped. Defending the school district was attorney and former school board member Joseph Alioto, subsequently mayor of San Francisco.

[23] SFUSD, "Report of the Ad Hoc Committee," April 2, 1963, pp. 7-8, emphasis supplied.

routines, the new policy had no practical effect. Moreover, Cobb's tacit support for the superintendent's refusal to release a racial census of the pupil population led the district's critics to charge him with "bad faith." "All we get from San Francisco after repeated correspondence, visits and conferences are policy statements, not facts," members of the black community complained.[24]

Indeed, the recommendations of the Ad Hoc Committee served to sustain the district's recalcitrant educational doctrine. The factor of race, although made visible, was never given real weight. A concern for relieving the effects of racial segregation was not reflected in any change of policy. On the contrary, desegregation— assignment of pupils by race—continued to be opposed by the administration.

The district's resistance stimulated stronger actions by the opposition. A consortium of civil rights groups, including the NAACP, the Bay Area Urban League, and the Council for Civil Unity, asked the California Fair Employment Practices Committee (FEPC) to investigate hiring practices in the San Francisco schools. Other pressure tactics were applied. NAACP lawyer Terry Francois, now a member of the San Francisco Board of Supervisors, introduced a resolution to require election of school board members, revoking the 40-year-old provision of mayoral appointment. Twenty-one civic groups combined to form a unified pressure group, the Coordinating Council for Integrated Schools. They attacked the educational and administrative considerations cited by the district as tactics of obfuscation, defensive measures undertaken to disguise a basic unwillingness to cooperate. The Committee on Direct Action was organized, and 100 people, bearing banners, marched for two days outside the offices of the school administration.[25]

This mobilization of concerted energies finally forced a response, albeit weak and belated, from the district. On the advice of the superintendent, the board offered to hold public hearings on the issue of "racial imbalance," and arranged to have the hearings conducted under the auspices of the city's newly formed Human Rights Commission.[26] The board's objective was to defuse the controversy,

---

24 Dr. Price Cobbs, a black psychologist not related to the Director of Human Relations, quoted in the *San Francisco Examiner*, April 8, 1965.

25 *San Francisco Chronicle*, August 3, 1965.

26 The Human Rights Commission was established in 1964 by Democratic mayor John Shelley, and consisted of 15 appointed members whose charge was "to equalize economic, political and educational opportunities." Section 12 A of the Administrative Code of the City and County of San Francisco.

and to ascertain the basis, if any, of a public consensus.

The responsibility for reshaping this policy was thrust on the school board in no uncertain terms by Spears' surprise announcement in August 1965 that he intended to retire at the close of the 1966-67 school year. Spears had publicly staked his professional integrity on the issue of a racial count, and it had become both a strategic and a symbolic target for the opposition. The pressures of the previous years, however, had succeeded in breaking down his resolve *not* to release figures describing the schools' racial composition. Forced to capitulate, Spears chose to step down as the district's leader. Despite loss of his authority, he nevertheless reiterated his position regarding the irrelevance of racial statistics and continued to defend the district's neighborhood school policy on educational grounds.

> The number of whites in a school has no bearing on the quality of education . . . . It behooves all parties now to reveal their sincere interest in protecting the learning situation.[27]

With Spears' departure, however, activists were determined to seize the opportunity and pressure the board to enact a new racial policy immediately, to the effect that "ghetto schools are educationally indefensible."[28] If this position was adopted, the board would have to undertake the desegregation of the schools.

But the school board gave no indication that it would endorse such a policy. Instead, an alternative consensus was sought by means of the Human Rights Commission's public forums. However, this attempt to display a broad spectrum of opinion, and thereby neutralize the more extreme points of view, did not succeed. Both the NAACP and CORE boycotted the meetings, maintaining that new policy directions should have been clearly stated prior to public discussion.

At the forums, a variety of views and some serious proposals for limited experiments with integration, such as extended neighborhood schools and paired schools (so-called Princeton plans), were presented. However, the administration argued against all such community-sponsored proposals. None of the suggestions, according to the superintendent, would have a significant effect on the district's racially isolated schools. Moreover, when board member

---

[27] Dr. Harold Spears, quoted in the *San Francisco Examiner*, August 5, 1965.

[28] Lois Barnes, chair of the NAACP Education Committee, quoted in the *San Francisco Examiner*, August 17, 1965.

Reynold Colvin suggested relocating all pupils from such schools, in effect closing the "ghetto" schools, he was reminded by Human Relations Officer Cobb that the black community in Hunters Point had just voted heavily in support of a local bond issue that included funds for building two new schools in that neighborhood. In addition, the superintendent pointed out, severe overcrowding would result if black children were moved to schools in adjacent areas, and the mixture of black pupils with the Hispanic children in the nearby schools would exacerbate educational problems. The attempt to negotiate administrative objections and to achieve consensus through public hearings thus foundered.[29]

By this time (1965), the schools of San Francisco were not alone in experiencing the shock waves of political conflict and social change. Controversy over school integration had become a major political issue across the nation. Both in the South and the North, school officials were engaged in political struggle, effectively ending the longstanding separation between education and politics. Despite strenuous institutional efforts to confine and delimit the issue, the winds of change could not be contained. Social and demographic shifts—the influx of nonwhite and ethnically diverse pupils into northern city schools—had produced educational problems that were bound to become political issues. Moreover, the direction of change was liberating, *not* repressive. In 1964 Congress passed the Civil Rights Act, and the Elementary and Secondary Education Act (ESEA) followed in 1965. Title I of ESEA included funding for educational programs meeting the special needs of poor and minority children. These actions signalled the beginning of a period in which policies reflecting public complacency and administrative neglect of the disadvantaged were no longer acceptable.

In San Francisco, Spears' retirement marked the end of an era in which the public schools had enjoyed the privileges of professional autonomy. Although the Board of Supervisors rejected Francois' proposed charter amendment to create an elected school board,[30]

---

[29] San Francisco Human Rights Commission, transcript of the Joint Conference on Racial and Ethnic Distribution of Pupils in the San Francisco Schools, Vol. I, August 23, 1965; Vol. II, August 26, 1965. (The author attended both meetings as the representative of the local chapter of the League of Women Voters.)

[30] *San Francisco Examiner*, August 7, 1965. Mayor Shelley had opposed the Board of Supervisor's proposal as "retrogressive." Future school board member Lee Dolson had argued that election was no guarantee of political persuasion, and he had reminded the supervisors that early in the century an elected school board had excluded Chinese children from the public schools.

and thus for the time being remained wedded to the continued separation between education and politics, the wall of professional sovereignty constructed to guarantee this separation was crumbling. Members of the school board were now directly exposed to the political crossfires that were searing the nation. Without the protection and authority of the district's longstanding leader, Harold Spears, the board and the school district became increasingly vulnerable to the militant forces of social change accompanying the advance of civil rights.

3

The Politics of Desegregation

The best way to keep your bad deeds from the knowledge of others
is not to commit them in the first place.[1]

The release of a racial census in 1965 revealed the predicament
of the San Francisco schools. First of all, it made clear that the
problem of racial imbalance was not severe in the secondary
schools: black students attended all eight district high schools, in
proportions ranging from four percent to 34 percent of the total
high school population; and of the fifteen junior highs, only two
had black student bodies in excess of 50 percent. Rather, racial
segregation and isolation were problems mainly in the small
neighborhood-based elementary schools. Although black pupils
composed only 28 percent of the total enrollment, they made up
more than 50 percent of the student body in 24 of the 95 elementary schools, and there were 17 schools with white student bodies of
90 percent or more. Thus 43 percent of the elementary schools
were racially imbalanced with respect to black and white pupils.
There were also 14 schools with Asian (primarily Chinese) populations exceeding 30 percent, and several schools with concentrations
of Hispanic and other nonwhite pupils.

In one assessment, the situation was quite hopeful: 76 percent of
the black elementary school pupils were in racially mixed schools,
compared to only 14 percent in St. Louis, for example.[2] To
integrate the remaining 24 percent however, would require imaginative redistricting and some busing of elementary pupils for purposes
of racial balance, an action that remained repugnant to the school
administration. The proceedings of the Human Rights

---

[1] Chinese proverb, citation in Ming-shih (Taipei, 1963), quoted by Ray Huang,
1587, A Year of No Significance (New Haven: Yale University Press, 1981), p. 60.
[2] Robert Crain, *The Politics of School Desegregation* (Chicago: Aldine Press, 1968),
p. 88.

Commission-sponsored conferences revealed that the administration was unwilling, and the community unable to come up with an acceptable comprehensive plan or even a promising approach toward a general solution. A core of NAACP activists believed districtwide busing was the only way to assure equal treatment for black pupils, but other groups, such as the Black Panthers in ghetto areas of Hunters Point and the Western Addition, were moving toward community control as a more effective strategy. (On this basis, the black community, including the NAACP, had lent its support to a recent school bond issue that included funds for the construction of new schools in all-black neighborhoods.)

It was inevitable that a school board disposed toward consensus and cooperation, and unused to exercising leadership over school policy, would find this issue too thorny to disentangle and resolve. Moreover, the rejection of the charter amendment on the method of selection of the school board served as a vote of confidence for the present members to continue cautiously, maintaining their pursuit of an acceptable compromise.

Crisis and Opportunity

Accustomed to leaning on the administration, the board requested the outgoing superintendent to develop a set of feasible plans for eliminating racial imbalance in the elementary schools. Nothing came of this request, however. The administration's resistance to assuming responsibility for altering its neighborhood school policy was bolstered by a favorable report from the California FEPC, released with the concurrence of the Human Rights Commission. Their racial census of school district staff showed an imbalanced distribution, but no evidence of discrimination. Among the tenured certificated staff (teachers and administrators), five percent were black; among classified staff (clerical and custodial personnel), 22 percent were black. (At that time the city's black population was 11.8 percent.) But progress in the hiring of black teachers was demonstrated by the fact that six percent of the probationary teachers (those likely to become tenured) were black.[3]

Some months later, in April 1966, frustrated by the administration's sluggish response, the board signed a contract with Stanford Research Institute (SRI) for a preliminary study to investigate the "feasibility" of school desegregation in San Francisco. The

---

[3] *San Francisco Chronicle*, August 7, 1965.

school board undertook the SRI study in part to satisfy its critics that something was being done, and in part because it was now preoccupied with a more immediate and pressing responsibility: the selection of a new superintendent. Always a key board function, under the circumstances, this task was a particularly critical one. At stake was the district's safe passage through the political crisis threatening its autonomy.

Along with the standard professional criteria developed for selecting Spears' successor, the board stipulated a more unusual qualification: "the ability to communicate before taking action."[4] Presumably, board members were reacting to Spears' close-to-the-chest style of leadership. But their conception of the requisites of leadership revealed lack of understanding and political naivety. That Spears did not "communicate before taking action," was because he had the authority to do so. Moreover, he recognized the threat to institutional autonomy posed by the schools' involvement in social and political issues, and perceived the potential danger of single-minded activist groups. He termed the schools "sitting ducks" for those with quick solutions to complex problems.[5] Had the board better understood these matters, it might have conducted its search for new leadership accordingly.

Spears' departure offered the opportunity to seek out a leader with political imagination and courage, someone with whom the board could work constructively to mobilize the energies of the school community. The ability to exercise leadership, in particular the ability to tackle political and organizational hurdles and to align institutional conduct to new ends, was now critical. Because the board failed to develop an appropriate concept of leadership, members set about selecting a chief executive distinguished from his predecessor by a somewhat "looser" style of communication, but in all other respects an adherent of conventional patterns of school administration. Fear and abhorrence of political entanglement were so deeply rooted, and the apparatus separating education from politics so embedded in professional standards of conduct, that the opportunity to adapt to the extraordinary circumstances of the mid-sixties was lost, not without consequences.

In the transition between administrations, autonomy was not the only value at stake. Institutional authority also was jeopardized. The trust and loyalty vested in the outgoing superintendent by his

---

4 *San Francisco Chronicle*, May 22, 1966.
5 Quoted in the *San Francisco Examiner*, August 17, 1965.

staff were suspended upon his departure. With the appointment of his successor, Dr. Robert Jenkins, an outsider, there followed a jockeying for position among various inside contenders. The new superintendent's "open" even "permissive" attitude encouraged administrators' ambitions and loosened the constraints of conventional career patterns. In addition, central control over staff at the school sites, including teachers, began to weaken. The schools' formerly solid structure was showing signs of cracking.

First, the growing conflict between the school district and critics of its racial policy was dissolving the distance between the institution and the community, and actually drawing them closer together. Members of the school board experienced new obligations for policy and were engaged in taking the measure of public sentiment. While leadership was still beyond their role expectations, they could envisage more collaboration with their chief executive. School critics also had gained confidence in their capacity to change the direction and focus of institutional policy.

Secondly, the school administration, in order to defend itself against outside pressures, was being forced to rouse itself from complacency and develop responses, other than capitulation. Pressures to consult with community representatives, and to include parents and teachers in decision-making mounted, shaking up established routines. These changes, on the one hand, promised to erode the self-protective distance that had prevented the schools from seeking the benefits of closer contact with the community. On the other hand, there was great risk that certain fundamentals of organization, such as attention to the schools' distinctive mission and the creation of incentives for organizational cooperation, would go unattended. Lack of leadership in developing responsiveness and shaping participation engendered serious institutional costs, including the weakening of morale.

But institutional considerations were not pressing issues at the time. On the contrary, they were regarded as hindrances to change. What was striking about public education in the late sixties was the extraordinary outpouring of enthusiasm and energy in pursuit of social ideals, at the expense, if necessary, of institutional integrity. Until then, schools were rather routine places to work. For students, excitement was associated with Halloween parties, high school dances, and football rallies. But when public attention began focusing on education, illuminating the otherwise ordinary process of teaching and learning and highlighting the social and political meaning of schooling, those involved in schools discovered new worth in their work and in their studies. The everyday reality of schools lost its dull, taken-for-granted quality. What was happening in classrooms suddenly mattered, and the social significance of their daily tasks made a difference to those connected with schools.

For one thing, more idealistic people were attracted to serve on the school board. Normally, such service was performed as an act of civic duty narrowly conceived, not for personal satisfaction nor for the realization of any foremost social purpose. A different set of motivations, however, was evident in the three highly charged, politically minded people chosen by the mayor in the fall of 1966. The mayor was still following the usual pattern, choosing representatives from the three religious faiths, at least one woman, and a representative of the black community, but the new nominees did not just accept, they aggressively sought their appointments to the board.[6] Each brought a sense of mission and dedication to the ideals of racial justice and equal opportunity. From their perspective, the schools as a public agency had a definite obligation to help poor and minority children, an obligation that deserved precedence over established educational priorities and practices, such as neighborhood schools.

Secondly, the public schools began to attract better educated, more committed staff, teachers who welcomed the opportunity to work with parents and children from the black community and who believed all children should achieve mastery of basic skills. School staff also expected their daily work to be interesting and personally rewarding.[7] Among the administrative staff, individuals were being recognized on the basis of their effectiveness in stimulating more imaginative, less rotelike approaches to learning: curriculum specialists were trying new techniques and developing new curriculum materials that aroused enthusiasm; supervisors were redesigning programs to meet the provisions of new federal laws and regulations affecting the education of Title I eligible children; special assistants, some drawn directly out of classrooms, were promulgating the human relations side of good teaching, as well as the need

---

[6] Replacing Mrs. Draper, Mr. Moore, and Mr. Stratten were University of California Professor Laurel Glass, M.D., Dr. Zuretti Goosby, an articulate young black professional, and Alan Nichols, a lawyer and leader of the Council for Civic Unity.

[7] The author joined the elementary division in the fall of 1968, along with 200 other new teachers, including young men seeking an alternative to the Vietnam War draft. Many teachers considered themselves to be members of a domestic War on Poverty or Peace Corps.

for adequate materials and support. Being an active member of the school system had become an exciting association, full of challenge and opportunity.

In some ways the most remarkable development was the extension of the experience of participation to those usually excluded from school affairs altogether: the parents. The professional management model of schooling had not wanted or needed parental involvement. There were rituals of parent participation, of course (open house, graduation ceremonies, the summoning of parents when a child drastically misbehaved), but from kindergarten on, every child knew that there was no real regard for parental authority in the schools, that only what "teacher says" counted. PTA mothers in middle-class schools assisted with field trips and helped support the school library, but the PTA had no distinctive role in the direction of school affairs. (The PTA was not even among the civic groups the mayor ordinarily consulted when nominating new school board members.) Now, however, PTAs were beginning to take a fresh interest in their schools and in school policy. In addition, several hundred volunteers, in conjunction with the introduction of federal support for early childhood education, were mobilized to assist in initiating Head Start programs in a selected group of schools.[8]

Motivated fathers as well as mothers were drawn into school activities. Groups of parents began forming at various school sites, some building on existing PTA councils, others creating new school or neighborhood associations. They were not interested in conventional kinds of parent participation (providing the cookies for school parties), but rather in exerting influence over school affairs, including curriculum and pupil assignment. They met in homes as well as on school sites to consider how to make the schools more responsive. One neighborhood group, Ocean View, Merced Heights, Ingleside (OMI), received a three-year federal grant from the Department of Health, Education and Welfare, (HEW) to develop ways to arrest housing deterioration and white flight. The energies of this racially mixed group were largely focused on school

---

[8] These became the nucleus of an organization called the Education Auxiliary, made up of volunteers who gave their time and talents to make school days more than the routine "reading, 'riting, and 'rithmetic" of the recent past. The author was personally involved in establishing this organization. Many schools since the late sixties were enriched by the range and assortment of activities introduced by these "outsiders," such as science experiments, photography, mural painting, and excursions to the country.

improvement.[9] A similar project was established in the Hunters Point area, an all-black community, following a rash of riots in 1966. With Title III money, an educational improvement program, the South East Educational Development (SEED) was initiated in eight elementary schools.[10]

Spokesmen for these and other grass-roots school-community associations regularly attended school board meetings, making their presence and needs visible. During the course of the SRI feasibility study, parents all over the city followed its progress and reviewed its recommendations for school desegregation. The media assigned special reporters to cover school developments, contributing to public knowledge about school affairs and furthering the sense of the schools' importance. At the time it seemed as though the San Francisco school community was going to embrace the early American practice of direct democracy and make its decisions at town meetings like those that impressed De Toqueville. The outpouring of interest, energy, and enthusiasm was an unprecedented happening, and one which school officials could neither fathom nor control.

Disarray and Withdrawal of Energies

Who would have suspected the apparently solid structure of the schools to be so porous after all, and so precarious? The administration's mode of command was derived from a theory of bureaucratic authority that stressed internal control mechanisms and prescribed procedures. Officials were not accustomed to public challenges, community intrusions, or school crises. The administration had no management techniques to handle the kind of crises that were beginning to occur. For example, in 1967, parents and community activists in a black neighborhood organized a boycott to force the removal of the principal and several teachers suspected of racism. This created a situation outside normal routines, and therefore without precedent. The community appealed directly to

---

[9] "Our struggle and efforts were for desegregated schools, early childhood programs, after-school programs operated by the community, multiethnic teaching staff, innovative curriculum, more parent participation and involvement, hot lunches, improvement of school property . . . " *OMI News*, Vol. 6, #9, pp. 4-5.

[10] Arthur Hippler, "The Game of Black and White at Hunters Point," in Howard Becker, ed., *Culture and Civility in San Francisco* (Chicago: Aldine Press, 1971). Also testimony of Reverend Charles Lee, Director of SEED, in U.S. Congress, *Hearings of the Senate Select Committee on Equal Educational Opportunity*, Part 99, 1971, pp. 4277-4282.

school board members, bypassing the administration, and they agreed, as an exception to the general rule prohibiting the board from interfering with administration policy, to try and arrange a settlement. In this case, the board's venture worked: new staff, satisfactory to the community, were assigned to the school.[11]

The school climate had changed. There was a fresh infusion of energy and an upsurge of interest in the public schools. It was a phenomenon for which the conventional administration was not equipped. In this respect, Jenkins, the new superintendent, was no more capable than his predecessor. Although the superintendent was different, his response and that of the administration was "more of the same." Those who hoped for boldness and new directions were disappointed by Jenkins' first major move, which was to conduct another series of public forums, ostensibly to receive public reactions to the completed SRI Report, but in effect to delay mobilizing the school district and guiding it in new directions.[12] The SRI Report, which emphasized both the educational importance and the feasibility of desegregation, afforded an opportunity for decisive action, but Jenkins failed to seize it.

The Jenkins years, 1967 to 1970, were extremely critical ones. As the structure of the schools began eroding, the system's distinctive features became blurred and unrecognizable. Like another historic turning point, "it was the best of times; it was the worst of times." There was turmoil and confusion, but also excitement and hope for reforms that would substantially improve educational opportunities for minority group children. Out of the disorder, many believed, the school system would emerge more just.

This hope was matched in its intensity by fears that such change would be both harmful and costly. At the public forums convened by the Jenkins' administration, the impatience of prodesegregationists for the first time was met by an equally extreme and vocal opposition. Parents opposed to school busing were not sure whether the new administration, like the old, reflected their

---

[11] The boycott occurred at John Muir School, and was organized by the Hayes Valley School Committee, a black community organization. *San Francisco Examiner*, March 9, 1967. The author's first teaching assignment resulted from the staffing changes that were put into effect as a consequence of the parents' boycott and the board's intervention.

[12] The original contract with SRI contemplated a systematic community review to be conducted by the consultants. This provision was altered, following Spears' retirement, to allow the new superintendent to undertake his own review. Stanford Research Institute, "Improving Racial Balance in the San Francisco Schools," 1967.

resistance, and they began to organize and speak up. One of the antibusing leaders, Teamster Union president Jim O'Rourke, insisted that parents had a constitutional right to enroll their children in schools of their choice and to resist school assignment by race.[13] The city's new mayor, Joseph Alioto, allied himself with this emerging resistance, and soon proved to be a highly articulate spokesman for the status quo of neighborhood schools. He repeatedly threatened to use whatever powers he had to prevent busing in San Francisco.

Confronted by polarized positions on either side, an embattled school board and administration pursued a zigzag course of action. On the one hand, to appease the prodesegregation critics who urged that immediate steps be taken to reduce racial imbalance, the board adopted a policy statement favoring limited redistricting and busing of pupils provided it could be accomplished in a manner both "reasonably feasible and acceptable."[14] A 32-member Citizens Advisory Committee (CAC) was appointed, and a task force of teachers and administrators formed to develop a specific plan, utilizing findings of the SRI Report.[15] However, when it was leaked to the press that the CAC was preparing to propose that a cluster of racially balanced schools be formed in one neighborhood, the Richmond District, on an experimental basis starting in 1968, and that busing would be used there, the school board, to appease the immediate outcry of the opposition, withheld its support from the proposal and postponed consideration for at least another year.

At the end of that year, the CAC, to avoid wasting time, recommended that two neighborhood school clusters be implemented at the same time, starting in 1969, one in the Richmond and the other in the Park South District. These experiments, the CAC claimed, would provide tangible evidence of the district's willingness to move toward meaningful desegregation.[16] But when the board met to consider this recommendation, instead of the customary heated debate, there occurred an unusual outbreak of violence. The disrupters, members of the local Teamsters' Union, had to be forcibly removed from the scene. Police guards were subsequently routinely assigned to prevent any recurrences. Even so, the board was

---

[13] *San Francisco Chronicle*, June 11, 1968.

[14] *San Francisco Chronicle*, June 5, 1968.

[15] The SRI Report had made no recommendations, but rather presented a range of policy options for various degrees of racial integration of the schools.

[16] The CAC's proposal was included in the report entitled *Educational Equality/Quality (EEQ)*, Report #2, February 1969.

threatened with major public disruptions should it approve any form, however limited, of school busing.[17] Thus warned, the board delayed taking action and proposed instead that still another year be devoted to detailed planning and preparation for the two school complexes.[18] The board also insisted that Jenkins obtain additional funding to insure that quality of education in the proposed school complexes not suffer. "The plan must mean better education for all the children involved," according to board member Reynold Colvin, a promise made to assuage the fears of those considering flight from the schools.[19]

The CAC meanwhile sought to involve everyone in the two neighborhoods, including those hostile to the complex concept, in developing the specific plans needed for implementation of the experimental desegregation program. Literally hundreds of people gathered weekly to debate and decide issues of pupil assignment, staffing, transportation, curriculum, communications, etc.—the kinds of administrative details normally reserved for the professionals. This was done partly to bypass the caution and hesitation of the administration, and partly to try to meet specific objections of those opposed to the busing plan. The meetings also generated their own momentum: ordinary people, fascinated with this opportunity to redesign school routines, enjoyed the vicarious experience of participating in changes that would make their children's lives richer and more interesting, or so they thought. Meanwhile, Mayor Alioto continued to insist that no form of busing, however limited, was acceptable and to maintain that "the majority of parents don't favor this plan, nor do the majority of teachers and principals."[20] Behind the scenes attempts by school officials to soften his adamant position failed.

In a dramatic public confrontation, Alioto appeared before the school board to urge the members not to proceed any further with their plans.[21] Angered by this use of political clout, NAACP president Charles Belle threatened retaliation in the form of a

---

[17] *San Francisco Chronicle*, March 19, 1969.

[18] The proposal ironically was titled "Time for Action," *EEQ Report #3*, May, 1969.

[19] Minutes of the School Board, March 30, 1970. A poll of parents in one of the schools to be included revealed that most parents were already planning to place their children in nonpublic schools if they were not satisfied with the quality of the proposed integration program. "Letter to Dr. Jenkins from the Madison School PTA," March 6, 1968.

[20] *San Francisco Chronicle*, February 4, 1970.

[21] Minutes of the School Board, February 20, 1970.

lawsuit to force the board to proceed not only with the two complexes, but with districtwide desegregation as well.[22] This escalation of the conflict proved fatal. Suddenly the plans and hopes for realistic reforms were placed in jeopardy, and neither the school board nor Superintendent Jenkins could control the situation. "Bringing politics and the judiciary into educational decision-making will damage the schools irreparably," predicted Alan Nichols, then president of the board,[23] but by now it was to late to escape these consequences of failed leadership.

Outside funds for the "quality" components of the school complexes did not materialize as Jenkins had promised, causing consternation among teachers and parents who had counted on these resources to support the innovative educational programs needed to attract and retain the white middle-class population, while upgrading opportunities for minority children.[24] Without the funds to support these educational components, the school board faced a Solomonic dilemma: Should it reduce the scope of the plan and focus available resources on one school complex, or implement both, but without extra funding? The first alternative was selected. After anguishing sessions with parents' advisory councils in both neighborhoods, the board decided to proceed with full implementation of the Richmond District Complex only.[25]

Mayor Alioto immediately reacted by urging parents opposed to the plan to bring suit enjoining the district from proceeding with "forced busing."[26] He also promised to introduce and fight for a charter amendment eliminating the existing method of school board appointment and, in effect, terminating the existing board. In turn, members of the board vented their anger and frustration by demanding Jenkins' resignation, charging him with failure to reach an effective compromise. Finally, the NAACP, disenchanted with the board's vacillations and apparent impotence, filed their threatened lawsuit in federal district court demanding not only the implementation of both school complexes, but also the desegregation of all the elementary schools of San Francisco.[27] "I had hoped we might avoid this," NAACP president Charles Belle told Jenkins, "but the mayor has turned desegregation into a political and

22 *San Francisco Chronicle*, February 4, 1970.
23 *San Francisco Chronicle*, February 6, 1970.
24 Minutes of the School Board, March 30, 1970.
25 Minutes of the School Board, May 27, 1970.
26 *San Francisco Chronicle*, June 4, 1970.
27 *Johnson* v *SFUSD*, N.D. Calif. (June 24, 1970).

emotional battleground . . . . We'll get an instant solution in federal court."[28]

By mid-1970, as a consequence of these dramatic and rapid-fire events, the school district was in turmoil. A new superintendent had to be hired immediately by a board that itself might be replaced under the pending charter change. There was the NAACP lawsuit to defend, as well as the one urged by the mayor to stop the implementation of the Richmond District Complex. Communication between Jenkins, the board, and the staff had broken down, disrupting lines of authority. No one knew who was in charge or what would happen next. Administrators and teachers held their own meetings and strengthened their organizations in preparation for the uncertain times ahead. Parents and students in the two neighborhood complexes, as well as others in the community previously untouched by the controversy over school desegregation, were suddenly aware that what was happening was likely to have an immediate and direct impact on their lives, drastically altering established patterns and expectations.

With the announcement of the NAACP lawsuit, board president Nichols submitted his resignation. Acknowledging his defeat, painfully aware that the board and the administration had failed to resolve the controversy, Nichols also expressed serious misgivings about the involvement of the court, which he had been unable to prevent. "Relying on the court is not the best method to achieve what should be the common goal—fair and equal educational opportunity."[29]

The withdrawal of leadership, symbolized by Nichols' resignation, marked the collapse of the board's inept, albeit sincere, efforts to respond to the issues of race and education. This responsibility, thrust upon the board in the wake of Spears' departure, was beyond its political competence and experience. Board members were no match for Mayor Alioto, whose vocal opposition had escalated the community conflict and made accommodation impossible. They lacked the political experience (for so long eschewed as a source of corruption) needed to guide social change and, as a result, had to confront personal failure; individuals on the board were among the first members of the school community to experience heartbreak and disappointment as the consequences of their failure unfolded.

---

[28] As reported by Jenkins in a personal interview.

[29] Nichols, quoted in the *San Francisco Chronicle*, June 25, 1970.

Desegregation by Default

The selection of a new superintendent now seemed the best hope for the troubled schools. The teacher organizations urged the board to select Milton Reiterman, director of the personnel division, a capable young administrator with leadership potential. Together with two other senior staff persons, he had emerged as the de facto leader following Jenkins' forced resignation. A committee of the board, however, despite lack of time for a proper search, once again chose an outsider, Dr. Thomas Shaheen, impressive for his forthrightness and a man who exuded an air of conviction. Attracted by Shaheen's vitality and his earthiness, the board did not perceive the enormous difficulties an inexperienced outsider, no matter how winning his personality, would have in mobilizing districtwide and community support at this time.

Pressures on the board and the superintendent were already considerable, but during the next two years, 1970 to 1972, they became overwhelming. One issue, however, was finally resolved: with Shaheen's appointment, the board's wavering stance toward desegregation came to a standstill; a clear commitment to pupil assignment by race was now the majority position. The federal district court in 1970 heard board members Laurel Glass and Zuretti Goosby testify that racial discrimination existed in school practices, and a liberal board majority implicitly charged the new superintendent to proceed as rapidly as possible with the elimination of racial imbalance.

Shaheen, convinced that desegregated schools were inherently good schools, immediately set about trying to convey this belief to the school staff and the community. At the same time he attempted a major administrative shakeup to increase the percentage of minority administrative personnel. This move was intended to expedite the implementation of desegregation, and also to create a new staff dependent on and therefore presumably loyal to Shaheen. (Had the board chosen Reiterman, no such action would have been necessary; Reiterman already had a strong following among the younger administrators.) While the federal district court deliberated over the merits of the NAACP lawsuit, and the community controversy over busing continued to rage, the new superintendent was putting his full energies into a major effort to create a multiethnic administrative staff, thereby also ingratiating himself with community activists.

Divisions both within the administration and teaching staff over the implementation of desegregation made it extremely difficult for the superintendent to maneuver, however. Teachers wanted direction and assurance that their work was appreciated and would be supported. The average teacher's basic concern for maintaining classroom order, teacher representatives argued, was an important starting point for in-service training to address anxieties about how to handle multiethnic elementary classrooms. The superintendent's approach, however, was to confront such concerns through encounter group explorations of attitudes and perceptions, rather than in terms of educational methods and practical techniques. Teachers believed that to dissolve racial discrimination and improve the educational opportunities of minority children required more than sensitivity training. Thus an antagonistic relationship quickly emerged between Shaheen and the teacher groups.[30]

Even more serious was the commotion created within the ranks of the administrative staff by Shaheen's plan, announced in the spring of 1971, to demote 125 tenured administrators, all of them white, retaining for his central office staff equal numbers of personnel from various racial backgrounds.[31] Criteria for the so-called "deselection" included an unusual qualification, namely, sensitivity to the racial and ethnic needs of students, as well as the usual ones of experience and competence. Some 121 of the demoted administrators demanded a hearing under the due process provision of the California Educational Code, and the School Administrators Association filed a charge of racial and ethnic discrimination against the school district with HEW. Attorney for the board, Irving Breyer, one of the three top-ranking administrators considered de facto leaders of the district after Jenkin's resignation, refused to support Shaheen's action, and instructed the board to seek outside counsel to represent it.

Administrative opposition succeeded not only in thwarting Shaheen's plan, but also in undermining his authority as the district's chief executive officer. The hearings failed to substantiate the racial and ethnic categories chosen by the superintendent for

---

[30] Shaheen hired a special consultant-psychologist, Dr. Marshall Rosenberg, to facilitate staff meetings, retreats, and community encounter sessions. Mike Miller, "The Tenure of Tom Shaheen" (San Francisco Federation of Teachers, unpublished pamphlet, January 15, 1972).

[31] *San Francisco Chronicle*, March 9, 1971. This incident is described in Earl Raab, "Quotas by Any Other Name," *Commentary* 44 (January 1972): 41-45.

special dispensation. Moreover, inaccuracies in the ethnic data, such that 26 persons were improperly classified, caused confusion and embarrassment. The state hearing officer postponed action until fall, but by that time, frustrated by the delay, dismayed by the expense of the hearings, and fearful of a negative ruling, the board voted to suspend the plan.[32] Besides stirring up staff and community suspicions regarding Shaheen's motivations, his professional competence, and his leadership, "deselection" as an attempt to promote equal opportunity for minorities thus served to create dissension between Shaheen and the board.

Compounding these difficulties was the administration's cavalier response to the federal court's deliberations in *Johnson*, the desegregation case. Hearings on the NAACP lawsuit, filed in June 1970, were rapidly concluded, and Federal District Judge Stanley Weigel stated that he would announce his decision sometime during the 1970-71 school year. In the meantime, he strongly suggested that the district begin immediate preparations for elementary school desegregation.[33]

Shaheen, preoccupied with other matters, such as the administrative deselection, at first ignored this suggestion. Finally, in response to pressure from community activists, he proposed that responsibility for planning districtwide desegregation be handed over to a new Citizens Advisory Committee (CAC) which the board would appoint, and which would work closely with staff on the details of the plan. Shaheen chose a relative newcomer to the administration, Don Johnson, to be staff director (bypassing Isadore Pivnick, the director of the earlier CAC, the group that had helped plan the two neighborhood school complexes). Considerable time was then spent in selecting members of the new committee, but since only persons partial to desegregation were willing to serve, the membership was hardly representative of the spectrum of community opinion. The committee had barely been formed, let alone settled down to work, when, on April 21, 1971, Judge Weigel announced that he was preparing a ruling that would require desegregating all the elementary schools by September.

Despite the judge's advance warning, the court order, issued on April 28, "stunned school officials."[34] The newly constituted CAC was aghast. A hastily assembled and inexperienced staff had not

32 *San Francisco Chronicle*, May 27, 1971.
33 *San Francisco Chronicle*, September 22, 1970.
34 *San Francisco Chronicle*, April 28, 1971.

even begun to gather the necessary pupil data, and it would take months, the CAC insisted, for preliminary statistical models to be available for study and consideration;[35] moreover, there were no guidelines for the development of a districtwide desegregation plan. Members of the committee, familiar with the SRI report's recommendations, immediately set to work drafting guidelines, and because of the time pressures, the CAC, without public discussion, and prior to the collection and analysis of demographic data, quickly adopted them as the framework for the desegregation plan.

The guidelines included the State Commission on Equal Opportunity's recent formulation of racial balance, namely, that racial balance is achieved when the distribution of pupils at any individual school does not deviate more than 15 percent from the district's overall racial distribution. Although the court's ruling presumably would apply only to black pupils, not only black, but also Asian, Hispanic, and other ethnic minority pupils were thus included by definition in the concept of racially balanced schools. In addition, the guidelines stipulated (1) the use of compact attendance zones, similar to the extended neighborhood concept developed in the two school complexes; (2) assignment of pupils such that the distribution of the burden of busing would fall equally on everyone (every child would be bused for several years to one elementary school, but also, either before or after this term of busing, assigned to a second school within walking distance); and (3) non-English-speaking pupils could be excused from racially balanced classrooms and placed in special classes for the purpose of achieving basic competence in English.[36]

Meanwhile, when opponents of desegregation realized that the fate of the elementary schools was in the hands, not of the board or superintendent, but rather of the ordinary (and prodesegregation) citizens appointed to the CAC, they protested angrily and tried to disrupt the committee's proceedings. The most dramatic display was staged by a group of 300 Chinatown parents, irate over the prospect of enforced participation in a citywide distribution of pupils that would violate their ethnic community.[37]

Nevertheless, on June 3, 1971, under the pressure of the court order, the school board adopted a plan for the desegregation of the elementary schools, hastily drawn up by the CAC, and by no

---

[35] *San Francisco Chronicle*, April 26, 1971.
[36] SFUSD, "Progress Report of the CAC," May 6, 1971.
[37] *San Francisco Chronicle*, May 26, 1971.

means, even within that committee, regarded as the most desirable plan.[38] The board and the superintendent accepted the citizen committee's recommendation without even examining the merits of the alternative plans included in the CAC's report. Preoccupied and distracted, the board and the administration neglected their most urgent responsibility: namely, the development of a politically feasible desegregation plan integrating the court order with educational policy so as to preserve the integrity of the school system. The administration, concerned with other agendas, and the board, overwhelmed by the emotional turmoil that enveloped the district, thus abandoned their responsibility for safeguarding the integrity and distinctive competence of the schools. The policy of desegregation and the demoralization that followed its implementation were not fortuitous and could have been prevented. They were the unfortunate consequences of leadership that failed to take responsibility for relating changes in school practices and organization to the achievement of educational ends.

Although short-lived, the CAC became so politicized that *not* becoming involved with it seemed the best way for school officials to avoid controversy over (as well as responsibility for) the plan. The board's stance could be characterized as "defensive avoidance."[39] But practically, the court had to be satisfied, and time was running out. Thus any opposition was easily dismissed.

The district's hasty and irresponsible preparation of the plan ordered by the court was symptomatic of the disarray into which school affairs were dissolving. In the spring of 1971, just before Judge Weigel announced his decision, the teachers called a strike.[40] In part they were reacting to Shaheen's lack of support for staff concerns. That fall, at the start of his term of office, the new superintendent had made the rounds, visiting every school site. He had talked to staff, and heard their complaints about lack of supplies and the absence of direction and guidance for the tasks of teaching, which were becoming difficult to manage during this unsettled period. Extensive surveys documenting the nature and scope of the problems were completed, but nothing was being done. In addition, the strike occurred as an act of solidarity with teachers

---

[38] For details on the plans and the history of the CAC, see Stephen Weiner, "Educational Decision-Making in an Organized Anarchy" (Ph.D. Diss., Stanford University, 1972).

[39] Irving Janis and Leon Mann, *Decision-Making* (N.Y.: Free Press, 1977), p. 112.

[40] Of the district's 4,655 teachers, 1,455 went out on strike; also two-thirds of the students stayed home.

nationally who were emerging as an organized force of workers demanding collective bargaining rights. Local leaders, such as James Ballard of the American Federation of Teachers (AFT), were speaking out against paternalism and giving voice to the pent-up frustrations of working under a closed bureaucratic system. And finally, the strike was, in part, a reminder that without support for classroom teaching, the commotion and clamor over improving educational opportunities was just so much empty talk.

Despite the strike, elementary teachers were not included in the desegregation planning that was going to affect their assignments as well as the children's. The CAC developed a proposal for desegregating the teaching staff, and so did the administration. Neither consulted the Negotiating Council, a body established under state statute to settle disputes between teachers and the administration. Under the plan the school district adopted, and following the CAC's suggestions, teachers were reassigned on the basis of seniority and race. There was no consideration given to the social networks within schools that provide important support for instructional tasks, and sustenance for morale. Instead, like soldiers, teachers were given their assignments and told to report to work.

Planning for desegregation was not concerned with how teachers would meet new classroom challenges, deal with confusions over assignments and busing schedules, and cope with anxious or hostile parents. That teaching is the kind of work that requires a certain ésprit de corps was a consideration that in the press of events was forgotten or overlooked. Those teachers most sympathetic to the purpose of the court order—improving racial justice in the schools—were among the most frustrated for they understood that what was happening was not the carrying out of justice, but rather the brutal effects of expediency.

Poor administration, disaffected teachers, classroom disorder, and public dismay—these are classic indicators of schools in trouble. All these conditions materialized during Shaheen's term of office (1970-72). Would a different superintendent improve matters? Almost everyone in San Francisco thought so. Shaheen had become the focal point of the community's mounting frustration and anger. When it was leaked to the press that he planned to take a vacation shortly after the opening of school in 1971, just as the desegregation program was about to get under way, teachers publicly demanded his resignation and a local columnist insisted that Shaheen owed the citizens an apology for his "effrontery" and "lack of decency."[41] The replacement of the school superintendent

---

[41] Guy Wright in the *San Francisco Examiner*, September 5, 1971.

became an issue in the November election, in which Joseph Alioto was reelected mayor (and the attorney for the Chinese protesters, Quentin Kopp, was elected to the Board of Supervisors). In January 1972, the school board asked Shaheen to resign. Unlike Jenkins who stepped down quietly when asked, Shaheen refused to do so and instead took steps to contest the board's action. To the end of his two-year contract, when he had no recourse but to leave, Shaheen remained convinced that although he had lost the board's confidence, he could persuade the community to accept him.[42]

Since Spears' departure, the school board had taken more responsibility for school policy, but persisted nevertheless in upholding the practice of formal deference to the administration. For example, the board had initially supported Shaheen's "deselection" and had complied with his proposal that a group of citizens, not the administration, take responsibility for the planning of districtwide desegregation. As Shaheen's actions became increasingly intolerable, however, this practice broke down. Members of the board divided into two factions: some remained loyal to the superintendent, while others became willing to over-rule the administration, and, casting aside conventions of caution and deference, to risk conflict and disgruntled public reactions. At this point, the pattern of governance by which an elite, appointed school board provided the schools with insulation against the intrusion of conflict politics came to an end.

One cost of Shaheen's stubborn refusal to step down was the creation of a dual administration, further exacerbating the disarray of school affairs. While the superintendent occupied himself with public encounters around the city (at a meeting in Chinatown, he was chased away under a barrage of rocks, a scene viewed on national television by millions of Americans), Assistant Superintendent Milton Reiterman and his two cohorts assumed de facto command. The "triumvirate" exercised decision-making power over budgetary matters and personnel, two key areas of administration; but without accountability to a line of command, their authority became susceptible to abuse. The intrusion of board members, in efforts to control a growing arbitrariness in matters of program budgetting and personnel appointments, was praised by some and

---

[42] In a newspaper article published after his resignation, Shaheen claimed that the real reason he was ousted was his commitment to integration. But the board members who demanded his resignation were also committed to integrated schools at that time. *San Francisco Examiner*, August 25, 1972.

criticized by others. Thus problems of poor management, a divided administration, and a board tempted to "meddle" in the details of school operation were Shaheen's legacy and played a major role in the deepening school crisis.[43]

First Phase of Demoralization

To what extent was the requirement of desegregation responsible for the administrative problems and the other troubles that were frustrating the energies of school participants? Was the schools' disarray caused by the court order? In the next chapter, I shall argue that the disruptions that accompanied desegregation and complicated its implementation had a more complex set of causes. In any case, as we have seen, disarray and political turmoil *preceded* the desegregation of the elementary schools. Lacking leadership, the school system began unraveling prior to desegregation, as its autonomy, the organizing principle upon which the system depended for its smooth-running operation, eroded. The breakdown of professional autonomy, as a strategy of legitimation and defense mechanism, precipitated the crisis of authority and the weakening of organizational structure.

The civil rights movement touched on a fundamental weakness, namely, the school system's structured incapacity to respond to the criticisms of new social groups and forces. When subjected to criticism, Superintendent Spears could not justify "racial imbalance" and unfair treatment of black children. Neither, however, would he accept the charges and provide an "educationally sound" remedy. Subsequently, the political fumblings of the board and Superintendent Jenkins as they attempted to establish a consensus for new policy exacerbated community conflict, and under Shaheen, not only was school organization damaged, but the erosion of educational competence had begun. Thus, before desegregation policy became a reality, institutional integrity was undermined and weakened, creating the conditions for demoralization.

The critics and then the courts began intervening in school policy. The orderly practices of administration and the routines of everyday school life were shattered by political activity and

---

[43] This charge was made by the Grand Jury in a special Interim Report, issued as a vehicle for formulating an agenda for Shaheen's successor, as yet unnamed. (A civil Grand Jury is an old tradition in San Francisco city affairs.) City and County of San Francisco, "Interim Report of the Grand Jury," 1972.

conflicts within the ranks of upper echelon staff, and by an upsurge of teacher militancy. At the school sites, teachers, parents, and even pupils were no longer deferring to centralized authority; instead, these normally passive constituents were actively participating and attempting to influence budgeting, staffing, and other decisions. The curriculum was expanding into nontraditional subject areas, such as black and Asian studies, and there was an unprecedented openness and excitement about learning. The disarray signalled a radical shift and was accompanied by hopes as well as fears for the schools' educational mission.

In any case, demoralization is not a necessary outcome of disarray. Periods of crisis can be occasions for a renewal of the dedication and commitment needed to realize a revitalized institutional mission. Out of disarray can emerge new patterns of concerted energies for the achievement of ends. Although these opportunities existed, the institutional leadership needed to understand and seize them was not forthcoming. The issue of equal opportunity was a challenge, but it was not a source of inspiration for local school policymakers. Rather, it precipitated the erosion of school organization and professional authority.

The ability to maintain the educational outcomes of the recent past (unsatisfactory as they were in terms of equality of opportunity), let alone to establish higher levels of aspiration and educational achievement for all pupils, was severely impaired. The social organization of the schools was strained by the turmoil of the decade-long struggle over the nature and extent of the schools' social responsibilities. The resultant frustration, confusion, and disarray constituted fertile breeding grounds for the withdrawal of energies.

The interest and enthusiasm of board members, staff, and parents that, throughout this period, had infused the schools with ideas and energies began to slacken. Political conflict and division, social unrest, and insufficient attention to the basic tasks of schooling were impoverishing the human investment needed to support the enterprise. Personal energies are a kind of institutional capital. Their withdrawal left the schools bankrupt.

Shaheen's early loss of credibility was a serious setback for the school system. His policy of "deselection" was a critical factor in the withering of staff support. It is not simple to accomplish organizational change; forcing it to happen, as Shaheen tried to do, was bound to fail. In withdrawing their loyalty from him, the staff lost the sense of identification with their leader, a significant component, albeit one taken for granted, of their relationships with prior superintendents. Instead of nurturing and concerting the energies that were available throughout the school district, Shaheen's policies undermined the cooperation of his associates and his constituents.

Withdrawal and alienation were the responses not only of staff, but also of the minority communities whom, paradoxically, Shaheen was trying to help. Leaders of the SEED Project, which had, since 1968, helped stimulate a sense of community spirit and pride in the Hunters Point neighborhood schools, when seeking new funding sources, received no cooperation from the school district and they eventually became disillusioned. "The SFUSD looks at community programs as some kind of bastard," a spokesman complained bitterly. "They choke you to death. They do everything to program you for failure."[44] Without funds, SEED had to discontinue the project, which, in its three years, had demonstrated promise of upgrading the educational performance of black children.[45]

Other ethnic groups also began charging the school district with acting in bad faith. The Mission Coalition, an umbrella organization representing dozens of Hispanic groups, filed a lawsuit charging discrimination in 13 predominantly Spanish-speaking schools. The specific complaint was that, over a period of years, compared to the district's average per school expenditures, lesser amounts were spent for teacher salaries and educational materials in those schools. It was further charged that efforts to negotiate issues of equalization with the staff had proved futile. Again, Shaheen lacked the authority and political skills needed to achieve cooperation.

The disaffection of the Chinese community became evident when a lawsuit was filed on behalf of Chinese-speaking pupils charging the school district with discriminating against the non-English-speaking population. A federal district court judge ruled in the schools' favor, rejecting the claim that non-English-speaking pupils were being deprived of equal access to the benefits of schooling. However, the case was appealed and eventually reached the Supreme Court, which ordered the district to provide relief.[46]

---

[44] Reverend Charles Lee, SEED Project Head, quoted in the *SEED Newsletter*, February 1970.

[45] SEED's Third Year Report concluded that first-grade pupils were achieving higher median reading scores, ibid., pp. 36-38; also the Hearings of the Senate Select Committee, March 1970, pp. 4285-87.

[46] *Lau v Nichols*, filed in U.S. District court in May 1970. The Supreme Court ruling came down in 1974.

Throughout the extensive period of litigation, there was hostility toward the school administration on the part of the Chinese community. Shaheen in particular was regarded with great disdain by the Chinese: a school leader who could not command the loyalty of his own staff had little chance of earning respect from the traditional Chinese.

Finally, in the beleaguered Richmond Complex, where a demonstration of the promise of desegregation was actually taking place in 1970-71, there was deep disappointment. Parents and teachers were at last putting into practice the dreams and plans of the preceding years, but the reality was something else. The "Adventure in Living," as it was advertised, was to have included a community resource center, special science and media equipment, and, above all, exemplary cooperation among diverse ethnic groups working in harmony toward the goal of "quality-equality" education. However, for various reasons, this "adventure" turned out to be altogether routine and discouraging. Too many distractions elsewhere in the school district prevented attention, let alone a special spotlight, being directed onto this model program. Besides, given the lack of resources, nothing really different was happening in the classrooms to inspire a move either for or against full-scale desegregation. Given nothing "radical" to protest, the threat of boycotts by resistant parents never materialized.[47] (The only protest was a "sit-in" by a group of 100 or so Chinese families demanding bilingual classes.) Both the public's fears and the hopes of desegregation proponents thus dwindled. Within the Complex, energies were diverted from the in-depth participation of the recent past, and redirected to old patterns of limited, PTA-style participation at individual school sites.[48]

The Richmond Complex became just another special program, competing for limited resources and attention along with all the other programs in the school district. Its status as a demonstration of the problems and potentials of desegregation was not recognized, nor accorded any more special privilege than SEED's demonstration of how to create an effective black community school improvement program. In the turmoil of the times, it was impossible to recognize and reward promising educational developments, and, lacking reinforcement and resources, such projects deteriorated.

---

[47] SFUSD, "Report on the Planning and Implementation of the Richmond Complex," prepared by Laurel Feigenbaum, 1971, p. 37.
[48] Ibid. pp. 42-46.

Disheartened, participants withdrew their energies from the schools and looked elsewhere for more satisfying engagements.

Shaheen's unpopularity and ineffectiveness were factors in the alienation of staff and community. The school board, particularly in its response to the prospects of court-ordered desegregation, was also the cause of much discouragement, especially among those who had, for some 10 years, been involved with issues of civil rights. By delegating its responsibility to the CAC, and charging this citizen group with the task of preparing a response, the board lost the respect routinely granted trustees of the public interest. Moreover, the board's lack of attention to the details of the CAC's recommended plan discouraged responsible participation in the schools. In retrospect, a member of the CAC reflected that, instead of serving together with school officials, the citizen group had been used as "front-men" to bear the flack, discharge their duty as quickly as possible, and disband. Their mission was not given the attention and consideration it deserved. Administrative expediency and the board's unwillingness to cope with the controversial details of the districtwide desegregation plan cost the school district the potential contribution that citizens can make to public policy when their energies and talents are recognized and appreciated.

Individual members of the board were among the first to suffer the consequences of alienation. Their disaffection had begun with the filing of the lawsuit, when board president Alan Nichols, in despair over the rupture of the political process, resigned. Not long after, the labor representative who had served for ten years, Edward Kemmitt, also resigned. In November 1971 the electorate overwhelmingly approved Mayor Alioto's charter amendment creating an elected school board, and at that point Laurel Glass resigned.[49] Three other board members, including Mrs. Lilienthal and Dr. Goosby, chose not to run rather than expose themselves to likely defeat in an election.[50] Thus by June 1972, the members of

---

[49] A year earlier, a similar measure failed to pass because it called for election by districts; San Francisco is partial to citywide local politics. See the *San Francisco Chronicle*, November 4, 1970. In 1971, the electorate confirmed three new mayoral nominees to the board, all of them opposed to desegregation. They were George Chinn, the first Chinese-American ever to serve on the school board (replacing Laurel Glass); Dr. Eugene Hopp, a former chairman of the local Commonwealth Club's Education Committee (replacing Alan Nichols); and a new labor representative, John Kidder.

[50] Howard Nemerovsky, who had recently replaced Reynold Colvin, also chose not to run, but David Sanchez, who succeeded Adolfo de Urioste, was among those elected to the school board in 1972.

the board who had been most active in shaping events during the sixties were no longer in office. By choice and by circumstance, they abandoned their efforts and their aspirations for the public schools.

Along with the withdrawal of energies on the part of school and community leaders, there was a dramatic rise in the incidence of school violence and vandalism. Principals, teachers, and pupils no longer felt involved, and their schools became just a place to which they were assigned to go every day. No longer a source of social value, buildings ceased being cared for and maintained. Vandals broke windows and trashed offices. Little attention was given to prevention and punishment, to the control of vandalism through social control and vigilance.

In 1970 the Grand Jury's investigating team issued a scathing report calling attention to the lack of discipline, the rampant use of drugs, vandalism, violence, and truancy prevalent in the San Francisco schools, but in the absence of leadership, nothing was done about the situation.[51] Apathy and alienation at the school sites, symptoms and consequences of the withdrawal of energies, were becoming serious and debilitating problems.

Summary

To assess the impact of desegregation on demoralization, I have analyzed the character of the relationship between the schools and the civil rights movement. In recounting the events of the sixties, I have argued that the principle of professional autonomy, separating the schools from politics, was responsible for (1) defensiveness on the part of the school administration regarding the accountability of the schools for social issues; and (2) inexperience and ineptness on the part of the school board in coping with the politics of desegregation, such that despite their sympathy for the cause of civil rights, they were unable to realize aspirations to assist blacks and other minorities. Further, I have shown how opportunities to rise to the political challenge were missed, and how leadership failed to harness the social ideals of the sixties as vehicles for concerting the aroused energies of the community. Instead, a decade of political

---

[51] City and County of San Francisco, "Report of the 1970 Grand Jury." Until that year, the Grand Jury had concentrated on such matters as the budget, and rising costs. But in subsequent years, issues of discipline and pupil achievement were paramount.

strife ended in turmoil and disarray. These conditions precipitated
the disaffection of participants and the withdrawal of their energies.

This first phase of demoralization was an effect of the schools'
structured incapacity to respond to the legitimate social and educational issues raised by the civil rights movement. A diagram of the
dynamics revealed by my analysis, is as follows:

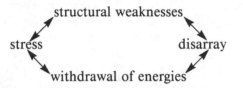

Some form of stress, in this case the pressures of the civil rights
movement, aggravated structural weaknesses, namely the rigidity
and political inexperience that were by-products of the schools' historic reliance on the principle of professional autonomy. Unable to
adapt politically, the schools suffered a crisis of authority and
leadership. The resultant disarray, despite the opportunities it
offered for a more positive outcome, exhausted the energies of
major participants and community supporters, producing the first
phase of demoralization.

The dynamics continued as stress in the form of generalized anxiety further weakened the capacities of the school system. School
participants became critically affected, in that they were increasingly unable to concentrate on their educational tasks or to invest
their work with meaning. We now turn to the heightened effects of
stress on everyday life in the schools.

Part II: DYNAMICS

4

Loss of Institutional Coherence

School is a place where children sit and listen, and wait, and raise their hands and pass out paper. School is where friends are made, where tests are passed and failed, where imagination is unleashed and skills acquired. But it is also a place where amusing things happen and yawns are stifled, and recess lines form.[1]

Part I described the encounter of the San Francisco public schools with the civil rights movement, and identified weaknesses of political and administrative leadership that led to crisis and disarray. Due to the failure of leadership and the structured incapacity to adapt to the significant social forces that were sweeping the country, the schools suffered a substantial withdrawal of energies. Desegregation of the schools, I argued, was not the cause of demoralization. Rather, school leaders, believing that the well-being of schools demanded strict autonomy—i.e. schools ought to be removed from politics and sheltered from social responsibilities—failed to respond in a timely fashion to the changes called for by the civil rights movement. The salient issues of the sixties—racial equality and civil rights—pressed hard on officials whose political sensitivity, skills, and experience were not adequate to the challenge of leadership, and who thus allowed the integrity and competence of the schools to deteriorate.

Part II examines the dynamics of demoralization in the San Francisco schools. Deterioration of the conditions essential for learning, I will argue, degraded the schools' public image and eroded participants' sense of personal worth. As pupils and teachers became frustrated in their work, as principals neglected the

---

[1] From the adaptation of Philip Jackson's *Life in Classrooms* (N.Y.: Holt, Rinehart & Winston, 1968) in Broom and Selznick, *Sociology: A Text with Adapted Readings* 5th ed. (N.Y.: Harper & Row, 1973), p. 364.

educational aspects of school management, as the administration and school board became so distracted they were unable to concentrate on the system's educational goals, the result was internal fragmentation and loss of institutional coherence, the second phase of demoralization. Orderly patterns fell apart, routine lines of communication were disrupted, and people began to lose their sense of purpose. Disruption of the schools' social structure deadened the spirit of dedication necessary to infuse the everyday life of the schools with meaning and purpose.

In this chapter, I analyze disruption as it affected the regularities of schooling at the elementary level. Disruption throughout the school district is the subject of Chapter 5. Disruption and a loss of coherence, I suggest, disconcerted the administration such that, instead of insuring the maintenance of resources and the conditions essential for learning, normal institutional oversight lapsed and school leadership pursued an opportunistic and ultimately self-destructive course of action. At the school site level, this entailed a failure to protect and safeguard the essential regularities of schooling.

Regularities of Schooling

The conditions for learning involve a basic tension between the need for order and the need for freedom. A balance must be struck that provides a sense of openness while avoiding the risk of disorder. Rules and regulations limiting behavior are necessary to protect the learning environment. These need not be repressive or stultifying. Nevertheless, schools require a reasonable amount of order to ensure civility of conduct. Such order need not be imposed, but rather can be constructed in response to the particular needs of the group situation.

Regularities of school life contain both customary routines, evolved over experience and embedded in the school's culture, and innovative patterns, developed in response to changing needs. Let us take a brief look at some of these regularities.[2]

---

[2] The discussion that follows is based on the author's experiences as a classroom teacher in the elementary schools of San Francisco from 1968 to 1972. The perspective is similar to that of sociologist Philip Jackson, whose study of classrooms (*Life in Classrooms*, ibid.) emphasized the "hidden curriculum," the rituals and routines that compose the background or taken for granted aspects of school life.

Daily Routine

Going to school occupies roughly six hours a day, and involves continuous contact for pupils and teachers. Children are expected to arrive on time, teachers to complete their lessons within fixed time intervals determined by the school schedule, janitors to clean the cafeteria and yard areas after lunch, and so on. Every room is equipped with a large clock that rings to announce the times for recess and dismissal as well as the beginning of the school day.

But despite its familiarity, classroom activity is complex and opaque; it involves a subtle blend of formal lessons and informal exchanges. Teachers are expected both to socialize and instruct pupils, and for their efforts, they expect to receive instrumental and expressive rewards. The tensions, satisfactions, and anxieties of the classroom impart a special character to the school day. It is unlike life at home, and also unlike working life. This is because learning—what is supposed to happen in schools—is a relatively open-ended process involving a complex entanglement of diffuse ends and means, and a variety of methods and activities. Learning poses a challenge to which the response has been the construction of definite routines and ceremonies whose purpose is the regulation of daily school life.

The regulation of the school day affects the educational function of schooling by limiting or supporting opportunities for learning. A school schedule, for example, can either enhance or undermine learning. The schedule is necessary to divide the school day into discrete units, so as to offer a diversity of daily lessons and activities. In an elementary school, every day can be the same (reading, spelling, arithmetic, social studies, etc.), or a weekly schedule can be prepared with daily variations in the order of subjects. The teacher can prescribe the order, or the teacher and the class together can develop a satisfactory schedule. But there are limits to the possibilities of accommodating the curriculum to the schedule. For example, it is not satisfactory to teach arithmetic all day for eight weeks, and then move on to spelling. Nor is it possible to keep pupils at their seats for a whole morning without physical activity. Children need nourishment at regular intervals, and they have to chat and play with their friends. Developing a schedule that is sensitive to the particular needs of a class of pupils, given their ages, their maturity, and the life patterns of their families requires effective classroom management skills.

A standardized curriculum has evolved to assist the average teacher. It establishes the scope and sequence of the subject matter to be covered within the school schedule and enables the teacher to structure the time so as to balance the human elements of classroom life with educational requirements. Changes in either the standard curriculum or the school schedule create disturbances in the classroom and place learning in jeopardy. For example, if the day is shortened, or if lunch is postponed, or if a classroom or playground is unavailable, lessons suffer and the curriculum has to be adjusted. Similarly, if new subjects or methods, such as new math, computer-assisted instruction, or foreign languages, are added to the curriculum, new schedules have to be evolved accordingly. Teacher resistance to new curriculum is not necessarily evidence of reluctance to introduce new learning materials or methods; more often, it is a natural reaction to the anticipated difficulties of readjusting a carefully crafted daily schedule. If changes are required in both curriculum *and* schedule, classroom management is likely to get out of hand; energies necessary for learning must then be diverted to the tasks of coping and trying to reestablish sufficient order for instruction to continue. Even slight instability causes difficulties for the achievement of a satisfactory balance between order and learning.

Organization of Classes by Grades

Elementary school children are grouped by age and assigned to grades. Six-year-olds are in first grade, eleven-year-olds in sixth grade, etc. A typical elementary school contains grades 1-6, plus an additional class (kindergarten) for children under age six who attend school usually for half a day.

Every school contains at least one class per grade; larger schools have two or more classes at each grade level. Teachers specialize in working with particular grades. If enrollments are high one year and a new first-grade class is formed, rather than transferring an upper-grade teacher, the principal will ask that a new first-grade teacher be assigned to the school. As every parent knows, socialization and instruction of a six-year-old is quite different from that of a youngster aged ten. Similarly, the daily difficulties and tasks of teaching a first-grade class are quite unlike those of working with fifth graders, even if some of them are reading at a first-grade level. Teacher specialization is an important corollary of the organization of classes by grades.

Space and Materials

Each elementary school class is assigned a room, and this space becomes the group's "home" for nine months. Every nook and cranny of the room becomes familiar, as do the common areas within the school—the bathrooms, hallways, yards, offices, etc. It matters whether one's school life is spent in a large sunny room or in a detached and dismal bungalow. Within a given room the spaces occupied by individual children also matter: front or rear desk, by the window, next to the door—each location has its special attributes and social meaning.

The room's furnishings are vital to the conduct of class activities: a flag to salute, maps and blackboards, desks and chairs, paper, pencils, books. Classrooms in the sixties, reflecting a more affluent society, commonly contained TV sets (for educational programs) and enrichment materials such as games, library books, science projects, and plants. Such items relieved the spareness of the standard furnishings. Some classrooms were even more personalized, with teachers and pupils adding wall decorations or creating special areas by using rugs or grouping desks and tables. Setting up classroom hobby or craft projects, such as photography or ceramics, was also quite common.

Even so, classroom space and equipment have limited flexibility. To make the classroom comfortable and conducive to learning calls for considerable ingenuity and constant vigilance. A teacher who is unmindful of the spatial and material aspects of classroom management is likely to have difficulty maintaining a learning atmosphere. Feelings are hurt and fights erupt when the classroom situation is insensitive to children's needs for personal space and materials. Such tensions distract attention from lessons. Moreover, if suitable materials are not provided, or are unavailable, teaching and learning suffer. Given the limited elasticity of these requirements, even minor shortages or mishaps can cause disruption: a lost ball, not enough books to go around, a stolen lunch or broken window—these ordinary vicissitudes of classroom life are difficult enough to cope with. Extraordinary disruptions, such as vandalism or violence, can make life unbearable and classroom learning impossible.

School Climate

Another dimension regulating the quality of school life is the school climate. A school can feel cold or warm, and its atmosphere can be strict or permissive, traditional or modern. The school principal's personality, administrative practices, and style of communication usually set the temperature and tone that controls the school's climate.[3] Within this setting, teachers and pupils work out arrangements that determine their classroom climate.

The principal's role is central because she (or more typically, he) has the formal authority for the school's performance within the school district, as well as the responsibility for its standing in the community. The reputation of the local school, for many parents, is an important consideration in establishing residence.

But school climate is also affected by the prevailing social climate. In the sixties egalitarian trends favoring a flattening of the traditional hierarchical structure of schools were in ascendancy. Principals were becoming involved in districtwide policy decisions, and teachers began participating in school-site decisions, such as personnel assignments, allocation of rooms, selection of materials, and daily schedules. The rudiments of decentralization were taking shape.

In the classroom, pupils' talents and interests were no longer ignored, but rather were taken into account in selecting materials and activities. Teachers, seeking the joys of discovery for themselves, began venturing into less conventional subject areas. Individual personalities and resources were called upon to create nontraditional, innovative learning environments, instead of repeating the same practices year after year.

This was the time when there was strong interest in so-called "open classrooms." Many teachers and parents found attractive the inherent optimism and enthusiasm for learning that were premises of this movement. Open classrooms assume that the innate curiosity of the child is a sufficient motivation for learning. Rather than relying on discipline and drill to subdue the child's supposedly instinctive aversion to learning, the "open classroom" called for the provision of supportive and stimulating environments. Within these nontraditional learning settings, children were expected naturally and eagerly to learn basic skills, without the need for repetitive

---

[3] Mary H. Metz, *Classrooms and Corridors* (Berkeley: University of California Press, 1978), p. 4.

drills and the constant monitoring and directing of each step in the learning process.

A corollary of this expectation regarding the nature of learning was a shift in the customary authority relationships between teacher and pupil. While still maintaining a distinctive status, teachers who opted for "open classrooms" relinquished their role as mentors, and assumed new roles as facilitators and even colearners. Their pupils, no longer regarded as mere receptacles of knowledge, acquired new status in recognition of their active participation in the learning process. In the theory of the open classroom, teachers and pupils join together in classroom experiences and share the "joys" of learning.

Innovations, such as "open classrooms," had a liberating effect on classroom climate. In contrast to the dreary routines of conventional school life, reproduced like clockwork from one class and grade to the next, in which the only new interest consisted of changes in the makeup of the class, and for pupils, the identity of the teacher, the new pedagogy opened fresh vistas and promised to make every day's work vital and interesting. Stimulation in the classroom shifted pupils' attention away from whisperings and small-scale conspiracies about tricks to play and mischief-making after school. Lessons themselves evoked interest, and there was laughter and fun in class, not just at recess. Instead of one teacher for the entire year, elementary pupils might have a team of two or more teachers, each with different talents and personalities. New options, such as games and manipulative materials, supplemented standardized textbooks to inculcate concepts and develop skills; audiovisual techniques replaced routine lessons, meeting individual needs through a multisensory approach. Recognition of individual differences included teachers as well as pupils. There was a new and exciting challenge in discovering and cultivating these differences.

But despite these trends toward less hierarchical and nontraditional schools, the difficulties of sustaining an atmosphere conducive to learning and responsive to individual interests and participation remained. Resources, although more abundant, were far from sufficient to motivate the average teacher to adopt innovations such as team teaching. Instructional change required more than an ordinary capacity for adapting to the ups and downs of group life, in which a certain number of pupils enter or leave during the school year, some are absent or not feeling well on any particular day, some can be relied upon for preparing classroom materials and participating in shared activities and others cannot, and a few always have special educational needs or handicaps. Given these contingencies, and if neither pupils nor teachers are personally engaging, and, in addition, if there is little interest in shared decision making, innovations quickly reverted to traditional and rigid ways. In the face of such vicissitudes, the atmosphere of oppression so often complained about reasserted itself. Gifted teachers, always in scarce supply, gravitated toward other options, and under more than ordinary stress, educational expectations dissipated. For typical teachers and pupils, it was easier to sustain a climate requiring minimal performance and therefore perceived and experienced as boring and oppressive. However, it is increasingly recognized that such a climate is not as conducive to learning as one which sets higher standards.

The ethos of the school neighborhood is another controlling factor in determining climate. Tensions between parental and school attitudes toward what is to be taught and how to teach it tend to be resolved in the community's favor, not the school's. A school that is comfortable with open classrooms, lots of field trips, and mastery of the techniques of photography is not likely to receive the resources necessary for such a program in a community that values the 3 Rs. But in a large school district, there is usually a sufficient variety of neighborhoods for principals and teachers to find a school where the pedagogical climate is congenial. San Francisco by the late sixties had a number of innovative programs as well as traditional elementary schools.

Conclusion

Controlled by the climate, limited by spatial and material conditions, confined by the school schedule and by grade organization, the regulation of elementary classroom life poses a constant challenge. Achieving the kind of order that facilitates learning requires resources of sensitivity and skill, and calls for the capacity to cope with the twists and turns of daily life among a lively group of children. The precariousness of this optimal order is a fact of elementary school life. Minor distractions can be absorbed, but major disruptions seriously interfere with and undermine the functions of schooling. The impact of a major disruption is bound to have serious consequences for learning.

Disruption of the Elementary Schools

In the fall of 1971, as ordered by the U.S. District Court, the elementary schools of San Francisco were desegregated. The desegregation plan, hastily drawn up by the Citizens Advisory Committee and immediately adopted by the school board, was an educational disaster. Changes in the structure of the elementary schools were conceived and implemented without consideration for the precarious order upon which learning depends. Disregard for school regularities and for the physical and social conditions essential to learning undermined staff performance and morale. Frustrations in the classroom, disorder within schools, conflict and confusion among administrators and school leadership, created severe disorganization and a preoccupation with short-range survival.

The Horseshoe Plan and Racial Balance

The desegregation plan called for grouping the city's 96 elementary schools into seven contiguous zones drawn in a horseshoe pattern around the city—hence the designation "Horseshoe." Crosstown busing was avoided because each zone contained a sufficient racial mixture of pupils such that pupils could be reassigned in ratios proportional to the city's racial population, give or take 15 percent (the formula for racial balance used in California state guidelines) *within* each zone.[4] As an illustration, given that 28.7 percent of the elementary population was black, a school, regardless of zone, enrolling between 13.7 percent and 43.7 percent black children was considered racially balanced with respect to blacks; similar calculations were carried out to determine if the school was balanced with respect to white, Chinese, Japanese, Korean, Filipino, Spanish-speaking, American Indian, and other nonwhite pupils, the eight other population groups involved in the desegregation. Aside from their potential for thus producing racial balance in each school, the seven zones were otherwise quite various: some contained more schools and more pupils than others, and in several low-income families predominated.

The zone arrangement took into account the city's major roads and freeways, as well as natural features, such as Golden Gate Park, that demarcate various neighborhoods. Not given the weight they warranted, however, were ongoing neighborhood efforts, such as OMI. At that time OMI was trying to stabilize a racially mixed

---

4 Title V, California Administrative Code, Section 14020-21, repealed in 1972.

residential area, but despite this promising development, its schools were divided between two zones, and black children previously attending integrated neighborhood schools were bused into ghetto areas. Similarly, in Hunters Point, the schools were split between two zones, effectively ending the innovative SEED project. Community action in both areas was thus diluted.

The Horseshoe plan was strictly a busing plan, aimed at remedying racial imbalance in the schools. It was not concerned with the values of school-community involvement. Moreover, it took for granted the continuity of the schools' educational programs, in effect reversing former superintendent Spears' position. The reader will recall that Spears was not willing to concede the educational worth of eliminating racial segregation. He assumed that standard programs of instruction, whether conducted in all-white or all-black schools, were sufficient, and that, so long as everyone, regardless of race, had access to the schools, norms of equal opportunity were satisfied. The Horseshoe Plan, on the other hand, assumed that desegregated schools would automatically improve educational opportunities for blacks and other minorities. Planners failed to recognize the importance of maintaining the social conditions, including school-community support, that facilitate learning. Both sensitivity to race and attention to the requisites of learning were called for, but Horseshoe's preoccupation with racial balance not only took the instructional program for granted, but disrupted its underpinnings.

In September 1971, when Horseshoe began, over half the elementary school population of 48,000 pupils was re-assigned to a different school from the one they had attended that June. Computers had been busy all summer working out the specific details, and shortly before school opened, families were notified by mail where their children would go and whether they would walk or ride the bus. Even youngsters assigned to the same school were confronted with major changes. Previously, all the elementary schools contained classrooms for grades K-6. Brothers and sisters, ages five to 11, attended the same school. Now, however, a returning second grader (age seven) found a school with only grades K-3; if he had older siblings, they were assigned to an upper-division, grades 4-6, school. Maintenance crews had been busy all summer, moving desks from school to school, installing toilets and sinks, and exchanging supplies. The separation of the elementary grades into two divisions, intended to make busing more equitable (every child would walk to one school and ride the bus to the other), had the unintended effect of creating specialized primary and upper-division schools. Instead of one or two classes for the second grade in a given school, there were now three or four classrooms full of seven- and eight-year-olds, and no older children. Regardless of whether pupils attended new schools or old, they thus found themselves in physically and socially new environments.

To achieve racial balance and for efficient use of the busing routes, all the appropriately aged children on a block were assigned to the same school. Children from adjacent blocks, however, might be assigned to different schools. Thus to move two Chinese students living on the same block to an elementary school where Chinese students were needed to achieve a desired racial balance, all the other non-Chinese students on that block were also assigned to that school, but a Chinese friend across the street could be assigned to a different school.

Among the many new faces on the school grounds, it was not easy for young children to find their friends from last year's class. Also, not everyone was returning to the public schools. Many parents had decided not to go along with the desegregation; they had either taken their children out of the public schools or moved away. Over the summer, the elementary school population dropped from 48,312 to 41,544, a loss of 16.1 percent.

Resistance to the desegregation plan was sufficient to damage the expected outcome of racial balance. Instead of a 34.5 percent white population, the schools' overall percentage of white elementary school pupils dropped to 30.1 percent.[5] In particular, white families refused, on the whole, to send children to schools in the Hunters Point area. Also, because large numbers of black Hunters Point children were assigned to Sunset District schools, many white families in that neighborhood opted for private schools. For their part, black parents whose children were assigned to older schools in the center of the city, the Mission District, instead of to new schools recently constructed in Hunters Point, also objected. In the city's Chinatown resistance was not only fierce but well-organized: 76 percent of the expected pupil population boycotted the public schools. The children were diverted to community-sponsored schools. Chinese mothers stood on street corners and in front of the public schools, recruiting children as they arrived to board the buses. Thus, at the outset, one-third of the elementary schools were imbalanced, according to the guidelines, with respect to one or more

---

[5] SFUSD, "Active Fall Enrollment," October 1975, Table IV, p. 9.

racial groups. Only Zones I and VII, which corresponded to the established Richmond and Park South school complexes, achieved the desired racial balance.[6]

Teacher Reassignment

In addition to pupil racial balance, the Horseshoe plan called for racial distribution of the teaching and administrative staff of the elementary division. Changes in staffing assignments were made to improve racial balance, but with little regard for the social networks that compose and support school climate. Similarly, the identity and self-worth of individual teachers were not serious considerations. Insofar as these matters bear upon school performance, their neglect contributed to an erosion of morale and the undermining of educational quality.

Teachers' organizations were not involved in planning the desegregation of the certificated staff. This was done by a central administration that showed little regard for social relationships within schools. Teachers' grade specializations were also not considered. Rather, teachers were reassigned on the basis of race and seniority, but because of the preponderance of white teachers (in 1970 the certificated staff was 80 percent white and only five percent black), it was seniority, not race that accounted for most of the reshuffling.[7]

The break-up of the elementary schools into primary and intermediate schools posed a major dilemma: Should teachers stay in a familiar school setting, even if it meant teaching a different grade, or should they remain with the grade they knew best, which might entail moving to another school? During the summer of 1971, teachers agonized over this question, only to discover that transfers were being made without consulting them. The inequity of the procedures, their disorderliness and arbitrariness were denounced by the teachers' union, but to no avail.

What happened was that schools designated for the primary grades (K-3) tended to hold their senior staff members. Given the uncertainties of moving to a new location, upper-grade teachers preferred to stay with their school even though it meant working with

---

[6] SFUSD, "Status Report of the Office of Integration," January 1975, pp. 18-19.

[7] By 1975, with affirmative action, the proportions were 71 percent white and 10 percent black, and this remained basically the same through the rest of the decade. Percentages of other racial groups also remained below 10 percent. SFUSD Memo, "Affirmative Action Policy," June 3, 1975.

younger children than the ones they were used to. The reverse was not the case, however. Most of the teachers in the intermediate (4-6) schools, anticipating discipline problems and heterogeneous classes, wanted to leave. Upper-grade teachers with seniority forced out the less experienced primary-grade teachers who had no choice but to accept upper-grade openings.

This extensive staff shake-up had several consequences. First, classroom teachers and principals did not experience the desegregation of schools as a challenge to their ideals and skills, but rather as an arbitrary exercise of administrative power. Even before school opened, the local teachers' organizations called for the resignation of Shaheen. The superintendent, even if he had tried to mobilize support, was in no position to offer leadership, given his lack of credibility in the district. And administration officials, preoccupied with the myriad details of preparing for the opening of school, had not taken time to formulate educational goals and objectives for this major change of organization. There was no rationale or sense of mission to which the staff could respond. Everyone knew about the court order, but its purpose had not been translated into organizational doctrine.

Secondly, the transfer of teachers did not give significant weight to grade-level expertise. On the contrary, the situation exploited and exacerbated fears and anxieties evoked by the prospect of drastic changes in the practical conditions of teaching. Experienced upper-grade teachers chose to stay in primary schools because they believed it would be easier to manage the younger children. Despite the educational consequences, the administration allowed them to do so. In retrospect, it appears that more attention was given to the logistics of moving school equipment than to the schools' instructional priorities.

Finally, given the extensive dislocation of physical and human conditions, the preparations for the opening of the school term were totally inadequate. Teachers had only a few days to meet together as faculties and to prepare their rooms before classes began. Those assigned to a different grade had virtually no time to study the curriculum and learning materials. Teachers complained that they were treated as deployable front-line soldiers, assigned without regard for their professional skills, and commanded to carry on without a clear understanding of their mission. While most obeyed, they felt ill-treated and harbored resentments. Teachers felt the coercive impact of the court order; they did not experience its potential empowerment.

Ironically, during the previous year, an entirely different process had resolved similar problems with positive results. The 20 schools in the Richmond and Park South complexes had also been divided into primary and intermediate facilities, and there too staff had been reshuffled. However, sound planning and supportive services, in a context of community participation, had produced satisfying, if short-lived, changes in those schools. Teachers had been given a choice as to whether they desired to participate or not. (Only a few opted out.) A task force of experienced teachers was organized and given responsibility for providing in-service training during the year preceding desegregation. Each classroom teacher was awarded a budget and invited to consider and choose new curriculum materials to help motivate and interest students. Finally, before school opened, there was a summer workshop (optional), and a weekend conference (required) to stimulate a sense of community and shared purpose among all those undertaking this exciting educational endeavor.[8] The teachers in those schools were not only prepared, they were eager to confront the challenges of working with racially balanced classes. Teacher training continued throughout the school year, and the task force was helpful in securing resources and administrative support for the school program. During the height of the controversy over desegregation in 1970-71, the complex schools lost only five percent of their expected pupil enrollment, and the following year, as Zones I and VII respectively of the Horseshoe Plan, they were the only zones to maintain the desired racial balance.[9]

Lessons from this successful experience were not applied to the districtwide desegregation. Nor was there appreciation of the considerable value of the complexes as models for successful desegregation. Teachers in the complex schools received their transfer notices along with all the other elementary staff. No special weight was given to sustaining the impetus and protecting the investment made in planning and implementing desegregation in those schools.

---

[8] As a member of the teachers' task force, the author helped promote and plan these instructional events, including the weekend conference that was held, at district expense, at Asilomar. The chair of the teachers' task force was Janet Benson, a seasoned classroom teacher, officer of the California Teachers' Association, and, because of her exceptional character, an inspiration to the faculties of the 20 schools.
[9] SFUSD, "Status Report of the Office of Integration," p.10.

Classroom Conditions

School life became very different. The neighborhood school had been a place children walked to and from, many returning home for lunch as well. Traffic guards, boys and girls in the sixth grade, stood watch on street corners, helping younger children cross safely. On rainy days, traffic monitors in yellow slickers, their shoes tucked into roomy rainboots, stood guard, their vigilance impressing upon younger children the message that school was an important place where it mattered that one came and went safely, and on time. Now approximately one-third of the children arrived by bus, the buses were frequently delayed, and they, not the children, were responsible for being on time. Arriving late was no longer a personal offense; it was a common occurrence and source of interference with the school schedule.

Classroom routines were substantially altered by the advent of busing. Given that many youngsters could be expected to arrive late, teachers rescheduled their daily routines of attendance and postponed the first group lesson. Instead of a general class exercise, teachers offered opening activities where it did not matter if everyone participated or not, and in which latecomers would not cause a disturbance. The first lesson of the day no longer took advantage of the fresh energies of the early morning. Instead teachers and pupils just marked time until everyone arrived. Quality instructional time was reduced, and the seriousness of schooling undermined.

In addition, under the Horseshoe Plan, nothing was done to make the older school buildings more attractive or to humanize the larger schools designated for the intermediate grades. Within each zone, it was these larger schools, with 12 or more classrooms, that were selected to house the older children. With few exceptions, these were multistoried brick or stucco buildings, surrounded by cement yards fenced off from surrounding homes or buildings. Such schools did not lend themselves to the flexible use of space. Reconstructing the routines of school life in these buildings was particularly difficult.

The older children could not understand why their school life so completely changed over the summer, just as they were acquiring upper-grade status, becoming school leaders, and looking forward to graduation from elementary school. Why were their expectations disappointed? Why was important information they had acquired regarding specific school rituals, what to expect from their principal, how to get along with all the different teachers and even the janitors all suddenly made useless? Many nine- to 12-year-olds approached their new assignments with understandable wariness, and even anger. Teachers, many of them having worked only with younger children, and themselves feeling disgruntled, sought in vain for advice or assistance in how to negotiate with these older and more hostile youngsters. But there were no faculty support systems to turn to, and principals had their own problems providing for the safety of children on the buses and in school corridors.

Prior to desegregation, teachers were accustomed to having classes of pupils with more or less similar skills, e.g. a class of fourth graders who could all read at about the same grade level and who had all mastered a certain amount of arithmetic. This was the case even in schools attended primarily by black children, where, however, teaching levels were lower than in schools with predominantly nonblack or non-Hispanic children.[10] Mixing the pupils, particularly in the upper-grade schools, meant that every classroom of pupils contained a much wider range of skills than teachers were used to. Such pupil diversity made teaching harder, and also required a greater range of materials, as well as more proficient classroom management skills.

But when upper-grade teachers looked for instructional materials suitable for pupils who were below grade level, they discovered that over the summer all the primary-grade books had been moved, along with the smaller desks and toilets, to primary school sites. With principals and teachers on summer break, the building custodians had been assigned the logistical tasks, and while they could not have been expected to be aware of the educational needs, the administration's negligence is not so excusable. Thus the upper-grade teachers, many of them inexperienced, had to face difficult and undesirable situations, and they had to do so without appropriate books and supplies.

Such mindless provisioning of the schools had not occurred in the reorganization of the complex schools because there teachers had the opportunity and the incentive to select the range of

---

[10] In 1969-70, the composite grade six achievement score for Lafayette School (4.7% black) was 6.9. (A score of 6.2 was the average sixth-grade achievement score, according to standardized tests.) In Anza School (89.5% black), the composite score for the sixth grade was 4.1. In 1970-71, when these schools joined the Richmond complex and their student bodies were integrated, Anza's scores rose to 6.4, and Lafayette's dropped to 6.6. The average sixth grade score for the entire elementary division those years was 5.2 and 5.3, or approximately one year below grade level. The successful grouping of schools like Anza and Lafayette seemed promising at that time. (Data from district records.)

classroom materials they expected to use. Materials and supplies were chosen and moved thoughtfully, and there were more than enough, so that if one particular book was not satisfactory, e.g. a programmed reader, the teacher could turn to others. The difficulties and challenge of integrated classrooms were similar in both situations, but in the complex schools, there were sufficient resources to support the effort and teachers were prepared for the diversity of needs they encountered. A year later, with the district-wide dispersion of teachers and materials, upper-grade teachers were at a considerable disadvantage. They were left to struggle and cope with whatever was available, getting by on a day-to-day basis until they could "beg, borrow, or steal" suitable learning materials, or until principals could arrange for school-to-school transfers.

Principals

When the Horseshoe Plan began, only 52 of the 96 principals remained with their schools. Like teachers, principals were also reassigned for purposes of racial balance, although the high proportion of white principals (82 percent) made the concept of balance pointless.[11] Those with tenure preferred moving to the primary schools. However, the intermediate schools attracted some more ambitious, as well as less experienced principals because there was a drastic change in the role of the elementary school principal at this time.

This role shift was due in part to changes in the structure of the elementary division entailed by the Horseshoe Plan. While the elementary division was retained as an organizational entity (there was an assistant superintendent for the elementary schools, and various subject-area supervisors), a new administrative unit, namely the zone, was created to accommodate the Horseshoe Plan, and each of the seven zones had its own administrator. Zone administrators were responsible for the logistics of the desegregation plan, which included implementing pupil and teacher assignments, monitoring bus routes and schedules, transferring supplies, and so on. Their authority over these matters was not clearly defined, however, and therefore principals had to figure out which channels—the Horseshoe zones, or the central administration—to use to solve particular problems. Was securing books a logistical problem or an instructional task? When proper channels were not used, internal

---

[11] In 1970, 82 percent of the field administrators were white, compared to 8 percent black. SFUSD, "Affirmative Action," p. 6.

politics made the principal's predicament confusing and often frustrating.

Loss of their accustomed support had the effect of forcing principals to become "entrepreneurs," in the sense that they personally had to seek out qualified teachers, secure supplies, locate resources, argue on behalf of their school's needs, etc. Many principals were disinclined to work this way, preferring the more routine bureaucratic procedures with which they were familiar. Many therefore chose to leave: in 1970-71, 10 percent of elementary principals took early retirement (before age 55), compared to only two percent in 1969-70.[12]

Another aspect of the principal's role that changed at this time was the relationship between the principal and the community. Whereas the principal of a neighborhood school could become fairly well acquainted with local parents and knowledgeable about particular problems and needs, under Horseshoe there was no easily identifiable school neighborhood. Children walked or were bused to schools from several residential areas, and with the shift of their children, parent groups, such as PTAs, lost their sense of school identity. There was some effort to constitute parent councils at the zone level, similar to the complex schools' parent council, but the energy and interest for this kind of intradistrict participation was not mobilized, and, in any event, the zone councils were too distant from school-site problems. Within each school there was now a wide range of educational concerns, from those of non-English-speaking children to the gifted and the handicapped. The principal not only had to procure additional resources so as to arrange a little bit of something for everyone, but also had to proceed without the backing of a school constituency.

The resourcefulness of the principal became critical to the viability and quality of the school program. In relation to the teaching staff, the principal's role shifted from that of instructional leader to that of site manager. Ensuring the safety of the children and the building became a key function; it was the principal who met the bus when it arrived in the morning, and who guided the children aboard at the close of the school day. Securing adequate supplies and materials was another task: bargaining, pleading, and illegal exchanges became acceptable strategies at a time when writing up an order was hopeless. Establishing special classes in the school to

---

[12] These figures are estimates provided verbally by the former director of personnel. He claimed that personnel records for these years were not available.

relieve teachers of children with exceptional problems (from speech handicaps to discipline), and encouraging teachers to participate in in-service training sessions, called for advocacy and politicking. Finally, principals had to make special efforts to mobilize community support and interest. But these were not the competencies required for promotion to principalship in the past. Since most of the elementary principals were trained for and tenured in a very different role, it was a rare school that benefited from such management.

School Conditions

School site leadership suffered, and so did physical maintenance. School janitors used to be permanent members of the school staff; they played an important part in maintaining school discipline. Janitors kept an eye on pupils in the yards and corridors, and they saw to it that balls were not thrown through windows, that yards were not littered nor walls defaced. Pupils knew the school janitor and this face-to-face relationship helped control behavior and sustain standards of cleanliness. But at the time of desegregation, to cut back costs, janitors were assigned to crews that covered the maintenance needs of several schools each day. Responsibility for the school building and grounds shifted from a person-centered approach to a segmental one. The effect was that no one was really responsible, and consequently even the newer buildings began to deteriorate.

Conditions in most schools were described as "chaotic." Shortly after the desegregation plan went into effect, the education reporter of the *San Francisco Chronicle* spent several weeks observing a number of schools, and he claimed that while there were no longer "good" versus "bad" schools, a sense of disruption was pervasive.[13] The changes produced by the Horseshoe Plan ruptured the social networks that supported the schools' instructional tasks. Without matrons and janitors to monitor the halls and toilets, these became trouble spots. Disturbances outside the classroom and in the yards had repercussions on classroom behavior. Principals had more discipline problems than they could manage, and also more difficulty contacting and working with parents. Uncivil behavior thus often

---

[13] Ron Moskowitz in the *San Francisco Chronicle*, February 24, 1972. Also by Moskowitz, "San Francisco, California: Where San Francisco Went Wrong," in Harris et al., *The Integration of American Schools* (Boston: Allyn & Bacon, 1975), pp. 62-72.

was overlooked or left up to the individual teacher to discourage. Only the most skillful teachers, by closing the door and concentrating on the immediate situation, could reconstruct the routines that support learning. No wonder the newspaper reporter concluded that "it all depends on the teacher."

But it was unfair and unrealistic to have relied on the capacities of typical teachers for achieving institutional competence. The instructional routines a teacher creates depend on the school climate and the structural conditions of the system. They are further limited by the teacher's personality and talents, and by the youngsters in a given class. There are teachers who thrive on relating to the bright, curious youngsters who respond well to encouragement and can be challenged to excel; their classrooms are lively and filled with creative projects. Other teachers work best with quiet, shy children who learn through careful guidance and patient instruction; in their classrooms, proprieties are important, such as fairness and politeness. Loud, unruly children are a challenge to another type of teacher, one who is dedicated to finding ways to reach and sustain their interest in school; to convert such children into learners provides these teachers with great satisfaction, and their classrooms convey a sense of the mission required to instill self-discipline. All teachers do their best when there is a match between their needs and interests, and those of the children. This is most clearly observed in secondary schools where teachers interact with several tracks of students daily, but with varying success, depending on the match between the groups' characteristics and their own.

To construct a comfortable and educationally viable climate in an elementary classroom composed of diverse pupils posed an entirely new challenge to most teachers at the time the Horseshoe Plan was put into effect. Every teacher knew this implicitly, and it was understood that the task would be less difficult, if perhaps less rewarding, in the primary schools. With no incentives to draw them to the intermediate schools, talented and effective upper-grade teachers chose to work with younger children, leaving the most difficult discipline problems to less experienced staff. Failure of foresight in this matter thus resulted in a weakening of the educational program.

Conclusion

The school district's lack of preparedness with regard to the changes entailed by the elementary school desegregation disrupted school programs and undermined essential conditions of learning. A special purpose organization, such as the elementary division of a large school district, cannot simply be ordered to accomplish social change or to achieve ends such as racial justice. Abstract goals have to be translated into organizational programs, and implemented concretely. Desegregation called for organizational sensitivity and guidance, not mindless compliance with legal formulas. The busing plan, implemented without regard for the social structure and the everyday routines of classroom life, was not sufficient. Maintaining the precarious balance between the goals of order and education is difficult at best. Under the circumstances accompanying elementary school desegregation in San Francisco, it became impossible.

Under the Horseshoe Plan, pupils were mixed, teachers and principals reassigned, and the grade structure and physical plants of the elementary division reorganized. Only the standard curriculum was held constant, on the assumption that the teaching and learning process would continue regardless of the disruption. Quality of instruction, however, is highly sensitive to fluctuations in school conditions. Under the circumstances, only the more remarkable classroom teachers were able to sustain a viable learning climate, and there was no school that had the resources to serve as a model for the others. The complex schools, which might have been looked to for this purpose, were absorbed into the general districtwide plan. The Frederic Burke School, used as a demonstration site by San Francisco State University for purposes of training student-teachers, was also incorporated into the Horseshoe Plan as an ordinary upper-grade school, and its faculty dispersed.

A school climate conducive to learning is a highly fragile outcome, dependent on care and nurturance; it does not just happen. Without such care, schools that had been effective in specific community settings (in middle-class neighborhoods, and in ghetto areas such as Chinatown) were disrupted. The components of those schools (their teachers, principal, pupils, custodial staff, materials) were dispersed and fragmented. No organizational models were available, nor did any emerge, to give direction for an educationally sound adjustment to the new conditions. Instead, the elementary division suffered from disorientation and loss of structural coherence. This entailed frustration and anger at a system that had failed to provide resources, guidance, and leadership. Coping with the difficulties of managing daily tasks consumed energies and frustrated cooperation. Principals and teachers used whatever influence they had to improve their assignments and to secure resources for their own schools and classrooms. A survival mentality prevailed.

5

Opportunism and Drift

Our schools, instead of directing the course of change, are themselves driven by the very forces that are transforming the rest of the social order.[1]

The upheaval within the elementary division sent repercussions throughout the school system. The fragmentation of energies that characterized the elementary schools quickly spread, infecting everyone involved with the San Francisco schools. We now explore several aspects of districtwide disruption and disorder, beginning with the administration of the Horseshoe Plan. Who was responsible for implementation, and how were desegregation policies and procedures managed, evaluated, and changed? What happened when a desegregated class of sixth-grade pupils advanced to the seventh grade? How did elementary desegregation affect the high schools?

We then examine various community reactions to desegregation. How was the plan received not just among the black and white populations, but also within the Chinese, Hispanic, and other ethnic minority communities? Finally, we look at how the politics of desegregation affected the character of school board leadership.

Administrative Neglect and Distraction

The plan for elementary school desegregation was conceived and carried out with minimal regard for preserving educational competence. The administration was so distracted and preoccupied with other problems that it failed to perceive the harmful consequences of its neglect. As noted, no special priority was given to the planning effort. Subsequently, responsibility for

---

[1] George S. Counts, *Dare the School Build a New Social Order?* (N.Y.: Arno Press, 1932/1969), p. 3.

implementation was assigned to a new and quite isolated department, named the Office of Integration. This office was not attached to the elementary division, nor was it under the supervision of Dr. Cobb, the director of community relations. Having been created by outsiders—the Citizens Advisory Committee (CAC)—the Horseshoe Plan was treated as a stepchild within the administration. However, the person appointed to direct the office, Don Johnson, was personally committed to the Horseshoe Plan. He believed it was the best plan, from the point of view of racial balance, and he was determined to enforce it.

Under Johnson, enforcement of the Horseshoe Plan became the special mission and responsibility of the office of integration. The specific requirements of the plan—zone structure, new grade organization, pupil assignments, busing routes—generated the everyday tasks of the office staff. However, neither the director nor the staff had any control over the kinds of difficulties and frustrations experienced at the school sites in the effort to reconstruct viable educational environments. From the outset, these kinds of concerns were divorced from the problems of enforcement, and, as we shall see, advocates of alternative social and educational solutions to the schools' problems, such as bilingual programs, found themselves at odds with the Office of Integration.

A key function of the Office of Integration was policing the traffic in out-of-district transfers. The staff had discretion to issue individual transfers from Horseshoe-assigned schools to students who, for health, family, or other reasons, requested permission to remain in their neighborhood schools. Horseshoe could not accommodate more than a modest number of such transfers, however, without jeopardizing the goal of racial balance. Nevertheless, in 1972-73, deluged with requests, all signed by a few Chinese physicians, Johnson's staff granted hundreds of permits allowing Chinese children to return to their neighborhood schools (a political strategy for ending the school boycott by the Chinatown community). But as the schools in Chinatown became again predominantly Chinese in population, the racial balance of the other schools zoned with them was undermined. Forced to compromise, the Office of Integration was impotent to control the erosion of the Horseshoe Plan.

The director found the situation intolerable, and, charging political interference, he resigned. Johnson claimed that without wholehearted and consistent enforcement, the plan was doomed. The predicament experienced by the Office of Integration typified the dilemma of enforcement in the absence of commitment. Isolated from the educational and political context of implementation, the Office of Integration lacked the resources for accomplishing its mission.

A Faulty Plan Applied Districtwide

Several years prior to elementary desegregation, a group of secondary school principals had recommended to the first Citizens Advisory Committee that the comprehensive high schools, which at that time served racially diverse student bodies, provide the nucleus of a revised set of feeder junior high and elementary schools whose student bodies would then be adjusted so as to improve their racial balance. This recommendation took seriously the need for articulation.between the elementary and secondary schools: first, the social and educational problems created by racial and ethnic diversity in the high schools would be identified; then, various remedies at the senior and junior high school levels would be initiated; finally, programs of the elementary schools would be redesigned so as to facilitate the goals of the secondary schools. This was an educationally based plan for districtwide desegregation. Racial balance at that time, however, was not conceived so strictly, and therefore no changes were proposed for high schools like Galileo, whose Chinese population of 60 percent would have exceeded the plus or minus 15 percent state guidelines.[2]

The second CAC, the committee charged with preparation of the elementary desegregation plan, had no time to think about the secondary schools. In any case, the court had only considered and found racial discrimination in the elementary schools, and the legal order was thus limited to them. The Horseshoe Plan was therefore adopted and implemented without regard for its adaptability to the secondary division. Despite the threat of another lawsuit specifically concerned with the secondary schools,[3] the school board encouraged the administration to move slowly with regard to secondary school desegregation, on the one hand, reasoning that with more time a better plan might have been devised for the elementary schools, and on the other hand, reluctant to commit the district to undertake full desegregation until the elementary case, then under appeal, was decided in court.[4]

---

[2] In 1965, of the 3,000 students enrolled at Galileo, 60 percent or 1,800 were Chinese. SFUSD, "Racial Estimates," November 1965. By 1972, of a total of 2,500 pupils, 50 percent or 1,260 were Chinese. SFUSD, "Data Report," 1972.

[3] *O'Neill* v *SFUSD* (N.D. Calif. May 5, 1972).

[4] Minutes of the Board of Education, July 11, 1972.

Carlos Cornejo, the administrator who replaced Don Johnson as director of integration, lasted only one year in the position. He was frustrated not only by the futility of enforcing the Horseshoe Plan in the face of steady resistance by the community, but also by the difficulties he experienced in the effort to articulate the elementary and secondary schools so as to achieve a totally desegregated school system.

The organizational separation between the elementary and secondary divisions created special difficulties for such articulation. Ordinarily, student assignments to secondary schools (except for Lowell and O'Connell, the academic and vocational high schools) were based on so-called "feeder" patterns: several elementary schools served as "feeder" schools for large and centrally located junior high schools (grades 7-9) and, similarly, several junior highs provided the population for the seven comprehensive high schools (grades 10-12), which were located throughout the city. When the first class of desegregated sixth graders entered junior high in the fall of 1972, they were assigned in exactly this way. Black pupils who had just attended racially balanced schools for the first time reentered a segregated situation and continued their education in predominantly black neighborhood junior high schools.

It took the district over two years to prepare a plan for secondary school desegregation. A key difficulty, given the size and location of the secondary schools, was maintaining continuity of student bodies between the Horseshoe schools and the secondary division. The zones created by Horseshoe had little bearing on the existing feeder patterns and did not take into account the size or location of the secondary schools. There was no readily feasible transition between Horseshoe and the secondary division. But to abandon Horseshoe and totally redesign elementary desegregation appeared too great a task, not to mention a concession of defeat to the program's detractors. On the other hand, to adhere to the zone structure meant perpetuating the flaws and deviations of the elementary plan. A compromise was adopted that was designed to improve, not eliminate, racial imbalance in the secondary schools, and at the same time achieve as much continuity as possible, within the restrictions of plant size and location.

Again, as with the Horseshoe Plan, educational aspects of the new arrangements were not a consideration. To minimize disruption, however, implementation of the secondary school plan was phased in over a three-year period. The pupils who entered desegregated intermediate schools as fourth graders in the fall of

1971 were thus the first group of youngsters assigned to a desegregated seventh grade. Their upper-grade classmates that year (1974-75), now eighth and ninth graders, remained in the same feeder schools to which they had been assigned after completing the sixth grade; only when they moved on to high school was racial balance taken into account in their assignment. 1977 was the first year the entire school district expected to come under planned desegregation. By that time, however, the Horseshoe Plan was being deliberately dismantled.

Among the unanticipated consequences of desegregation, as we have noted, was the use of out-of-district transfers, or as they were later labeled, temporary attendance permits or TAPs. (When the desegregation plan was formally abandoned, there was a further change of nomenclature: the requests were designated "optional enrollment requests.") The number of TAPs issued to the first group of desegregated seventh graders was greater than the number of pupils scheduled to be bused, and therefore predominantly black schools, such as Pelton Junior High, remained segregated (71 percent black). Every transfer request was honored.

The Office of Integration's third director, recognizing the futility of trying to enforce the Horseshoe Plan and achieve articulation between desegregated elementary and secondary schools, announced a retreat from these aims. Thus the district's originally weak commitment to these goals dissipated even further. The monitoring and supervision of the pupil reassignment plan became a hollow operation: by 1975, even if all pupils in the district were compelled to attend the school to which they were assigned, the goals of racial balance could not be realized, given the basic flaws of the original plan.[5]

Thus undermined, the policy of school desegregation became blurred and ineffectual. The trappings of the Horseshoe and secondary school plans continued. Annual reports were dutifully prepared detailing the extent of the deviations from the goals of racial balance. But compliance was no longer taken seriously. The number of racially unbalanced elementary schools steadily increased: from 38 in the fall of 1971 to 43 or almost half the

---

[5] SFUSD, "Status Report," January 1975, p. 90. Of the 43 elementary schools that were out of balance, 14 were predominantly Chinese, 12 were black, nine Hispanic, and five white. In 1975, of a total student body of 72,400 the percentages of these major racial groups were Chinese 16 percent, black 30 percent, Hispanic 14.5 percent, and white 25 percent.

elementary schools in 1974. Similarly, despite desegregation, 10 out of 17 junior high schools remained racially unbalanced.[6]

Other Agendas

During these years (1971-75), the matter of racial balance was only one of several major issues confronting the school administration. Other concerns competed, mitigating against enforcement efforts. One such concern was the safety of school buildings.

School Reconstruction. In April 1971, shortly after the court announced its decision regarding school desegregation, the school board's buildings and grounds committee reported that 63 of the district's schools failed to meet the state's earthquake safety standards. The immediate closure of six highly unsafe structures was recommended.[7] A year later, following an extensive school survey, it was definitively announced that 56 schools (four high schools, eight junior highs, and 44 elementary schools) were unsafe and, unless repaired, all of them would have to be closed.[8] That fall, after repairs forced the closing of three elementary schools, elaborate preparations began for a major bond issue to raise the funds necessary to repair all earthquake-vulnerable buildings in the district.[9] This included plans for relocating hundreds of pupils who would be displaced by the reconstruction of unsafe schools.[10] Thus, at the same time that the Office of Integration was revising the elementary school assignment plan for the following fall, staff of the assistant superintendent in charge of buildings and grounds were selecting sites for the first phase of a major reconstruction project.

School safety took precedence over racial balance. Despite its flaws, the Horseshoe Plan continued to be implemented without major changes in the zone structure or feeder arrangements in anticipation of the significant reallocation of pupils entailed by the closing of 40 elementary schools.[11] Suggested changes to improve the effectiveness of the desegregation plan, such as reassigning children residing in naturally integrated neighborhoods to their local schools, were out of the question. Of 14 elementary schools located in racially diverse neighborhoods, seven were on the list for demolition and reconstruction.[12]

---

[6] Ibid., p. 10.

[7] *San Francisco Chronicle,* April 23, 1971.

[8] Minutes of the Board of Education, June 15, 1972.

[9] Minutes of the Board of Education, October 10 and November 14, 1972.

[10] Minutes of the Board of Education, January 9, 1973.

[11] Minutes of the Integration Committee, May 16, 1973.

[12] Minutes of the Integration Committee, November 5, 1972.

In November 1973, the city passed a $37.8 million bond issue for school reconstruction. While the school board was considering proposals for secondary school desegregation, administrators were putting the final touches on the plans and the timeline for school closings, double sessions, and the so-called "staging" of school populations at alternative sites, all of which would significantly interfere with the school assignments aimed at improving racial balance. Decisions about school closings were made on the basis of engineering and contractors' recommendations without involving the school communities affected.

Adherence to the aims of racial balance was provided for but in a most mechanical manner, as follows: Based on Horseshoe's pupil assignment scheme, classrooms of pupils from one of the 44 elementary schools designated for reconstruction were moved intact, teachers and books included, to various other buildings with sufficient space to "stage" them for the duration of the reconstruction. These other classrooms were not necessarily in the same zone. In blatant violation of one of Horseshoe's principal guidelines, namely, that the burden of busing be shared and kept to a minimum, children from unsafe schools were bused all around the city. Moreover, because construction timelines did not necessarily coincide with the school year calendar, classes were moved sporadically; there was no concern for continuity of school routines.

Schools placed on double sessions remained under one principal's supervision, but classrooms dispersed to other schools were temporarily assigned to the staging site principal. In Zone II, for example, pupils from four of the seven primary schools were transported to four other schools during the reconstruction of the unsafe buildings; only one of these schools was in the same zone. However, administrative juggling made it possible for pupils from two intermediate schools in the same zone to be housed in available space in the three remaining primary schools.[13]

The racial makeup of schools during this period was one thing on paper where, despite the actual distribution of pupils, what counted was their original Horseshoe assignment; in reality, because

---

[13] In my interview with Mrs. Lilienthal (school board member from 1958 to 1972), she related a painful personal experience with the school desegregation plan. Her six-year-old granddaughter, after a successful start in a Zone II primary school, to which she was bused from her neighborhood, was reassigned the following year (during school reconstruction) to a Zone III school on the opposite side of the city. When this happened, her parents, worried about what further changes might occur, decided it was time to place her in a private school.

racial balance depended on the effects of the makeup of specific classrooms at the relocation sites, its extent was not strictly known. School safety took precedence over racial balance, and, one might add, justifiably so. However, the school safety program could have served as an opportunity for redesigning the original plan, attending to its basic flaws and ameliorating some of the distress it had produced. Instead, school reconstruction introduced yet another cycle of disruptions for pupils and school staff to cope with.

One reason for keeping the Horseshoe zone structure intact, at least on paper (because in reality the "staging" of classrooms throughout the city reflected indifference to the zone concept), was that it had become a known quantity to the administration. The potential threat to centralized authority that the zone concept embodied was never realized: zone administrators became defined as staff, not line officials and their powers thus remained limited and temporary; parent zone councils similarly were not delegated any real decision-making responsibilities. Not surprisingly, the costs of the busing program doubled during the reconstruction, even as the number of empty seats multiplied and the bus runs became increasingly one-way, moving minority children out of ghetto areas without bringing in nonminority children. Despite the additional expense, however, retaining the zone structure helped the administration maintain its control.

School reconstruction, however, was time-limited. Once completed (it took approximately a year to remodel each elementary building), the program came to an end. All the schools affected became safer and more attractive sites for learning. Moreover, the success of the 1973 bond issue was positive reassurance that voters still cared about the public schools. Nevertheless, for an already weary and disoriented school community, the disruption could not have happened at a less opportune time. Following as soon as it did the 1971 upheaval of desegregation, it drew energies away from the purposes of this major project, and deepened tendencies toward fragmentation and drift.

Special Programs. Another distraction on the administration's agenda during this time was the district-wide development of special programs. In part a response to the difficulties of coping with the heterogeneity of the desegregated classrooms, in part a response to previously unrecognized educational needs, there was a sudden and amazingly rapid growth of special programs, especially in the elementary schools.

Prior to 1970 there were two major types of special education, both funded by state aid: one for children classified as educable mentally retarded (EMR), and one for children identified on the basis of individual intelligence tests as gifted. A small number of emotionally disturbed children also were provided special attention in a program for the educationally handicapped (EH). Teachers for the gifted and EH classes required no special license and were selected on the basis of interest and seniority. Only the EMR children, a majority of whom were black, were separated out and grouped in distinctive classes, taught by specially credentialed staff. Starting in 1971, however, concurrent with the implementation of Horseshoe, 13 so-called "total impact" classes were established, approximately two per zone, to meet the educational needs of gifted children, most of whom were white. The following year, the number of classes doubled, and by 1974, one out of every two elementary schools had a special class for gifted children.[14]
For purposes of enrolling in such a class, TAPs were readily dispensed.

There was also a rapid increase in the number of special classes for children identified by psychological tests as EH. Whereas in 1965 the total number of EH children identified was only 460, and their needs were met by special counseling or small group sessions, in 1971, 900 EH children were targeted; by 1972, there were 1,200. Special "total impact" classes were provided for these children, such that every elementary school had a program either for EH or EMR children, or for a new classification of children with learning problems who did not technically qualify for either of these programs, so-called learning disability grouped (LDG) children. Thus, ironically, while desegregation was being implemented with regard to racial differences, a new system of segregation was being

---

[14] The district received approximately $100 per gifted child from the state to help support its programs. In the 1974-75 school year, the racial composition of gifted classes was as follows:

Racial Composition of Enrollment in Gifted Classes		
	% Gifted	% Districtwide
Black	15.8	31.2
White	46.0	24.9
Hispanic	7.4	24.9
Chinese	17.5	14.1

Source: San Francisco Human Rights Commission, "Report on Programs for the Gifted," 1975, p. 4.

instituted with regard to learning abilities. This system reinstated an unofficial, educationally based racial segregation.

Concurrently added to the curriculum were special programs for the increasing numbers of non-English-speaking children in the schools. Some classes provided bilingual education in various languages, including Chinese, Japanese, Korean, Filipino, and Spanish. There were also classes in English as a Second Language (ESL), and intensive education centers for newly arrived immigrant children. These special programs were developed partially in response to another lawsuit against the school district.[15]

Under Title I of ESEA there was still another type of special program, compensatory education. This was intended for children from low-income families. After 1971 these targeted children were no longer concentrated in ghetto schools, and therefore the federal funds designated to supplement their schooling were widely distributed. But the administration decided to put "comp ed" programs only in schools containing 30 percent or more children eligible for Title I. This meant that many children who met the guidelines, but who were located in schools with fewer than 30 percent eligible pupils (approximately one-third of the total), did not receive the program's benefits. The dilution of the impact of Title I was a consequence of the guidelines used in drawing up the Horseshoe Plan, which did not take into account family income. However, Title I programs, where they did exist, were some compensation for low-income black and non-English-speaking children in schools that, in spite of Horseshoe, remained racially unbalanced.

Other kinds of special programs included: (1) children's centers, prekindergarten classes providing childcare for working mothers; and (2) early childhood education (ECE) programs, a state pilot program begun in 1973 to encourage parent involvement at the school sites. In addition there were alternative "community" schools for grades K-6, organized by parents and teachers interested in nontraditional methods; one school was initiated in 1971, and two others soon followed.

The Office of Integration was besieged by requests from parents seeking transfers into schools with special programs. Granting exceptions to Horseshoe assignments was allowed, encouraging expansion of special programs at the expense of racial balance. While each program offered some special benefit to a particular

---

[15] *Lau* v *Nichols*. This case is discussed at length in the next chapter. The defendant was Alan Nichols, president of the school board at the time the suit was filed.

child, the proliferation of programs resulted in fragmentation of the schools as a common enterprise.

To receive the benefits of bilingual education, for example, Hispanic and Asian children were separated from their black and white peers. Similarly, gifted and other special education children were set apart, recreating racial division. The staff of the elementary division likewise became separated into two competing groups: classroom teachers and special program teachers. Regular classroom teachers complained about the minimal attention and resources they received. Yet they were also relieved to have difficult and troublesome children removed from the classrooms. Special teachers, on the other hand, also complained because, along with their programs, they were shifted frequently from school to school. Their frustrations stemmed from an inability to develop satisfying staff relationships; they felt relegated to marginal status. Finally, various community groups that once had joined in support of civil rights and more equal educational opportunities for all children became splintered, and found themselves at odds over the distribution of resources. Special programs fostered special interests and undermined cooperation.

Accommodating all these special programs, as well as school reconstruction and desegregation, constituted a remarkable administrative juggling act. Safer schools and special classes were responsible actions, but they undermined desegregation. Moreover, while special education had advantages, especially for reaching non-English-speaking children, separating out gifted children deprived their classmates of the stimulation bright children can provide. (There is little evidence to indicate that their education or, for that matter, the education of EH, EMR, or LDG children, improves in a total impact situation.) However, the existence of such classes in almost every school put pressure on the classroom teacher to identify and label children for testing and possible placement in such classes, increasing expectations regarding their deviation from normal classroom conduct. It also diminished the teacher's sense of responsibility for reaching out to each child in the class. There is no question that individualized instruction is more difficult to achieve in desegregated classrooms. Special programs offered a way out for teachers whose efforts were not valued, supported, or guided during this period of extreme stress and dislocation. The school system sustained its juggling act but lost sight of the fundamental aims of the learning situation. This neglect undermined the schools' educational competence.

Erosion of Discipline and Community Support

Discipline is a chronic problem for schools. The disruption of school reconstruction, the proliferation of special programs, and the difficulties of enforcing desegregation had serious consequences for maintaining order. In the early seventies, the erosion of standards of conduct was, to many parents, the schools' most serious problem.

Parents of elementary pupils naturally worried about the safety of their children on the buses. In response, the district hired bus monitors to restrain unruly behavior and ensure safety during the daily ride to and from school. This considerably increased the expense of transportation, but was understood as an essential assurance for concerned parents.[16]

After the bus ride, however, in classrooms and on school grounds, safety continued to be a problem, as manifested by a dramatic rise in the rate of suspensions in the elementary schools. Suspension is a serious punishment, reserved for extreme misconduct, such as carrying a deadly weapon, assault, or arson; notice of suspension places a permanent black mark on a student's school record. A year prior to desegregation 490 suspensions were issued to sixth graders, 70 percent of them to black pupils.[17] But once desegregation began, the number of suspensions tripled, gaining the attention of the school board. But assuring safety on the buses was much easier than resolving the problem of discipline at the school sites.[18]

A certain amount of intractable behavior, most teachers agree, is inescapable. Apart from hard-core cases, however, the typical teacher tries to establish a classroom climate that discourages disruptive behavior without destroying individual initiative. But when pupils come to school with negative self-images and hostile attitudes, this objective is difficult to accomplish. Upper-grade pupils following desegregation, many believing they had little to lose in challenging authority, were always testing the teacher. When teachers permitted such testing, their classrooms experienced constant interruptions and stress. However, punishing every offense quickly exhausted teachers' small store of punitive resources, and did so at

---

[16] Minutes of the Board of Education, May 18, 1972.

[17] SFUSD, "ESAA Proposal," May 1973.

[18] Minutes of the Board of Education, February 21, 1973. Also the San Francisco Human Rights Commission, "Report on Suspensions," November 7, 1974, p. 6.

the price of securing cooperation in classroom activities. A small number of difficult children could be controlled, but large groups of hostile youngsters terrorized certain classes and even entire schools. In others, resorting to stringent controls converted ordinary schools into reform schools.[19]

A comparative survey of student attitudes during the 1972-73 school year (one year after the desegregation of the elementary schools), found the self-concept and motivation of black elementary school pupils strongly negative.[20] There was also no denying the rise in suspension rates, nor the evidence of continued low achievement of black pupils: the reading scores of black sixth graders were the lowest in the district.[21] Black community leaders complained that the district's liberal dispensation of TAPs contributed to these outcomes. Spokesmen repeatedly stated their opposition to the transfer policy, complaining that it resulted in one-way busing and diminished educational opportunities for black pupils.[22]

Given that the majority of black pupils did poorly in school, and that parents from the black community viewed with contempt the district's enforcement of desegregation, the discipline problems mounted. In the junior and senior high schools, the inability to maintain control became a major source of frustration. Violence, arson, and continuous classroom disruptions became increasingly serious, despite district efforts to separate out the more dangerous and disturbed youngsters. (Two small junior high schools and a senior high school were created for this purpose as alternative schools, and EH and LDG programs were introduced into the secondary schools.) Although juveniles represented only 22.5 percent of the city population, in 1974 they accounted for 36.7 percent of the total arrests for felony offenses (major crimes against persons and property). The police department estimated that 85 to 95 percent of purse snatchings involved teenagers and that 10 percent of San Francisco juveniles had police contact.[23]

---

[19] Various studies confirm these findings. See Mary H. Metz, *Classrooms and Corridors* (Berkeley: University of California Press, 1978), and the classic study of Ralph White and Ronald Lippitt, *Autocracy and Democracy* (N.Y.: Harper & Row, 1960).

[20] Jane Mercer, "Evaluating Integrated Elementary Education," unpublished paper prepared for the SFUSD, September 1973.

[21] In 1972, compared to a norm of 6.8, black pupils' reading scores averaged 4.6, while white pupils' was 7.04. SFUSD, "ESAA Proposal," 1973, p. 58.

[22] SFUSD, Minutes of the Integration Committee, January 17 and February 21, 1973. Also Minutes of the Board of Education, January 24, 1974.

[23] "San Francisco's Future: A Study of Youth Resources," report prepared for the San Francisco Junior League, issued by the San Francisco Mental Health Associa-

At the urging of the police Community Relations Division, and with funds provided by the California Council on Criminal Justice and the Comprehensive Employment and Training Act (CETA), in 1974 the district hired over 50 security guards to patrol the halls and yards of the secondary schools so as to contain and minimize disruptions.[24] Parents consistently complained about student injuries, lack of notification regarding dangerous conditions, and unsafe and unsanitary buildings, but it was not until a student was stabbed and murdered that preventive action was taken. At that time, the district revised its policy regarding teacher safety and also began reimbursing teachers not only for damages, but also for theft of personal property. Hundreds of teachers submitted requests for such reimbursement, and provisions for teacher safety became a standard negotiating item.[25]

An enterprising newspaper reporter spent three weeks in a city high school disguised as a student. Excerpts of his observations suggest a "prison-like" atmosphere, complete with an undercurrent of violence and indifferent teachers:

> I arrived for my civics class to find the students waiting in the hall. Vandals had sealed the door shut by pouring wax in the keyholes. Class was canceled . . . . Another day I saw a student sitting in the office, waiting for an ambulance; he'd been seriously hurt in a schoolyard fight . . . . During one of my classes a student hopped on a skateboard and rode out of the room. The teacher never looked up, nor did he say a word . . . . Twenty-four students were enrolled in the class, but average daily attendance was nine . . . . One day the teacher assigned homework, but no one bothered to do it . . . . The student body is made up of blacks, whites, Chicanos, Chinese and Filipinos. The whites linger around the steps from the courtyard to the third floor, the blacks near a second-floor entrance, a Chicano gang of about 50 members hangs around the courtyard. "You just don't mess with them, man," I was told.[26]

The 1973-74 annual report of major school incidents included 35 cases of assault with a deadly weapon, or approximately one per week; the same number of arsons; over 100 assaults against school staff; as well as 500 reportedly unprovoked attacks on students.[27]

---

tion, May 1976. San Francisco was not unusual in the amount of juvenile crime.

24 Minutes of the Board of Education, October 22, 1974.
25 Minutes of the Board of Education, August 13, 1974.
26 *San Francisco Examiner*, October 6-8, 1975.
27 SFUSD, "Annual Report of Major School Incidents", 1973-74.

Financial costs associated with violence and vandalism skyrocketed: the cost of liability insurance quadrupled due to the large awards for student injuries, and the costs of repairing damaged buildings and grounds was such as to prohibit routine maintenance.[28] Other costs, not measurable in dollars, but with discernible effects on the quality of school life for those who continued to attend and to operate the system, also mounted, although not all were affected. For teachers and children in the gifted classes, for example, most of them white, life was tolerably pleasant. Likewise, Lowell High School, which continued to accept pupils on the basis of achievement in elementary and junior high school, maintained high academic standards and kept its reputation for excellence. But for children assigned to EH classes, anxiety was a prevalent response—indeed the highest levels of school anxiety were found among black and Hispanic children who composed the majority population within these classes.[29] As for the students responsible for the widespread violence, of whom two out of three were black,[30] their future prospects remained as bleak as the unemployment rates for black youth. A majority of students and teachers were consigned to daily life in a school system under siege.

Community Response

The impact of districtwide disruption and disorder was felt especially in the black community of San Francisco. The pursuit of integration had bound together middle- and lower-class black families; its implementation drove them apart. Middle-class families joined the flight from the public schools, while the Hunters Point community adopted a posture of resistance to the district and, like the Chinese, began demanding TAPs to keep their children in neighborhood schools with special programs. Black leadership did not support the extension of desegregation to the secondary schools. The lawsuit filed by the NAACP in 1972 was not pressed, and consequently the school district desegregated the secondary schools voluntarily, not under court order. Not haste, but lack of political will and administrative neglect were responsible for the confusion accompanying desegregation of the junior and senior high schools.

---

[28] SFUSD, Minutes of the Buildings and Grounds Committee, October 25, 1972.

[29] Mercer, "Evaluating Integrated Elementary Education."

[30] San Francisco Human Rights Commission, "Report on SFUSD Suspensions," 1974, p. 6.

The dismay and disappointment of the black community had its counterpart in the liberal white community where hopes for racial justice and the desire for active participation in school affairs dissipated in frustration. A few parents, the remnants of the civil rights movement, became attached to the alternative community schools. Abandoning the effort to achieve "quality/equality" education in all schools, these bands of former activists focused their energies on improving the schools attended by their own children. They strived to make their schools places where individual differences were respected and personal talents recognized and given expression in the organization of learning, justifying their actions as setting an example for the future. This small-scale effort consumed all the energies for civil rights that remained.

The majority of parents had little choice but to endure the schools' difficulties and to buffer as best they could their children's exposure to the hazards and miseries of school life. Their concerns, like those of the remaining staff, were focused on trying to sustain faith in public education, despite the turmoil and disappointment of desegregation.

To keep community spirits up, the district's Office of Public Information tried to emphasize positive aspects of desegregation, such as the introduction of multiethnic curriculum materials, the availability of bilingual school aides, expansion of special programs, and the like. But as achievement scores fell, teachers and parents knew that the curriculum was being neglected. Danger and violence in the schools were visible, and support for public education was dissolving. Desegregation, school reconstruction, and the proliferation of special programs had disrupted school-community involvement, and the redistribution of pupils, teachers, and administrators fragmented and diluted the substance of the school program.

Between 1970 and 1975, school population fell 16 percent (from 82,033 to 68,862), and the racial composition of the schools shifted markedly. The proportion of white students declined from 46 percent in 1965 to 25 percent in 1975. During the years following desegregation, black students also began leaving the schools in significant numbers, but their proportion nevertheless grew from 25 percent in 1965, to 30 percent in 1975.[31] Upper- and middle-class families able to afford private schools increasingly withdrew their

---

[31] SFUSD, "Status Report of the Office of Integration," 1975; also "Fall Enrollment Report," 1975.

children.[32] Consequently, some schools had to be closed and new patterns of pupil and teacher assignment drawn up annually, only to be repeatedly discarded.

Financial Setbacks

Declining enrollments decimated the school budget. Throughout this period, in part due to state legislation limiting school revenues, budget and management difficulties beset the administration and school board, while the staff faced constant threats of layoffs. In 1972, the state legislature began passing a series of property tax laws with the dual aim of relieving the local property tax burden on homeowners and equalizing the distribution of school revenues statewide. Until then, San Francisco schools had been supported primarily by local property tax revenues. Because the property tax base in San Francisco, a major center of commerce and industry, was substantial, a relatively low tax rate was sufficient to raise school revenues that afforded a per pupil expenditure far exceeding the statewide average. In 1973, for example, assessed property value amounted to $36,023 per pupil; with a tax rate of 3.62 per $100 assessed value, the school district raised revenues of $1,934 per pupil. But state legislation to comply with the landmark *Serrano* decision[33] gradually diminished the district's reliance upon local property tax revenues. In 1978 the San Francisco tax rate was reduced to 1.21 per $100 assessed value.[34] Restricted resources together with inflationary costs resulted in annual budgetary nightmares.

Had the aftermath of school desegregation occurred in more tranquil and affluent times, it might have minimized the divisiveness and bitterness that accompanied efforts to achieve compliance with the court order. More money could have eased the situation, even if it did not resolve the underlying problems. As it happened, however, an increasing scarcity of resources compounded and aggravated the schools' difficulties.

---

[32] Despite declining birth rates, the parochial system maintained a fairly steady clientele. The Archdiocese schools experienced only a slight decline from a population of 24,000 in 1970 to 22,500 students in 1975. (Figures supplied by the Archdiocese in 1975.)

[33] *Serrano* v *Priest*, 5 Cal 3rd 584 (1971).

[34] San Francisco Public Schools Commission Report, "Fiscal Future," 1976.

School Board "Meddling" in Administration

The politics of desegregation did not cease with the filing of the NAACP lawsuit in 1970. Despite the intervention of the court, conflict over the extent of the school district's obligations with respect to civil rights and racial equality continued. Desegregation was a key issue in the mayoral election of 1971. The incumbent mayor, Joseph Alioto, a foe of busing, used the occasion to call for the resignation of Superintendent Shaheen. Also, Alioto, who had not been able to restrain his own nominees on the school board from supporting the two school complexes, now actively campaigned in behalf of a charter amendment replacing the appointed school board with an elected body.

In November, two months after the implementation of the Horseshoe Plan, the charter amendment passed and the old school board began to dissolve. Two members (Nichols and Glass) had already resigned. In selecting their replacements, the mayor had been careful to choose individuals acceptable to an antibusing constituency and, in June 1972, they were among the seven members elected to the school board by a public still angry at the political ineptness of the old board and disgusted with the so-called "Shaheenigans" of the superintendent.[35]

The first year of elementary school desegregation, 1971-72, found no improvement in a school administration preoccupied with internal problems. Despite Alioto's attack, Shaheen clung to his position, refusing to be the sacrificial offering, but he later relented and, in exchange for a substantial settlement, accepted the termination of his contract. Meanwhile Deputy Superintendent Reiterman and two other senior administrators assumed control of the day-to-day operation of the schools. In the summer of 1972, with the mayor's approval, a new superintendent, Dr. Steven Morena, a native San Franciscan and City College administrator, was selected.[36] The elected school board now began to take an active part in school

---

[35] In its annual report, the Grand Jury blasted Shaheen for administrative mismanagement, and the charge was picked up by the local papers. "Report of the Grand Jury," 1971. The new board members were mayoral appointees George Chinn, the first Chinese-American to serve on the school board (replacing Laurel Glass); Dr. Eugene Hopp, a former chairman of the local Commonwealth Club's education committee (replacing Alan Nichols); and a new labor representative, John Kidder. Also elected were Lucille Abrahamson, Lee Dolson, Charlie Mae Haynes, and David Sanchez.

[36] Minutes of the School Board, August 25, 1972.

affairs, taking advantage of Morena's lack of school district experience and the administration's confusion, as well as the general upheaval.

An elaborate committee structure was established whereby the myriad details of school management were carefully scrutinized before resolutions regarding their adoption were presented to the full board for approval.[37] Whereas previous boards had delegated their formal powers to the superintendent and the professional staff, the newly elected board took its public mandate seriously. At various times individual board members proposed their own budgets, administrative reorganization plans, and teacher assignment procedures as well as various special programs.[38]

Failure of leadership had cost the appointed board its legitimacy, and led to its demise. Electoral support, however, was no guarantee that public purposes would be better served or gain in authority. Some basic patterns of board decision making, set in motion by the appointed board, persisted. Individual board members had already begun to speak for special constituencies, and on their behalf, to challenge and frequently defy the administration. While the full spectrum of community differences may not have been represented by appointed board members, there was sufficient diversity to generate heated debates and bitterness over controversial decisions, such as proceeding with the two school complexes, appealing the *Johnson* decree, and supporting administrative "deselection." The elected board merely formalized this pattern. Given the highly charged political climate, neither type of governance structure was able to insulate the schools from excesses of public opinion, nor to buffer them from the pressures of special interests. On the contrary, the board served as a mirror reflecting community differences and lack of consensus. Caught up in the maelstrom of events, the board became increasingly shortsighted and neglectful of its institutional responsibilities.

The complexities of school management required the benefits of bureaucratic organization, such as an explicit public purpose, clear jurisdictions and channels of communication, merit-based personnel appointments, and routinized decision making governed by

---

37 Minutes of the School Board, October 10, 1972.

38 For example, Lee Dolson developed his own budget, Mr. Kidder prepared a teacher transfer policy and administrative chart, and Dr. Hopp was responsible for developing the total impact gifted program. Minutes of the School Board, May 11, 1972; August 9, 1972; April 19, 1975; and May 6, 1975.

rules.[39] Disarray and pressures for greater flexibility of response, however, diverted attention from these essentials of organization and eroded the line between administration and policy.

Members of the elected board aspired not only to set policy, but to direct the administration of the public schools. But unlike staff, the board lacked continuity of membership: of the seven persons elected in 1972, three were replaced in 1974, and by 1976 only two of the original group remained. Also, unlike the office of the superintendent, the presidency of the board was a nominal position that rotated among the members and carried no special authority. Finally, without independent staff of its own, the board remained dependent on the resources of the administration. It could and did hire outside consultants, and even relied on citizen committees to perform complicated staff work, such as the Horseshoe Plan. But these attempts to circumvent the staff usually backfired because their implementation depended on the cooperation of the administration.

Yet despite their lack of qualifications and resources, board members persisted in efforts to oversee the details of school operation. Their intrusion was noted by outgoing Superintendent Shaheen, who charged that board interference had hampered his administration.[40] Similar charges were made by Superintendent Morena, who, despite strong board support for his appointment, was unable to gain sufficient independent authority for his administration.

The burdens of staffing the numerous board committees, while juggling the major projects undertaken by the district during the early seventies—desegregation, reconstruction, special programs—strained administrative capacities. Morena suffered a heart attack, and subsequently urged the board to appoint Deputy Superintendent Lane DeLara outright. But preferring the confusion of official leadership, the board refused to do so and instead undertook a lengthy search for a successor, effectively forestalling an appointment for two years.[41] Meanwhile, administrative burdens took their toll on other senior staff members as well. Transfers and resignations for health reasons became common practice, causing

---

[39] These are Weber's famous elements of bureaucracy. See H. H. Gerth and C. Wright Mills, *From Max Weber: Essays in Sociology* (London: Oxford University Press, 1946), Ch. 8.

[40] Minutes of the School Board, August 25, 1972.

[41] Minutes of the School Board, June 6, 1974. Robert Alioto, no relation to the mayor, was not appointed until June 17, 1975.

confusion and uncertainty within the central office.[42] From 1971 to 1975, the school district was in effect leaderless, and its response to both routine and critical problems of school policy and management was guided not by policy, but by opportunism.

"Opportunism is the pursuit of immediate, short-run advantages . . . inadequately controlled by considerations of principle and ultimate consequence."[43] Lacking leadership, the district became vulnerable to the demands of special interests. Without purpose and clearly defined goals, there were no grounds for establishing priorities. Decisions were reached not on the basis of principles, but through the force of pressure politics.

Outcomes of Opportunism

The handling of the annual budget illustrates the pitfalls of the board's shortsightedness. Normally, the protection of scarce resources is almost a reflex action on the part of administration. In the face of the potential threat to school revenues posed by the *Serrano* decision, one might have assumed that on this essential issue the school district would muster itself and develop a strategy to defend its interests.[44] At the very least, the board could have taken the advice of management consultants, hired during Shaheen's final months, who had recommended that the district establish an Office of Budget and Management for long-range fiscal planning. But the board refused to approve the appointment of a staff director, and instead attempted to serve as its own budget manager. Then, despite state action that dictated a cautious approach to raising local property taxes,[45] the board, to support the 1972-73 school budget, proposed a tax rate increase. At the last minute, however, in response to the mayor's objections, special reserve funds were called upon instead. A politically undesirable action was avoided,

---

[42] Among the transferees were Carlos Cornejo, the second director of the Office of Integration, and George Karonsky, administrative assistant. Resignations included Irving Breyer, the district's legal counsel; Associate Superintendent of Instruction Howard; Associate Superintendent of Business Egly; and in subsequent years the director of the elementary division, Isadore Pivnick; George Boisson, Director of Personnel; and Associate Superintendent Reiterman.

[43] Philip Selznick, *Leadership in Administration* (Evanston, Ill.: Harper & Row, 1957), p. 143.

[44] *Serrano* v *Priest*, 5 Cal 3rd 584 (1971). This decision called for remedies to the inequities of per pupil expenditures in California, such that school financing would not depend on local property taxes.

[45] SB 90, passed by the legislature in 1972, limited the amount of money a school district could raise per pupil.

but the underlying problems of inflation, the multiplication of special programs, and the need for long-range fiscal planning were not addressed.

Over the next few years, substantial budget increases combined with reduced enrollments to produce a serious fiscal crisis. Under Morena, the board hired another consulting firm to develop a management system, but continued to reject the appointment of candidates for director, despite Morena's complaint that his staff lacked the qualifications to institute fiscal controls. At one point, he admitted that the administration could not even determine the exact number of certificated staff on the payroll.[46] Additional consultants were brought in to conduct a fiscal and position audit, solving the immediate problem, but there was still no director of budget and management, and no management system. The issue of administrative incapacity came up repeatedly, but the board refused to concede any of its fiscal powers.[47] Instead, submitting to the pressures of various interest groups, the board kept adding new programs, forcing the district to neglect routine building maintenance and to eliminate programs that lacked visible, political support.

During the 1974-75 school year, the district faced a serious deficit. A hiring freeze was put into effect, but the superintendent complained that efforts to contain costs, given the lack of priorities and the failure to develop a long-range fiscal strategy, were undermined by the board. Each board member had particular preferences, and all were included in the budget as it was finally adopted, despite the superintendent's strong objections.[48] The hiring freeze meant that two key administration positions would remain vacant (the director of the budget and an assistant superintendent of instruction), and that the volume of internal transfers to fill vacant positions would increase.[49] (Forty classroom teachers were appointed to fill positions funded by federal and state categorical aid programs.) However, the district was also forced to hire an

---

[46] Minutes of the School Board, November 14, 1972.

[47] Minutes of the School Board, December 19, 1972; March 27, 1973; and April 23, 1974.

[48] Board member Abrahamson supported funds for art projects, the volunteer program, career counseling, and the Exploratorium; Mrs. Haynes was an advocate of the Teacher Learning Center. Father Reed favored school athletics. Lee Dolson liked more data processing equipment; Kidder wanted an Asian-American specialist; Sanchez asked for more health and bilingual aides, etc. Minutes of the School Board, August 6, 1974.

[49] Minutes of the School Board, August 27, 1974.

additional 26 licensed bilingual and special education teachers to satisfy special program requirements.[50]

The district's budget crisis was compounded by the needs of these special programs. An anguished administrator described the dilemma he faced in the effort to meet federal program comparability requirements. Under Title I, schools were required to equalize per pupil expenditures before using federal supplementary funds for compensatory education. (Equalization refers to the expectation that there be uniform allocation of instructional staff and services per pupil, regardless of the size of the school or its educational needs.) But strictly preserving the ratios meant sacrificing administrative flexibility to accommodate the special needs of small schools and Title I eligible pupils throughout the district. Small schools tended to have higher staffing ratios because, regardless of enrollment, every school needed a clerk and a principal, and every school also received, according to need, the services of a librarian, speech therapist, psychologist, and curriculum specialists. Small schools thus distorted the basis for calculating comparability. Moreover, after desegregation, federal resources followed only a certain portion of Title I eligible pupils, those located in schools with concentrations of 30 percent or more. If the district tried to provide special assistance to pupils with educational needs in non-Title I schools, this also upset the comparability ratios. In addition, annual changes in the designation of Title I schools, due to reconstruction and pupil mobility, made it difficult to maintain consistent ratios. Together with the budget crunch, this constraint frustrated administrative efforts to sustain educational standards.[51]

By 1975, problems of school management began to overwhelm members of the board as well as staff. The committee system suffered from overwork and unexpected delays in the search for a new superintendent. In desperation, a group of concerned administrators urged the board to retain Morena, despite his failing health, so as to provide some measure of continuity. Their proposal was rejected. The board wanted new leadership, but to avoid criticism for making a poor choice, delegated the selection of a new superintendent, historically the central responsibility and prerogative of the school board, first to an outside consultant and later to a citizen committee.[52] Once again, weakness and opportunism prevailed.

50 Minutes of the School Board, September 24, 1974.

51 SFUSD, "Comparability Report," memo by Deputy Superintendent DeLara to the Board of Education, June 24, 1975.

52 Minutes of the School Board, March 25, 1975 and May 6, 1975.

Adrift in a Sea of Special Interests

The problems of budget management and the inability to set priorities left the schools with dwindling resources and no sense of future direction. Under the elected system, the administration lost the confidence of the board and the community, leaving the schools to cope on a day-to-day basis, staff and students ever on edge in anticipation of the next crisis.

As long as there existed a vocal and persistent pressure group, the board felt obliged to respond. Attention was paid to representatives of the zone councils, teacher organizations, and to community groups of every sort, regardless of whether their intentions were to complain, promote, or insist. The concerns of the administration—avoiding budget deficits, maintaining school property, issuing supplies in a timely manner, and sustaining educational standards—came to represent just another special interest, no different from other complaints and demands. Support for the administration's concerns amounted to no more than a "pet project" for one or two members of the board, along with girls' athletics, Japanese bilingual studies, drug education, ROTC, and countless other preferences.[53] The concept of "priority" lost its meaning.

The urgency of special interest issues distracted attention, diverted energies, and fragmented the sense of common purpose. In a context of commonality, differences—even conflicts—can be accommodated. But as this context becomes shattered, a plurality of interests gives rise to divisiveness. Thus reductions of staff and program necessitated by the school district's worsening fiscal situation were experienced as painful "cutbacks." Teachers vied with one another and with administrators over procedures for reducing staff. Program advocates, including students, fought over dwindling resources for their projects, becoming embittered when their battles were lost.[54] Meanwhile, unsupported by vocal interests groups, or because they were visible only from a long-range perspective, certain basic issues went unattended.

A Typical Agenda. Meetings of the school board lasted long into the night because, as the details of school operation became confused with policy, every item was deemed appropriate for

---

[53] Minutes of the School Board, June 27, 1973. These were among 18 special priorities listed during a prebudget hearing.

[54] Minutes of the School Board, January 28, 1975 and February 11, 1975. Teachers complained about loss of supplies and supportive services, students about loss of funds for music and other extracurricular activities.

consideration. The following scenario was typical:[55] First, there were reports from various board committees. Buildings and Grounds reported that parents were complaining about the disruptions caused by the school reconstruction program, and proposed hiring an outside management consultant firm to facilitate the program that evidently was experiencing delays and constant contract modifications. (This proposal was subsequently adopted.) Next the Personnel Committee described a recent study of the district's teacher transfer policy, and gave a progress report on principal selection. These were matters of interest to representatives of parents and the zone councils, as well as to principal and teacher organizations, all of whom made statements to the board, followed by discussion and debate, but no action. The Planning Committee then reported on various problems, such as providing food services, mishaps and breakdowns in transportation, and the general difficulty of anticipating problems ahead of time so as to avoid makeshift solutions. Finally, the Integration Committee proposed in-service training for secondary school staff. (This meeting was held just prior to the implementation of secondary school desegregation.) The proposal stimulated heated debate, and a resolution to rescind the decision to proceed with secondary desegregation was introduced, on the ground that its objectives would not be met, but at a subsequent meeting was defeated. The board then reviewed a long list of proposed budget items, listened to a report from management consultants hired to reorganize the central office, and approved a bond issue to raise funds for a central kitchen.

Notably absent from the lengthy school board agendas of this period were issues of personnel and program evaluation. Declining enrollments, portents of staff and program reductions, indicated the need for evaluation, but the issue failed to generate a constituency and was therefore neglected. Similarly, the district neglected standards and procedures for assuring staff competence. Neither teacher nor program evaluation had the support of a special interest group. The Integration Committee, its attention diverted by complaints and demands concerning pupil transfer policies, busing contracts, and problems of data processing, did not even discuss the Mercer study of the effects of desegregation on pupil and teacher attitudes. Likewise, although special reading programs were funded, their effectiveness was not evaluated. Neither these nor less sensitive curriculum matters received careful attention as to

---

[55] Minutes of the School Board, June 25, 1974.

their merits. Although questions were raised as to how federal- and state-funded programs were integrated into basic instruction,[56] the issue was never pursued.

Thus the school board's "priorities" were not based on informed judgments. Despite the decline in pupil achievement scores, and the accompanying rise in vandalism, the board did not begin to act on these matters until 1975, by which time they had become major sources of public embarrassment. There was no special interest group to speak for the schools' basic responsibilities for instruction.

The shortsightedness of school officials regarding key resources, such as revenues and personnel, is all the more striking in the light of the administration's capacity to undertake substantial obligations, such as the reconstruction of unsafe school buildings. This conscientious endeavor, however, failed to take into account declining enrollment trends. Unsafe buildings were brought up to earthquake-proof standards only to be closed down for lack of pupils, while other schools fell into disrepair due to vandalism and cutbacks in maintenance.

A prevailing pattern of opportunism accompanied disruptions in the classroom, and exacerbated the districtwide disorder that followed in the wake of elementary school desegregation. Opportunism and drift aggravated the schools' vulnerability to outside pressures. The school board, distracted by conflicting constituencies and careless of its basic responsibilities, capitulated to external pressures, neglecting the more precarious and undefended values of education. Failure of leadership constituted a fertile breeding ground for the deepening of demoralization.

---

[56] Minutes of the School Board, April 22, 1975.

6

A Crisis of Legitimacy

Legitimacy carries the lively seed of legality, implanted by the principle that reasons must be given to defend official acts. . . . Where reasons are defective authority is to that extent weakened and even des-
troyed.[1]

Withdrawal of energies, structural incoherence, lack of leadership, organizational drift—these are the features thus far identified
as elements of institutional demoralization. But organizational
dynamics are only part of the story. Institutional morale also
depends on the vitality and legitimacy of the values at stake. In the
early sixties, when our story began, the worth accorded to public
education was a significant source of morale, sustaining the efforts
of teachers, administrators, pupils, and parents. But as the clarity
and force of institutional purpose diminished, so did the quality of
participation and performance. In this chapter, we see how changes
in the values of schooling, interacting with the conditions we have
described, contributed to demoralization by eroding the grounds of
legitimacy.

Bearing in mind the political context (Chapters 2 and 3) and the
social conditions of the San Francisco schools (Chapters 4 and 5),
we next consider the values that give meaning and purpose to the
schools as a public enterprise.

- How did changing conditions affect those values?
- What justifications were given for major changes in school policy
  and organization?
- What was the basis for cooperation in implementing those
  changes?

To answer these questions, we focus on two entities that assumed
responsibility for assessing and judging the schools' performance.

---

[1] Philip Selznick, *Law, Society and Industrial Justice* (New Brunswick, N.J.: Transaction Books, 1980 [copyright Russell Sage Foundation, 1969]), p. 30.

In this and the next chapter, we examine the assessment of the San Francisco schools by the courts. Chapter 8 concerns the evaluation of the schools by a special state commission. Encounters with these external reviewing agencies reshaped the expectations of the San Francisco school community. Shared beliefs in the effectiveness and worth of the public schools were shaken by their criticisms and judgments. The values of schooling thus lost legitimacy for those whose efforts were essential for the achievement of organizational goals.

Educational Values and the Worth of Schooling

An historic activity such as schooling inevitably has many bases of justification, and over time accumulates multiple sources of worth.[2] But does such a plurality provide legitimacy? How does one ascertain and assess legitimacy?

Institutional Legitimacy and the Problem of Disarray

When the the legitimacy of an institution, such as the public schools, becomes problematic, it is institutional competence, i.e. performance in relation to needs and expectations, that is placed in question. The assessment of institutional legitimacy thus entails measures of public confidence and support, but to possess legitimacy in depth, institutions also have to meet reasonable principles of justification with regard to their policies and practices.

> The development of legality requires a richer doctrine of justification, one that permits appeal to public purpose and to the moral commitments of the community. But once that road is taken, the principle of legitimacy shades into a political philosophy. The polity becomes the touchstone.[3]

Institutions that deeply satisfy public needs, and do so in accordance with critical standards, pass muster. Accordingly, one can imagine an institution in organizational disarray—fragmented and incoherent—but still endowed with legitimacy in that its services are valued, and satisfy reasonable principles of justification. This imaginary situation is unlikely, however, because of the close

---

[2] Historian David Nasaw describes the schools as "contested institutions with several agendas and different purposes," *Schooled to Order* (London: Oxford University Press, 1979), p. 243.

[3] Selznick, *Law, Society and Industrial Justice*, p. 31. Also, Jürgen Habermas, *Legitimation Crisis* (Boston: Beacon Press, 1973), pp. 96-102.

connection between the rationality required for efficient organization, and the reasoning that elaborates principles of justification for concerted action. Rational authority, the basis of modern institutions, involves grounding decisions on rules, procedures, and principles. Moreover, unlike organizations based on tradition, modern institutions are open to challenge and criticism. When there is a question as to whether or not a decision has been made on the basis of official rules, or when organizational policy is open to challenge on grounds of faulty reasoning, then one can assume that rationality forms the basis of that organization's authority, and that its purpose is likewise "rooted and nourished in the light of reason."[4] On the other hand, an organization in disarray, its decisions reflecting opportunism and the domination of special interests, not the governance of goals or the regulation of rules, is not likely to be so sustained. In such cases, there are grounds for suspecting that organizational disarray is symptomatic of the erosion of organizational rationality and purpose.

Since the civil rights movement, disarray in the San Francisco schools permeated their organization and the values and standards by which performance was measured. School board members, administrators, teachers, parents, and pupils became confused and uncertain as to the public purpose of the schools, although well aware of the special interests schools satisfy. The fact that schools serve multiple and conflicting interests, however, is no sure measure of their general value. The process of justifying the purpose of the schools needs to take into account this plurality, but plurality alone is no guarantee of legitimacy.

The Values of Public Education

Historically, strong ideals of equality and social betterment provided justification for the development of public schools. Comparing past and present support for the schools, however, historians note serious weakening of the traditional American faith in public education.[5] Recent revisionist scholarship has placed public education's formative ideals under close scrutiny and found them wanting. According to the revisionists, the schools promised more than they delivered in terms of equal opportunity and social mobility, with the result that those favored by birth and fortune benefited

---

[4] H.H. Gerth and C. Wright Mills (eds.), *From Max Weber: Essays in Sociology* (London: Oxford University Press, 1946), pp. 329-41.
[5] David Tyack and Elizabeth Hansot, *Managers of Virtue* (N.Y.: Basic Books, 1982).

more than minorities and the poor. These critics of the schools, attempting to shatter the "myth" of the "common school," and, by calling attention to the issue of the schools' competence and public worth, to displace the schools from their pedestal of public esteem, thus contributed to the crisis of legitimacy.[6]

On several counts—mission, means, and ends—schools have lost credibility. In the past school leaders could point with pride to the swelling ranks of those passing through the portals of the public schools as proof of the schools' worth, and cite the contribution of the schools to the development of an educated citizenry capable of sustaining a democratic form of government. These historic justifications are no longer persuasive. Nor is the rationale developed by John Dewey, who cited the commitment to schools as the "paramount moral duty" of a society engaged in fulfilling its responsibility for assuring a civilized future. Not only is a sense of social obligation no longer keenly felt, but even more narrow grounds of utility offer insufficient support for a rational commitment to public schooling. Declining standards and test scores, problems of discipline, administrative incompetence, and political disarray make the choice to exit increasingly rational.[7]

Our own case study has demonstrated the disillusionment of those in close contact with the schools. Their experience, where it did not result in withdrawal, generated contempt for school leadership, frustration over efforts to sustain viable educational climates, anger over the loss of status and satisfaction that once accompanied school work, and despair in contemplating the future.[8]

This was not the state of affairs a generation ago. Until the late sixties, the San Francisco school system was a respected and stable institution, its contributions to civic and economic life taken for granted, its occupation satisfying if sometimes dull, its administration well-regulated, and its leadership trusted. But, as a result of

---

[6] See Michael Katz, *Class, Bureaucracy and Schools* (N.Y.: Praeger, 1971); also by Katz, *The Irony of Early School Reform* (Boston: Beacon Press, 1968). For a critique of revisionist history, see Diane Ravitch, *The Revisionists Revised* (N.Y.: Basic Books, 1977).

[7] See the discussion of this option, based on Albert Hirschman's *Exit, Voice & Loyalty: Responses to Decline in Firms, Organizations and States* (Cambridge: Harvard University Press, 1970) in Chapter 1.

[8] San Francisco was not unique in this respect. See the results of a statewide survey of teachers reported in the *New York Times,* September 19, 1982. More than half the teachers said they would choose a different profession, given the chance. A National Education Association poll confirmed that more than one-third of all teachers are dissatisfied. *Newsweek,* April 20, 1981, p. 65.

the charges and criticisms raised by the civil rights movement, an unexpected and dramatic shift in attitude occurred, undermining institutional legitimacy. Able neither to withstand the demands for change, nor to provide persuasive arguments to justify the status quo, the school board and the administration floundered, and their uncertainty and confusion undermined the foundation of their authority. The civil rights movement had struck a key weakness in school leadership, namely, its political incompetence. While school leaders vacillated, pursuing a zigzag course through the events of the sixties, activists were mobilizing political forces and developing strategies for intervention. Various minority groups, supported by civil rights advocates, believed that school reforms, including desegregation, would improve school performance and more fully realize principles of equality and social betterment. To invoke these values and achieve these goals, they sought the leverage of the courts.

The quest for new directions and purpose transported the schools away from the familiar forum of local politics into the special domain of the legal system. Our analysis follows this quest in the interplay between politics and law, and between issues of educational policy and those of social and racial justice.

The Schools in Court

Weakness in the school district's political capacity to cope with the powerful social issues of the period dovetailed with the development of an activist judicial system. This coincidence was dramatically evident as a procession of challenges to school policies wound up in court. In addition to routine legal complaints, such as breach of contract or the costs of personal injuries, starting in the late sixties the schools found themselves defending the legitimacy of numerous educational and administrative practices against constitutional and legal challenges.

Precedents for Judicial Action

This development was the consequence of emerging judicial responsiveness to social policy issues. Since one of the judiciary's functions is to clarify normative conflicts, pronouncing judgments that authorize or condemn individual or institutional conduct, the court's capacity to resolve disputes over values in an authoritative way became perceived as a valuable resource at a time when societal expectations were in transition. It was therefore not surprising that during this period the courts sought to respond. Furthermore, changes in legal process, instead of discouraging access to the courts, facilitated judicial decision making on a host of social policy issues.

The starting point for judicial intervention in social change was the unanimous *Brown* decision,[9] which shattered the nation's caste system by rejecting the legal basis for separation between blacks and whites. Forbidding segregation in the schools, the Supreme Court assumed moral leadership on this deeply rooted and divisive social issue. Later decisions confirmed the court's clear commitment to eradicating the formal practices of racial segregation in the schools, "root and branch."[10] But while racial inequality was the central focus of the court's concern, *Brown* and its successors reached beyond race, potentially engaging all questions regarding fairness and equal treatment in the schools. The court in *Brown* spoke of education as a critical function of government, such that any child deprived of adequate schooling could not be expected to succeed in life. This judicial language served as an invitation to a host of supplicants seeking relief from a variety of allegedly unfair school practices. Viewing *Brown* as an opportunity to convert their grievances into constitutional wrongs, the non-English-speaking, the handicapped, women students, poor students, and others began flooding the lower courts with lawsuits.

Local Actions

As early as 1962, eight years after *Brown*, judicial sanctions regarding the practice of racial segregation encouraged the San Francisco branch of the NAACP to file a lawsuit against the school district.[11] The NAACP's local action, alleging violations of the constitutional rights of black students, was stimulated by community opposition to the opening of Central Junior High School. The administration's plan for the school, the reader may recall from Chapter 2, involved an assignment of pupils likely to "tip" the school into becoming predominantly black. Community pressure, however, forced the administration to rescind this plan, and the district hired a black official to handle grievances. Subsequently, when the Ad Hoc Committee recommended that race be taken into

---

[9] 47 US 483 (1954).

[10] Landmark cases include *Green* v *County School Board*, US 430 (1968), and *Swann* v *Charlotte-Mecklenburg Board of Education*, 402 US 1 (1971).

[11] *Brock* v *Board of Education*, No. 71034 (N.D. Calif. Oct. 2, 1962).

account in school boundary changes, the NAACP lawsuit was allowed to lapse. However, a similar suit filed in 1970 led to the first federal court action requiring school desegregation in a city outside the deep South.[12]

The issue of racial imbalance in the schools, recalling Part I, was a longstanding political bone of contention between the school administration, the board, and the community. A liberal coalition had for years prodded the district to take action on this question, and while progress was evident, it was not enough to satisfy increasingly impatient black activists. Even while negotiations concerning school policies aimed at reducing racial imbalance were in progress, a team of NAACP lawyers hastily put together materials for a lawsuit that demanded "a preliminary and permanent injunction ordering the immediate and complete desegregation of the student bodies, faculties and administrative personnel in the public elementary schools."

At about the same time, another complaint against the San Francisco schools was filed in federal court, but by an entirely different set of plaintiffs, described by their attorneys as "unable to either understand or communicate in the English language."[13] Chinese for Affirmative Action, an activist group representing the plaintiffs, had been unable to persuade the school administration to attend to the needs of these non-English-speaking pupils of Chinese origin, 1,800 of whom were estimated to be enrolled in the city schools at that time. Their suit, *Lau* v *Nichols*, claimed denial of a meaningful educational opportunity; alleged violation of Title VI of the 1964 Civil Rights Act that bans discrimination on the ground of race, color, or national origin in any program receiving federal financial assistance; and demanded districtwide bilingual education taught by bilingual teachers.

The *Johnson* case was stimulated by Mayor Alioto's intervention, and the school board's subsequent hesitancy over the decision to proceed with the Richmond and Park South school complexes. The mayor had urged concerned parents to bring suit against the schools and, following his advice, they took their case to court.[14] In response, the NAACP immediately filed its suit, escalating the conflict over desegregation and placing its resolution squarely

---

[12] *Johnson* v *SFUSD*, 339 Fed Suppl. 1315 (N.D. Calif. 1971), vacated and remanded 500 F 2nd 349 (9th Circuit, 1974), complaint filed June 24, 1970.

[13] *Lau* v *Nichols*, 414 US 565 (1974), complaint filed March 25, 1970, p. A-2.

[14] *Nelson* v *SFUSD*, #618-643, Superior Court (June 15, 1970).

before the mediation of the federal court.

While *Johnson* was intended to force the school district to desegregate, *Lau* was conceived to redirect the district's attention to the needs of Chinese and other non-English-speaking ethnic minorities.[15] While these cases demonstrate the use of legal tactics in the struggle of minority groups to achieve political recognition, they also illustrate the complexity of the problem posed by demands for fair treatment of every pupil, regardless of race, ethnicity, or national origin, for among its pupil population, the San Francisco schools had nine distinctive minority groups.[16]

Johnson and *Lau* were just the beginning of a series of challenges to local school policies. In subsequent cases, a variety of plaintiffs criticized the schools for inflicting injustices upon them and depriving them of basic rights and privileges. Each challenge probed for the justification of particular practices and forced the school district to formulate a defense of its policies and procedures. The following brief exposition will illustrate the extent of the questioning, and the values at stake.

Educational Values Become Legal Questions

In 1971, a civil action suit, *Larry P.* v *Riles*, was filed on behalf of five black pupils who alleged violations due to the cultural bias of the IQ tests used to place them in classes for the mentally retarded, or EMR classes.[17] A preliminary injunction issued in 1974 forbade the further use of the tests in question and prohibited the placement of children in EMR classes on the basis of test results. This case questioned the legitimacy of the schools'

---

[15] A third suit, filed by a group of Hispanic activists, alleging inequities in expenditures and services in schools with predominantly Spanish-speaking pupils spoke to the needs of this minority group. The suit was subsequently dropped when the administration made concessions the community found satisfactory. *San Francisco Chronicle*, December 10, 1970.

[16] The categories identified by the school district, and their proportions in 1975, were Chinese, 16.2%; Japanese, 1.7%; Korean, 0.6%; Spanish-speaking, 14.4%; Filipino, 8.2%; American Indian, 0.4%; black, 30.3%; other nonwhite, 3%; and other white, 25.3%. SFUSD, "Status Report," January 1975. (White pupils were categorized as one of the nine minority groups.)

[17] F. Supp. 1306 (N.D. Calif. 1972). The suit was subsequently transformed into a class action on behalf of all black pupils in California classified as mentally retarded. An extensive series of trials began in 1977. A federal court decision in 1979 outlawed the use of the IQ tests, which the court found discriminated against black pupils and thereby violated both the Civil Rights Act and the Federal Education for the Handicapped Act. The State of California later appealed the ruling.

conventional use of intelligence tests as a means of sorting pupils into special programs. Had such tests become barriers, excluding certain groups from the benefits of schooling? Or were they a justifiable means of assuring more individualized attention for children with specific learning disabilities?

Also in 1971, there was a lawsuit challenging the operation of Lowell High School as an academic school on the ground that such a school violated rights to equal protection of students who failed to pass the school's special admission requirements. The suit was argued by counsel from the Youth Law Center, a federally funded legal assistance agency, on behalf of students who also claimed that Lowell discriminated against low-income students, certain minority groups, and females. The court, in denying the claimants' suit, held that the school district exercised its discretionary powers legitimately, both in operating an academic high school and in setting admission standards.[18] Also, since the high school enrolled pupils of all races, the court held that their disproportionate representation was not conclusive evidence of racially discriminatory intent. However, a Court of Appeals later required that the school district enforce its admission policies without regard to sex, even if this meant admitting a higher proportion of females.[19] (The district had previously set slightly lower admission standards for males to keep the student body equally balanced between males and females.)

The case placed in question the schools' authority to operate not just classes, but entire school programs that depend on special admission criteria. The arguments suggested that there were limits to such authority and that it was legitimate to question the rationale behind program requirements. Were academic admission criteria beyond the purview of the courts and completely at the discretion of school authorities? If not, to what extent did the schools' standards have to satisfy constitutional and statutory guarantees of equal protection?

In May 1972 in yet another federal court, the NAACP filed suit demanding desegregation of the secondary schools.[20] By the time the matter came to trial, however, there was no serious interest in pursuing the suit and the case was subsequently dismissed by both parties. Nevertheless, the case opened for questioning the issue whether, given the desegregation of the elementary schools, the

---

18 *Berkelman* v *SFUSD*, 501 F 2nd 1264 (1974).

19 This decision was based on Title IX of the 1972 Education Amendments.

20 *O'Neill* v *SFUSD*, #C-72-808 RFT (N.D. Calif. May 5, 1972).

district was still in violation of laws forbidding racial segregation. Was elementary school desegregation sufficient, or should every vestige of segregation have been eradicated by the school district?

Finally, also in 1972, a student who assumed the anonymous name of Peter W. Doe filed suit in superior court, charging the San Francisco schools with negligence and lack of proper supervision, instruction, guidance, and counseling—in short, with denial of a proper education.[21] This student, a recent high school graduate, albeit functionally illiterate, claimed that as a consequence of the school district's malpractices he suffered pain and mental distress, as well as the loss of earning capacity, and he demanded personal damages of $500,000. This malpractice case, like the Lowell High School case, was argued by attorneys from the Youth Law Center.

Thus, by the early seventies, a variety of school policy issues were transformed into legal questions, and the school district was becoming a familiar defendant in various courts of law, answerable there for its actions to attorneys and judges, while still accountable to the electorate and its constituencies. Having to defend itself in court entailed costs, but also had potential benefits. To the extent that it might vindicate its policies in court, the district would enhance its legitimacy. Also, to the extent that the courts could either disentangle and accommodate conflicting values, or define new ones in an authoritative way, stronger justifications for administrative policy would be available. In other words, there was reason to regard the schools' legal predicament as an opportunity to restore key elements of its educational and political competence.

The costs of litigation, however, were substantial in time, money, and energy—resources the school district could ill afford. Its difficulties were aggravated in 1973 (the year superintendent Morena had his first heart attack) when the school board's legal advisor resigned. A prolonged search for a replacement began, but it was not until August 1974, after a *Time* magazine article describing the besieged state of the San Francisco schools generated vocal outrage over school management,[22] that the school board finally hired a new lawyer. By the time he assumed his responsibilities, however, the most significant cases had been decided. Judicial review was already having widespread and devastating effects on everyday life in the San Francisco schools.

---

[21] *Peter W. Doe* v *SFUSD*, 131 Cal 854 (1976).

[22] *Time*, February 26, 1974.

7

The Ironies Of Legal Reform

Should there be a judge who, enlightened by genius, stimulated by honest zeal to the work of reformation, sick of the caprice, the delays, the prejudices, the ignorance, the malice, the fickleness, the suspicious ingratitude of popular assemblies, should seek with his sole hand to expunge the effusions of traditional imbecility, and write down in their room the dictates of pure and native justice, let him reflect that partial amendment is bought at the expense of universal certainty; that partial good thus purchased is universal evil; and that *amendment from the judgment seat is confusion.*[1]

In this chapter we follow three important cases—*Johnson, Lau,* and *Doe*—into the courts to examine the role played by the judiciary in educational policy making, and to find out what happened to San Francisco school policies as they became the subject of judicial review.

- Did recourse to the relatively distant and dispassionate legal process enhance the legitimacy of local school decisions?
- Did the assertion of rights and the legal critique of authority enrich civic participation?
- Did school policy, as reshaped by the court, result in more or less responsive and effective education in San Francisco schools?

Distortion of Educational Issues for Legal Action

When a claim is pressed in the form of a lawsuit, the issues at stake have to be formulated in terms of an available and authoritative legal doctrine. Ordinary claims, in other words, must be reshaped to fit a appropriate legal framework. The underlying policy issues are therefore potentially subject to distortion, depending on the state of development of the legal system at a particular time.

---

[1] Jeremy Bentham, *Comment on the Commentaries* (London: Clarendon Press, 1928), p. 214, emphasis added.

Each of our three cases involved a serious challenge to the school district's authority and the legitimacy of its educational policies. They differed, however, with respect to the legal frameworks and doctrines they invoked. In the process of reframing educational issues for legal action, each case distorted facts and issues. As a result, the courts' judgments failed to fully reflect educational realities.

The legal action in the *Johnson* case was reshaped to fit the constitutional doctrine of equal protection, as elaborated by the federal courts in the wake of *Brown* and later school segregation decisions. While no large city outside the South had yet been required by law to desegregate its schools, the Supreme Court had declared in 1967 that a "board must be required to fashion steps which promise . . . a system without a 'white' school and a 'Negro' school, but just schools." [2] A federal district court had also held that inaction by a northern city school board in the face of de facto segregation was tantamount to deliberate segregation.[3] Having this doctrine available greatly aided San Francisco NAACP lawyers in preparing their legal case, but it also required them to distort certain facts to make them fit the conditions contemplated by the evolving doctrine.

The facts, as gathered by local lawyers in the *Johnson* case, true as far as they went, emphasized the school district's reluctance to take steps to remedy racial imbalance in the elementary schools. Increases in the extent of school segregation between 1965 and 1970 were cited, and the pleadings documented the school board's repeated vacillation, and its ambiguous stance toward the condemnation of practices that perpetuated racially imbalanced school enrollments. Presentation of these facts distorted the actual record, however, because they excluded actions by the board, e.g., the closing of Central Junior High School and the extensive preparations for the 20 complex schools, which accommodated public demands for racial balance. The district's increasingly favorable attitude toward racial justice was not revealed and therefore not considered in the court's judgment.

The *Johnson* case also relied heavily on the findings of the Coleman Report as evidence that racial imbalance was the prima facie cause of the educational harm declared heinous by the Supreme Court. This claim involved a distortion of the Coleman Report's

[2] *Green* v *County School Board*, 391 U.S. 430 (1968).
[3] *Davis* v *School District for the City of Pontiac*, 309 F. Supp. (1970), aff'd. 443 F. 2nd 573 (1971).

more significant conclusion, namely, that school achievement is best predicted by socioeconomic background, not race.[4] Had the NAACP attorneys really attempted to identify the extent of educational harm suffered by black pupils in San Francisco, and then proposed a remedy, the emphasis on racial balance might have been considerably diluted and the educational consequences of the case made more central. One of the NAACP attorneys did attempt to raise questions concerning the educational consequences of racial balance, but, given the thrust of the plaintiffs' case, he was put down by the court.[5]

The *Lau* plaintiffs also rested their case initially on grounds of equal protection. However, with respect to claims concerning foreign origin or foreign language rights, there were not the same kinds of precedents as in the chain of decisions regarding racial discrimination. After a brief hearing, therefore, the case was dismissed by the district court, and the dismissal was later affirmed by the court of appeals.[6] Three years later, however, as a consequence of additional work performed by a host of legal experts, the Supreme Court issued a favorable ruling, but on statutory rather than constitutional grounds, citing Title VI of the 1964 Civil Rights Act.

The legal framework of the decision thus provided no standards by which to devise a remedy. When the case was remanded to district court for remedial action, its disposition became contingent on the educational policy of the HEW Office of Civil Rights, which was responsible for enforcement of Title VI. However, the language of Title VI, which provides that "no person . . . shall on grounds of race, color or national origin, be excluded from participation in, be denied the benefits of, or be subjected to discrimination under any program of activity receiving Federal financial assistance" offered little guidance for school policy.[7] The result, as we shall see, was a highly charged political confrontation between advocates of comprehensive bilingual-bicultural education (BBE),

---

[4] James Coleman et al., *Equality of Educational Opportunity* (Washington, D.C.: Government Printing Office, 1966).

[5] Memo and Order of Dismissal, June 27, 1978, Footnote 9. In an interview (April 7, 1975), the attorney, Edward Bell, said that he withdrew from the case at that point, disappointed with the court's attitude but not willing to risk an open controversy implicating the black community whose integrity, he felt, was vital to the larger social cause of racial justice.

[6] 483 F 2nd 791 (1971).

[7] 42 U.S.C.A. 2000 (d), Section 601.

and educators content with "pure and simple" training in English.[8] Recourse to the courts in this case, rather than solving a dispute, distorted and politicized the problems of educating non-English-speaking children.

Our third case, *Doe*, took a rather different legal course. No civil rights issues were raised because the equal protection clause does not protect persons from equal neglect. *Doe* was a private suit in tort in which the plaintiff's attorneys undertook to demonstrate educational malpractice. The complaint struck at a general educational failure on the part of the schools, but hardly one that could be characterized as discriminatory.

In each case, the legal framework distorted the policy issues. In *Johnson*, the focus on eliminating racial imbalance in the elementary schools obscured the effects of desegregation on the education of black elementary school children, as well as other minorities and secondary school students. *Lau* centered on the needs of non-English-speaking-Chinese children, but because its legal underpinnings were not supported by constitutional principles, the underlying policy remained obscure and controversial. Was national origin the criterion for identifying educational need and establishing special bilingual-bicultural programs? Or was foreign language to be the basis of plaintiffs' rights, such that the needs to be addressed were those of native, as well as foreign-born children with limited English? If the former, then a central mission of the public schools, the assimilation of foreign-born children, was placed in jeopardy. But if the latter, the remedy of providing remedial English sufficed. In either case, there was no constitutional argument to force the establishment of bilingual programs, as *Brown* forced the dismantling of southern dual school systems.

The precedent of *Brown* and its successors for the *Johnson* case was also far from clear. Since no cases involving northern school districts had as yet been reviewed by the Supreme Court, the extension in principle of the rulings requiring desegregation was far from obvious. Legal scholars then and since have argued that the de jure-de facto distinction was never clearly enunciated by the court, and that this lack of clarity has been responsible for a series of confused and misguided lower court decisions.[9]

---

[8] Deputy Superintendent Lane de Lara, quoted in Dexter Waugh and Bruce Koon, "Breakthrough for Bilingual Education," *Civil Rights Digest* (Summer 1974): 24.

[9] Frank Goodman, "De Facto School Segregation," 60 *California Law Review* (1972): 275-437. Also, Mark Yudof, "School Desegregation," 42 *Law and Contemporary Problems* (1979): 57-110.

Finally, because issues reshaped by a legal framework are more likely to be defined in terms of individual rights, rather than as social problems, they fail to generate a policy perspective. As class action suits, both the *Johnson* and *Lau* plaintiffs avoided this outcome, requiring the court to consider larger questions of policy and organization. However, *Doe,* a personal injury case, excluded a potentially large class of plaintiffs. Although Doe's attorneys, members of a public interest law firm, were no doubt aware of the case's institutional implications, they chose not to pose the issue in terms of multiple plaintiffs.[10] The more general issue at stake, educational negligence, was thus obscured by a single individual's private interests.

Adjustments to the Court's Competence

Although in a sense accidental, the legal frameworks and strategies chosen by the plaintiffs proved quite fateful. They determined the focus of the courts' attention and the scope of judicial inquiry. These matters, as we shall now see, were critical for the formulation of the courts' judgments.

Scope of Review

School policy that results from legal action tends to be constrained by the following dilemma: Either the court's attention is brought to bear directly on the educational issues at stake—but since this is an area where courts gravely doubt their own competence, the judgment is likely to defer to school authority—or the issues are legally couched so as to invite the court's scrutiny—but since this entails a distortion of the policy issues, the judgment is likely to neglect educational and social consequences. *Lau* and *Doe* were examples of the first possibility: in these cases, educational policy issues became the focus of inquiry, but the courts then acted with restraint, preferring not to intervene. *Johnson* exemplified the second option: here an elaborated legal framework gave the court confidence in its constitutional expertise, but the result was a blunt order that ripped apart the fabric of the schools.

---

10 Various legal commentators have pointed out that a better hearing might have been obtained had the suit been framed as a class action. See Note, "Educational Malpractice," 124 *University of Pennsylvania Law Review* (January 1976): 755; Steven Sugarman, "Accountability Through the Courts," 82 *School Review* (February 1974): 233.

In *Lau,* the complaint alleged that there were 1,800 Chinese-speaking pupils in the San Francisco schools "unable to either understand or communicate in the English language" and who were not receiving any special instruction in English, and another 1,050 pupils receiving limited help of only an hour a day of instruction, or less. The court was asked to order the schools to provide all these students with "special full-time instruction in English, taught by bilingual teachers."[11] In its defense, the school district insisted that it was perfectly aware of the language handicaps of these pupils, and many others with limited command of the English language, but that its resources were limited and therefore it could not expend more funds for these needs, given the many other competing and valid educational needs that had to be met.[12] The defense also noted the controversy among educators regarding the various advantages and disadvantages of two current approaches to teaching English to foreign language children.

One approach, English as a Second Language (ESL) stressed speedier learning through short, intensive classwork, supplementary to the normal curriculum. This approach benefited students who already had some knowledge of English. It also had administrative advantages because its costs were limited to training and assigning regular teachers to conduct the special classes. The other approach, the one advocated by the plaintiffs, called bilingual-bicultural education (BBE) involved having a bilingual teacher present all subjects. It required a curriculum that emphasized the national culture and heritage of a particular ethnic minority group, as well as the study of English. This approach called for hiring bilingual teachers in various languages and developing new curriculum materials. But the grouping of children for purposes of BBE conflicted with the purposes of racial desegregation.[13]

The federal district court, in the face of the explicit educational issues underlying this dispute, opted for judicial restraint and dismissed the complaint. The court pointed out that it was the educational needs, not the constitutional rights, of the plaintiffs that were in question, and that this was a matter for schools, not courts, to decide. Refusing to pass judgment, the court concluded that

---

[11] Complaint for Injunction and Declaratory Relief, filed March 25, 1970 in U.S. District Court, N.D. Calif., pp. A-2, A-3.

[12] Answer to Complaint, filed May 26, 1970. Also, Affidavit of Associate Superintendent for Instruction Edward Goldman, filed May 26, 1970.

[13] Affidavit of Acting Director of Research and Evaluation Yvon Johnson, filed May 4, 1970.

"the Chinese-speaking students . . . by receiving the same education made available on the same terms and conditions as the other students in the SFUSD . . . are legally receiving all their rights." [14] While granting that the BBE approach might have educational advantages for some non-English-speaking students, the court found "no legal basis to require it." [15] The court of appeals for the 9th circuit upheld the decision, pointing out that this was a case "calling for significant amounts of executive and legislative expertise, and non-judicial value judgments." [16] Even though the Supreme Court later found a narrow basis on which to grant a modified plea for redress, upon remand to the district court for remedy, the discretion of the school district to develop its own program of remedial English instruction was fully preserved. The scope of review was limited to enforcing the schools' responsibilities under Title VI of the Civil Rights Act.

Judicial restraint in matters of educational policy was also evident in the *Doe* case. The complaint charged the school district with negligence in failing to provide the plaintiff with basic skills.[17] Peter W. Doe (the young man's assumed name) had graduated from a San Francisco high school, but claimed he could not find employment because he was functionally illiterate. According to standard educational tests, Peter possessed an average IQ; yet he had the reading ability of a fifth grader. Nevertheless, according to school district records, he had satisfactorily passed all the necessary requirements for high school graduation. His suit asked the court to award him $500,000 for the personal injury he suffered as a consequence of the district's negligence and failure to provide him with basic literacy skills.

In sustaining the district's demurrer (a pleading that assumes the truth of the allegations but objects that there are insufficient legal grounds for redress), the superior court judge found no statutory basis for Peter's claim that schools owe pupils a duty to provide them with mastery of basic skills,[18] and the court of appeals affirmed this judgment.[19] Both courts were impressed by the absence of consensus among professional educators as to standards

---

[14] Civil No. C-70-627, May 26, 1970, p. 35.

[15] Ibid.

[16] 483 F. 2nd 791 (1973).

[17] First Amended Complaint for Damages, filed October 30, 1973, City and County of San Francisco Superior Court.

[18] Superior Court #653312, September 6, 1974.

[19] 131 Cal. 854 (1976).

for assessing competence.

> Unlike the activity of the highway or the marketplace, classroom methodology affords no readily acceptable standards of care, or cause or injury. The science of pedagogy itself is fraught with different and conflicting theories of how or what a child should be taught, and any layman might—and commonly does—have his own emphatic views on the subject.[20]

Given this highly uncertain state of affairs, the court felt unable to render an opinion, and therefore the result was to defer to the schools any further policy development on this educational issue.

In *Johnson*, the court was not so restrained in its judgment, because in this case the focus of inquiry was not educational needs, but individual rights. Here the court could rely on constitutional doctrine regarding the deprivation of rights, and reframe the educational policy issue in legal terms. The plaintiffs, relying on the 1968 Supreme Court decision that called for racially balanced schools,[21] asked for complete desegregation of the elementary schools and for assurance that the district would proceed with its plans for the two complexes. Citing recent litigation in Pontiac, Michigan, the NAACP attorneys claimed that the school district was guilty of de jure segregation because it had failed to take steps to eliminate racial imbalance, the existence of which was public knowledge, and had been furthered by construction of new schools in black neighborhoods. Facts regarding the extent of racial imbalance and a brief history of the school board's actions constituted plaintiffs' proof for these allegations. Although educational harm had been a consideration in the *Brown* decision, this theme remained an unexamined assumption in the evolving legal doctrine, and the *Johnson* arguments, which repeated the claims regarding the educational deprivation brought about by segregation, did nothing to further inquiry regarding this dimension of the issue. Early in the trial, when one of the plaintiffs' attorneys questioned whether racial balance would redress the *educational* handicaps of black pupils and urged stressing the inferior quality of ghetto schools

---

[20] Ibid. 862.

[21] *Green* v *New Kent County School Board*, 391 U.S. 430 (1968). "The notion of a unitary school system in which schools were not racially identifiable gradually came to be seen in terms of the dispersion of black children. Integration and desegregation came to be synonymous." Mark Yudof, "Nondiscrimination and Beyond," in Walter G. Stephan and Joe R. Feagin, eds., *School Desegregation* (N.Y.: Plenum Press 1980), p. 100.

rather than pupil attendance patterns per se, he was advised to withdraw from the case.[22]

Confident of its expertise and bolstered by a series of precedents, at least with regard to the desegregation of southern school districts, the federal court proceeded to pass judgment on the constitutional questions raised by *Johnson.* The court agreed with the plaintiffs' charges that the school district had engaged in de jure segregation, and went on to order the remedy of complete racial balance in the elementary schools, such that the "ratio of black to white children will be . . . substantially the same in each school." [23] Six weeks were allowed for the parties to prepare alternative plans for reorganizing the 96 elementary schools, with their 1,600 teachers and 48,000 pupils. We have previously discussed the flaws and consequences of Horseshoe, the district's plan. The NAACP also prepared a plan, utilizing outside consultants who spent 48 hours gathering their data. Their plan would have reassigned pupils taking into account factors not only of race, but also of socioeconomic background and levels of achievement, as gleaned from district records. The two plans were otherwise similar: both involved the use of attendance zones and two-way busing; both plans required the integration of all pupils, not just blacks, as well as the elementary staff; and neither gave any consideration to the educational consequences of such a massive reorganization.

Nor did the court. The parties having met the stipulated deadline, the court expressed satisfaction that the two plans before it met constitutional requirements, namely, racial balance. Accordingly, the court approved both plans, and gave the school district its choice of which one to implement.[24] Needless to say, the district chose its own plan, Horseshoe.

The school district, as we have seen, proceeded to enforce the legalistic formula approved by the court and embodied in the Horseshoe Plan. Thus the focus of inquiry, in this case constitutional issues, not the educational values at stake, was central in determining both the narrow scope of review and the hasty remedy. The result was a blunt court order, insensitive to the social and educational context, and a judgment that made no contribution to the legitimation of school policy.

---

[22] Transcript, August 12, 1970, p. 206.

[23] 339 F. Supp. 1315 (N.D. Cal. 1971).

[24] Transcript, June 24, 1971, at 1321.

Adversary Proceedings

Conventional legal wisdom assumes that the competence of courts largely derives from the virtues of adversary proceedings. Recent legal theory, however, proposes a contrasting "public law" model that is more appropriate under certain conditions.

> When the argument is about whether or how a government policy or program shall be carried out, the court is inevitably to some degree enlisted in the service of the legislative purpose. . . . Simple prohibitory orders are inadequate to provide relief. . . . The relief called for is an affirmative program to implement the purpose. The undeniable presence of competing interests of all sorts, many of them unrepresented by the litigants, requires that the program be shaped so as to take those interests into account.[25]

Although the *Johnson* case might have been better adjudicated from this "public law" perspective, in fact it satisfied none of the model's specifications. The policy issues raised were drastically narrowed in scope so as to fall within the confines of available desegregation doctrine. The court made no effort to respond to the specifics of San Francisco's residential segregation patterns, and appeared to ignore the multiracial, multiethnic composition of the schools. Knowledge of the history of the political dispute, and presumed familiarity with the local context did not widen the scope of judicial inquiry.

Instead, the court exhibited a distinct preference for simplified bilateral proceedings. Participation was limited to the two main parties (plaintiffs and the school district), and assumed the existence of a clear-cut conflict over specifiable matters of fact and rules of law. Only one group of racially mixed parents, Robert G. Nelson et al. was allowed to intervene. (They were the parties who, with Mayor Alioto's encouragement, had just filed suit in superior court to enjoin the school district from implementing the two school complexes.) The court permitted the Nelson intervenors to enter the case provided they limit their pleadings to this particular aspect of the dispute. Although attorneys for the Nelson group developed extensive legal arguments to demonstrate that racial imbalance in the San Francisco schools was not unconstitutional, the court, confining their participation, denied them the opportunity to present their materials.[26]

---

[25] Abram Chayes, "The Role of the Judge in Public Law Litigation," 89 *Harvard Law Review* (1976): pp. 1304-5.

[26] The gist of their argument is contained in the following statement (Intervenor's

After the trial was over, a group representing Chinese interests, angered by the hasty proceedings of the Citizens Advisory Committee and disturbed by the remedial plans being drawn up for the court's approval, also tried to intervene. They insisted on a hearing on the ground that children from Chinatown would be deprived of their constitutional rights by the *Johnson* remedy, which included reassigning substantial numbers of children to schools outside the Chinatown area. The attorney for the Chinese, Quentin Kopp, argued that the Chinese community, which in San Francisco had historically been subjected to various forms of discrimination, including at one time exclusion from the public schools, should not be further "subjected to a 'cure' they neither need nor want."[27] However, the motion to intervene was denied by the court. Kopp then sought a stay of the desegregation decree, also denied, and he appealed the district court ruling first to the court of appeals of the 9th circuit, and upon rejection there, to the Supreme Court. The high court ruling upheld the lower courts' denials, and gave as its reason the applicability of desegregation doctrine to all ethnic minorities.

> *Brown* was not written for blacks alone . . . . Our school desegregation cases extend to all racial minorities.[28]

This judgment finalized the exclusion of the aggrieved Chinese from intervention in a case where representation of their interests might have modified both the ruling and the remedy. However, three years later, these plaintiffs did obtain satisfaction when the court of appeals reversed the *Johnson* judgment and ordered that the Chinese be allowed to intervene on remand.[29] By this time, however, accommodations to the Horseshoe Plan had already been arranged outside the courtroom.

Additional parties entail additional work and they complicate simple adversary proceedings. However, insofar as the parties excluded from *Johnson* represented real interests, their exclusion

---

First Objections to Plan Filed on June 10, 1971, June 14, 1971, U.S. District Court, N.D. Calif.): "There is nothing whatsoever in either *Brown* or *Swann* which requires that justice be blind to the effects of institutional racism implicit in the notion that children are fungible commodities, or that Negro children must be in the company of white children before they may improve their achievement."

[27] Complaint of Plaintiffs in Intervention, June 18, 1971.

[28] 404 U.S. 1214 (1971).

[29] 500 F. 2nd 349 (1974).

deprived the judgment of participatory force and accuracy. Lacking fidelity to the factual situation, the order was bound to be weak.

Factual inquiry in *Johnson* was limited not only by the exclusion of third party evidence, but also because it consisted mainly of hastily compiled historical materials—perfunctory descriptions of the extent of racial imbalance in the elementary schools—summarily reviewed. In addition, two depositions were critical in establishing the factual basis of the ruling. The director of community relations testified that, although it had been district policy since 1965 to take considerations of race into account when redrawing school boundaries and selecting new school sites, other factors always outweighed the improvement of racial balance by these means. Board member Laurel Glass admitted that acts of omission, evasion, and delay on the part of the board had contributed to increased racial segregation.[30]

That was the crux of the evidence presented to the court. For purposes of a speedy judgment, moreover, the court took no initiative in soliciting more information. The *Johnson* court thus demonstrated little interest or understanding of the institutional factors necessary to shape a broadly remedial outcome, one that would speak to the values at stake. Rather, the court's conception of relief was limited to the undoing of racial imbalance. In framing a remedy to respond to the grievances stated by the plaintiffs, the court was not concerned with the larger, more complex purpose of the schools, but rather with the permissible range of its remedial powers. To establish the scope of its remedy, the court held back its decision until after the Supreme Court ruling in *Swann,* which, as it anticipated, set a precedent for lower courts to enforce racial balance through mandatory busing.[31] The imposition of this legalistic form of relief did more to frustrate than to enlarge educational opportunities for San Francisco's black pupils.

---

[30] Depositions of Dr. William L. Cobb and Laurel Glass, M.D., filed July 22, 1970 and July 14, 1970 in U.S. District Court.

[31] *Swann* v *Charlotte-Mecklenburg Board of Education*, U.S. 1 (1971), a highly controversial decision that asserted that "the nature of the constitutional violation determines the scope of the remedy," and then went on to require a full-scale busing plan to bring about districtwide racial balance. In this case, "the predominant concern of the court is the segregated pattern of student attendance rather than the causal role played by past discriminatory practices." Owen Fiss, "The Charlotte-Mecklenburg Case and Its Significance for Northern School Desegregation," 38 *University of Chicago Law Review* (1971): 704.

After ordering both parties to prepare plans to implement racial balance, the court conducted public hearings and informal sessions to consider the merits of the two remedies, but again with only the most narrow concern for remedial issues. Although the court had been far from hesitant to exercise its powers of judgment in its constitutional domain of expertise, it now displayed considerable reluctance to entertain any discussion of the district's difficulties, or to recognize deficiencies in its administrative and educational functioning that might impede the remedial process. At this stage, the court chose to defer entirely to the school district, regardless of its past history or current circumstances, and awarded it the full responsibility for implementation of the order.

Technically, the court did retain some oversight, but the judge adopted a passive stance toward all subsequent events, including the filing of the secondary school desegregation suit and the erosion of the Horseshoe Plan. In 1978, for lack of prosecution, the *Johnson* case was dismissed, and although the resources of adversary proceedings had hardly been fully utilized, this avenue of redress was then exhausted.

For Whom Do Parties Speak

One reason for restricting the participation of third parties is that courts normally lack the capacity to measure the representativeness of outsiders. This incapacity applies to the main parties as well.

The *Johnson* plaintiffs were six black elementary school pupils, chosen and represented by the local branch of the NAACP, assisted by a young solo practitioner. The districtwide remedy they sought nevertheless presumed that they were acting not as individuals, but as representatives of a larger class. Yet at no time did the court examine the grounds for this assumption. Had it done so, it would have discovered considerable disagreement within the black community with regard to the solution of racial balance.

The plaintiffs in the *Lau* case, 1,800 Chinese pupils, most of them native-Americans but non-English-speaking, claimed that all Chinese pupils were adversely affected by school policies.[32] But it

---

[32] Victor Low, *The Unimpressible Race* (San Francisco: East/West Publishing Co., 1982). The Chinese in San Francisco endured many years of discrimination, but this was not the basis of the claim in *Lau*. Indeed by 1970, Chinese pupils were among the school district's highest achievers, and according to the Mercer study, had a very high measure of self-esteem. Subsequent interpretations of *Lau* have largely affected the nation's Spanish-speaking pupil population. See Herbert Teitelbaum and Richard J. Hiller, "Bilingual Education: The Legal Mandate," *Harvard Educational Review* (May 1977).

was not clear whether they were alleging discrimination based on national origin or whether what distinguished the class of plaintiffs was a special linguistic inability. Further, it is doubtful whether the initial remedy sought—BBE taught by bilingual staff—was designed to teach fluency in English, or to inculcate cultural values, or whether it was simply a strategy for employing more bilingual staff. Courts have limited capacities for checking the credentials or ascertaining the basis of the interests that advocacy groups, such as the Chinese for Affirmative Action, claim to represent.

The *Doe* case posed the obverse of the same problem. Whereas the *Johnson* and *Lau* plaintiffs' claims to speak for classes of children appeared dubious, it was rather striking that the large (though likely embarrassed) class of potential plaintiffs to which Peter Doe belonged—the functionally illiterate—was not made a party to his complaint. Doe's attorneys, members of the Youth Law Center, were hardly unmindful of the case's social policy implications. Demonstrations of a more widespread pattern of educational neglect might have made their case more persuasive. Yet here an aggrieved individual who could truly have represented many ended up speaking only for himself.

The court did not try to evaluate the claims of plaintiffs. It also was unable to ascertain the constituency represented by the defense. In denying the Chinese group standing to intervene in the *Johnson* case, the court reasoned that its interests were adequately represented by the immediate parties. The court had in mind here not the plaintiffs, but the defendant. In taking for granted that the school district represented the main interests opposed to the plaintiffs' demands, the court failed to recognize the presence of the Nelson intervenors as evidence of conflict between the interests of the school district and at least some of the community.

That the school district in fact did not represent interests sharply at odds with those of plaintiffs was apparent from its actions. In the first place, it allowed the defense to be handled by a novice city attorney, who was also the defense counsel in the Nelson suit, where he had to argue *for* the district's affirmative obligation to seek racial balance. Secondly, no rebuttal evidence was submitted against the facts alleged to document a pattern of de jure segregation of black pupils.[33] Yet the school board had not only approved the voluntary Complex projects, but had hired Thomas Shaheen,

---

[33] Memorandum in Opposition to Motion for Preliminary Injunction, July 20, 1970, U.S. District Court, N.D. Calif.

who was committed to integration, to implement them. There was enough potential evidence to support a defense that the school district did *not* condone discriminatory policies, but the defense—by not even taking the trouble to point out that some decisions that resulted in racial imbalance, e.g., the decision to build new elementary schools in Hunters Point, had been reached with the full support of the NAACP and the local black community—conducted what amounted to a tacit acknowledgment of the plaintiffs' claims. In addition, the damaging depositions of the two school officials were not rebutted, but rather left standing as evidence of the district's lack of political will. Their testimony represented an implicit invitation to the court to intervene to settle a situation that had reached a political stalemate.

Its half-hearted defense reflected the ambivalence of the school board with regard to the rightness of its racial policies, and its disingenuous attitude toward its obligations. Only by an agonizing four-to-three vote did the board subsequently decide to appeal the court's adverse judgment, but when the court of appeals ruled in its favor some three years later, a new board opted not to press the position it had belatedly won in court.[34]

The trappings of adversary proceedings thus concealed an absence of genuine dispute between the parties. True, the desegregation issue was the subject of deep public controversy, but the real conflicts were not exposed in court because they lay elsewhere—not between the apparently adverse parties, but rather between both of them, on the one hand, and a number of other groups, including segments of the black community, several other ethnic minority groups, and a host of alarmed, but not necessarily racist, white parents. The school district was not the true representative of the multiple interests at stake in the controversy.

When institutional values are placed in jeopardy before the law, there is bound to be variation in the quality and representativeness of the defense. This variation is dependent upon the nature of the particular issue, the constituencies involved, and the institution's pattern of commitments. In the *Lau* case, the school district built a forceful and effective defense on behalf of the numerous categories of children with special educational needs, from whom scarce resources would have to be diverted if the relief requested by the Chinese was granted. (In 1973, the San Francisco schools contained over 9,000 students, from 15 different language backgrounds,

---

[34] 500 F 2nd 249 (9th Circuit, 1974).

in need of remedial English; moreover, language programs comprised only 62 of some 200 programs aimed at special educational needs.)[35] The educational focus of the *Lau* case gave the school district greater confidence in its abilities to resolve this issue, which, despite its political overtones, involved distinctive pedagogical and administrative interests. The unanimous decision of the Supreme Court in favor of the *Lau* plaintiffs in no way diminished the school district's authority to do the best it could in this case. Although inaction was forbidden, no particular action was required. Since the district had every intention of doing something, the decision was not experienced as a defeat but merely as a reminder and a validation of its multiple educational responsibilities.

In *Doe,* too, the district's defense stemmed from a compelling interest to avoid a liability that, by reallocating resources to former students, would have seriously impaired ongoing school operations. Moreover, an unfavorable ruling in *Doe* would have deeply discredited the schools. Here the defense had to be vigorous.

Limitations of Judicial Review

There has been, until quite recently, a tendency to extol the virtues of judicial review and to underestimate its limitations.[36] To allow the judge to make hard decisions relieves officials of their responsibilities, but as Jeremy Bentham long ago warned ("amendment from the judgment seat is confusion"), it is a temptation to avoid because of its costly consequences. Certain elements of legal process proved ill-suited for resolution of the complexities of the *Johnson* and *Lau* cases.

Objectivity

Adjudication offers the benefits of objectivity. Arguments are placed before the judge and he is required to justify his decisions by reference to evidence and reasoning. Judicial review is expected to be less subject to political influence and impartial.

To preserve judicial impartiality, each of the federal cases concerning the San Francisco schools, including the two desegregation cases, was heard by a different judge, responding to different

---

[35] SFUSD, "Bilingual Education: 1973 Census Report," 1974.

[36] For recent criticisms, see Alexander Bickel, *The Supreme Court and the Idea of Progress* (N.Y.: Harper & Row, 1970) and Donald Horowitz, *The Courts and Social Policy* (Washington, D.C.: Brookings Institution, 1977).

questions of law and different facts and oblivious to commonalities among the issues. The judge in the *Johnson* case decided to refuse the Chinese standing to intervene, and rejected their plea for a stay of the desegregation order in order to forestall a delay in the implementation of his decree. Meanwhile, considerable energies were being marshaled to reverse the *Lau* judgment so as to require special bilingual programs for Chinese children, circumventing the *Johnson* decision. These divergent outcomes were never clarified in court.

The Court's Own Timeline

The judiciary followed its own timeline. Although the *Johnson* case was tried in August 1970, a decision was not announced until April 1971—not because of the school calendar, but because the judge wanted to wait for the Supreme Court's ruling in *Swann*. In order to conclude the case, however, he then gave the parties only six weeks to submit their remedial plans. We noted earlier the consequences of this arbitrary haste and the destructive effects it engendered in the schools. Three years then passed before the 9th circuit considered the school district's appeal. By this time school desegregation doctrine had been modified by the *Keyes* decision, which required a finding of discriminatory intent.[37] On this basis, the case was remanded for reexamination. Had the court of appeals acted sooner, a retrial would have been pursued, at least by the Nelson intervenors who had prepared a set of demands for data they believed would have demolished the judgement of de jure segregation. By 1974, however, all parties to the suit were uninterested and disinclined to engage in further litigation.

Hearings and the Quality of Representation

In the *Johnson* case, failures of representation combined with the court's own predilections on matters of procedure and substantive law with drastic consequences for the factual and legal review. There was no trial in the case, i.e. no cross-examination of the factual allegations and virtually no oral testimony at the preliminary injunction hearings. The crucial legal issue—whether evidence of deliberate discrimination is a necessary determinant of unlawful segregation—was never considered. During the hearings, the judge asked instead, "Does not a school board, which for ten years has known of the existence of serious racial imbalance, have a positive

---

[37] *Keyes v School District No. 1, Denver*, 413 U.S. 189 (1973).

duty . . . to act effectively in the interest of eliminating that imbalance?"[38] Interviewed after announcing his decision, the judge replied, "Regardless of whether this is technically de jure or de facto, it is a situation of which no city should be proud."[39] It was precisely on this point that the 9th circuit reversed the judgment.

Judicial Resources

Courts can issue punitive judgments, but they are in no position to assist an institution with enforcement. In *Johnson,* judicial review lacked resources for implementation. The costs of compliance and the educational consequences of legal actions were not considered. Although court orders are not self-executing, the ability to comply was assumed. Implementation called for institutional commitment, but the court had no means of generating this commitment, nor was it capable of overseeing the process of institutional rehabilitation.

Ordinarily, legal action becomes an attractive prospect for seeking redress only after all other avenues—administrative hearings, political persuasion, and negotiation—have been exhausted. This reveals an important limitation: legal action is not appropriate for achieving ends that require genuine collaboration. In a complex organization such as the public schools, it was not enough simply to order desegregation. To achieve the ends of racial justice required leadership, sustained administrative action, and sensitivity to the persistent tensions between order and learning. These were not matters susceptible to the simple command of a court.

Pyrrhic Outcomes

For the plaintiffs, *Lau* and *Doe* ended in apparent defeat, *Johnson* in apparent victory. In retrospect, however, these three cases are striking for their pyrrhic outcomes. The teaching of remedial English and the setting of standards for high school graduation, although they "lost" in court, became matters of public concern and district action. A "victory" for racial integration, the *Johnson* decree never gained more than formal and shallow administrative compliance. Lack of support for the Horseshoe Plan, even in the black community, led to its eventual abandonment. In shaping the actual outcomes of these cases, administrative priorities and public

---

38 Transcript, August 12, 1970.
39 *San Francisco Chronicle,* May 6, 1971.

pressures, not judicial verdicts, were crucial.

Despite the district court's dismissal of *Lau,* there was widespread concern about the educational issues it raised. The school district had not been unaware of the language needs of Chinese and other non-English-speaking students. Indeed, three years before the *Lau* case was conceived, the district concluded that some 5,000 students (five percent of the total enrollment) needed special instruction in English.[40] Until that year, however, the California Education Code had required that "all schools shall be taught in the English language."[41] Legislation subsequently amended that requirement to allow instruction in the pupils' native languages "to the extent that it does not interfere with regular instruction of all pupils in the English language."[42] With this statutory permission, the school district quickly introduced ESL and BBE classes and set aside a small budget for teacher training and curriculum development.[43] The district court had noted these developments in its opinion, and so did the local newspapers. In urging expansion of remedial English efforts, one editor remarked, "Among the many duties of the public schools, one of the most basic is to improve the skills of students deficient in understanding and speaking English."[44]

The San Francisco Human Rights Commission, the local agency which earlier had sponsored the public forums on racial imbalance, voluntarily undertook to monitor the school district's remedial English efforts and to promote their expansion. And at about the same time, the Office of Civil Rights (OCR) of the Department of Health, Education, and Welfare (HEW) issued a memorandum defining its policy under Title VI of the Civil Rights Act and explicitly directing that

> where inability to speak and understand the English language excludes national origin, minority group children from effective participation in the educational programs offered by a school district, the school district must take affirmative steps to rectify the language deficiency in order to open its instructional programs to these students.[45]

---

40 SFUSD, "Bilingual Education in the SFUSD," mimeo, 1967.
41 California Education Code, Section 71 (adopted 1959).
42 Ibid., as amended in 1967.
43 SFUSD, "Chinese Bilingual Education: A Preliminary Report," 1968.
44 *San Francisco Chronicle*, June 12, 1970.

The director of the OCR announced that his office was undertaking a nationwide review of school districts to assess compliance with this requirement.[46]

In 1972, California passed a Bilingual Education Act that provided funds to satisfy the new federal regulations. The San Francisco school district was able to hire bilingual teacher aides and to appoint minority staff both to develop new programs and to represent the interests of various foreign language minority groups in budgetary hearings. The proportion of the student population in need of remedial English increased during the seventies, adding substantially to a constituency for these special programs. Thus, by the time the Supreme Court remanded the *Lau* case for reconsideration under Title VI, the OCR informed the school district that no particular changes were required, and that, in exchange for assurances that affirmative program efforts would continue, no sanctions would be imposed.[47]

The controversy between advocates of BBE and ESL was resolved outside the court. Under community pressure, the school board appointed a citizen's task force that hired special consultants to prepare a master plan. This plan recommended converting the school district into four separate language-based K-12 school complexes (Chinese, Spanish, Filipino, Japanese).[48] However, with the strong backing of the Human Rights Commission, the district declined to undertake such a radical departure from conventional instruction, and instead adopted a general statement of goals and objectives for an improved remedial English program.[49] Limited resources and competing needs supported this more modest resolution, which formed the basis of the consent decree.[50]

The *Doe* case similarly coincided with public concern over the educational issues highlighted by the plight of the plaintiff. The

---

[45] 35 Fed. Reg. 11595, May 25, 1970.

[46] HEW "News Release," May 25, 1970.

[47] Correspondence between Regional Commissioner Edward Aguirre and Superintendent Morena, March 1974. OCR and the Justice Department interpreted the *Lau* decision as requiring "a plan which promises reasonably . . . to provide equal access to the educational program for those who do not understand English." Statement of J. Stanley Pottinger, Civil Rights Division, before the House Committee on Education and Labor, March 12, 1974.

[48] Center for Applied Linguistics, and Citizen's Task Force on Bilingual Education, "A Master Plan for BBE in the SFUSD," February 1975.

[49] S.F. Human Rights Commission, "Statement and Resolution on ESL and BBE," March 1975; SFUSD, "Resolution on Bilingual Education," March 25, 1975.

[50] Civil #C-70-627, October 22, 1976.

aftermath of the legal decision followed a comparable pattern of arousal of public interest, the emergence of special constituencies, and measured response by the school district. What aroused public interest was the release in 1975 of results of the California state testing program that indicated that the average San Francisco twelfth grader's reading performance ranked in the 18th percentile of the statewide distribution. This meant that only 17 percent of twelfth graders statewide, including students from districts with similar socioeconomic background characteristics, scored lower than comparable San Francisco students.[51] Public alarm over this deplorable situation shook the district.[52]

At that time, the San Francisco public schools had no special requirements for high school graduation, nor were there any standards for advancing from one grade to the next. After *Doe,* however, a committee was appointed to study these matters, and promptly recommended that minimum requirements for promotion be established for all grade levels.[53] By then, the school board had selected a new superintendent, Dr. Robert Alioto (no relation to the former mayor), committed to the "back to basics" approach,[54] and he began to develop a new grade structure reorganization of the school system designed to provide better articulation for teaching basic skills. The adoption of his plan, he promised, "would signify the end of social promotion and meaningless diplomas." [55]

In contrast to the heightened activity that followed the *Doe* and *Lau* "defeats," the aftermath of the *Johnson* "victory" was notable for the frustrations and disaffection that accompanied the implementation of the Horseshoe Plan. Support remained weak in part because the suit had been conceived and prosecuted in relative isolation from a significant portion of the black community. Other minority groups, especially the Chinese whose hostility was vocally and visibly expressed, withheld support because they perceived the

---

[51] SFUSD, "Interpretive Supplement, Grade Twelve, California Assessment Program," 1975. The average level of twelfth-grade performance in districts comparable to San Francisco in socioeconomic indices ranged from the 26th to the 41st percentile.

[52] The publication of these test scores precipitated the movement that resulted in the appointment of the special state commission, discussed in the next chapter.

[53] SFUSD, "Report and Recommendations of the Educational Standards Committee," May 25, 1976.

[54] A contemporary argument for this approach was becoming popular: Frank E. Armbruster, *Our Children's Crippled Future: How American Education Has Failed* (N.Y.: The New York Times Book Co., 1977).

[55] SFUSD, "A Proposal for Educational Redesign," January 1978.

desegregation plan as jeopardizing the educational and political objectives of bilingual programs. We have already described the disruptions that fragmented the school district, and noted the school population decline and the difficulties of enforcing the desegregation plan. After five years of coping with these unrelenting conditions, the administration decided that it was time to develop a more realistic pupil assignment plan, one designed to capitalize on the currently fashionable "back to basics" trend.

The school district's new plan, called Educational Redesign, was announced in 1977. It called for abandoning both the zone concept and the formula for racial balance, the two cornerstones of Horseshoe. Instead of aiming for a racial distribution in each school that would reflect the districtwide racial population plus or minus 15 percent, the new guidelines called for each school to contain a minimum of four major ethnic groups, with the provision that no single group exceed 45 percent of the total school population. The revised grade structure involved eliminating the existing fourfold division (primary, intermediate, junior high, senior high), and replacing it with a threefold one (primary, middle school, high school). In redrawing school attendance boundaries so as to reduce pupil transportation, special dispensation was given to naturally integrated neighborhood schools. These logistical changes were coupled with educational plans, in particular the development of "magnet" schools, emphasizing some special curriculum, such as the "3-Rs," open classrooms, vocational training, and performing arts, so as to draw pupils from all over the city and also to attract back to the public schools students who had abandoned them for parochial or private schools.

The plan was discussed at public meetings held in various locations throughout the city. A number of parents opposed the proposed closing of 20 schools (included in the plan to reduce costs, and in recognition of declining enrollments), but the administration insisted that dwindling resources and fewer pupils made this move necessary. The most controversial feature of the plan was the pairing of three elementary schools in Hunters Point with schools on the naval base at Treasure Island, a known source of resistance to school desegregation.[56] The Hunters Point parents also balked, with

---

[56] Treasure Island parents had refused to send their children to San Francisco schools under the Horseshoe Plan, but eventually did so when the district assured them of assignments to nonghetto areas. *San Francisco Chronicle*, December 7, 1971.

the result that it was agreed to leave the schools in this community almost entirely black. With this glaring modification, the plan was adopted, and put into effect in the fall of 1978.

In June of that year, the *Johnson* plaintiffs challenged the Educational Redesign Plan in court. The national office of the NAACP, disturbed by the apparent apathy of the local black community and not willing to concede defeat in the first northern city under a court-ordered desegregation plan, assumed control of the prosecution. However, at this stage of the proceedings, the court chose to terminate its involvement, and did so by dismissing the original suit without prejudice. Inaction and lack of prosecution during the intervening years were the primary reasons the court gave for its decision. Also cited were the changed circumstances of the schools, including the decline in the white school population, and the popularly elected school board. Finally, the court noted that none of the original plaintiffs any longer attended a San Francisco public school.[57]

Thus the legal battle ended. One veteran of the long struggle to improve educational opportunities for black children in San Francisco commented, "I don't care any more that the schools are not integrated. The key thing I want blacks to look at now is the educational plan."[58]

Conclusion

Legal reform, at least in the *Johnson* case, was not a vehicle for improvement of the schools' educational obligations. By focusing on an artificial formula for the removal of racial segregation, the *Johnson* decree obscured the larger issue at stake, namely, the schools' responsibility for racial justice. What should the San Francisco schools have done at this time to overcome the impact of historic practices of slavery and racial discrimination? Was racial balance alone the answer? What else should the schools have been doing to enhance educational opportunities for children from every racial and ethnic group? The institutional changes stimulated by *Johnson* were hardly responsive to these issues. It was not surprising that a strong commitment to the provision of full membership in the community, establishing the expectation that all children

---

[57] Memorandum and Order of Dismissal, June 22, 1978, U.S. District Court, N.D. Calif., No. C-70-1331.

[58] Idaree Westbrook, quoted in the *San Francisco Chronicle*, January 19, 1979.

equally learn the basic subjects and disciplines, was not generated by this experience in court.

In *Lau* and *Doe,* while a few plaintiffs were rebuffed, and nothing like the sweeping and arbitrary changes of *Johnson* were imposed, these cases also provided no forum for the elaboration of goals for the schools with respect to the issues they did address. These issues and the changes that did occur after the legal action was concluded were precipitated by pressure groups and constrained by short-term administrative criteria. They were opportunistic solutions, not long-range decisions embodying a revitalized sense of mission. Graduation standards, for example, are not the equivalent of goals for a school system's educational program, nor are grade-level proficiency standards sufficient objectives toward those goals. The minimum standards by which third graders, starting in 1978, were tested as a basis for promotion to the next grade were not even grade-level norms.[59] Indeed, they were designed to identify only five percent of the pupils for possible retention, and thus to allow the promotion of a large proportion of below grade-level students.[60] Parents were misled to think that passing a proficiency test was consistent with achieving grade-level standards. Similarly, the satisfaction of high school graduation standards was no guarantee that students had acquired anything beyond minimum competence, if that.

The failure of legal arguments to reestablish more legitimate bases for school decision making was due in part to the kinds of incapacities cited earlier—simplifying issues for judicial review, failures of representation, and the like—but it was also a consequence of a more general limitation, namely, the application of abstract reasoning to the resolution of concrete social problems. One disheartened parent called attention to the irony of legal reform that could produce a plan as blunt and mindless as

---

[59] The tests were developed by local staff familiar with the typical reading problems of San Francisco pupils. While this method has the advantage of tailoring the tests to lessons taught in school, it has the disadvantage that no comparison can be drawn between the achievement levels of local pupils and national or state norms. See SFUSD, "Third-Grade Minimum Standards Test," 1977; also "Letter to Parents of Third-Graders," November 9, 1977.

[60] Nearly one-quarter of the 4,400 third graders tested in December 1977 failed the basic skills test. In May 1978 upon retesting, 95 percent of those who initially failed improved sufficiently to pass. A third chance was offered those of the remaining five percent who attended summer school, so that in the end only 400 third graders, or one percent were advised to repeat the third grade. *San Francisco Chronicle,* August 23, 1978.

Horseshoe. In a letter to a local newspaper editor, he said, "It is hard to believe that the Constitution requires fleeting mathematical perfection in preference to meaningful change . . . ." [61] Of course it was not the Constitution that required the Horseshoe Plan. This plan was the product of *legalism*, a mode of thinking uninformed by social and educational realities, and therefore unresponsive to the conditions that it so drastically transformed.

The inappropriateness of abstract reasoning for guiding social change was also present in the construction of the consent decree by which the *Lau* case was concluded. This decree illustrates the tendency for legal judgments to favor formal or procedural outcomes, rather than substantive ones. Procedural pronouncements do not call for concrete knowledge of institutional practices. In their broad sweep, they tend to neglect the specific details that constitute substance. Thus the *Lau* decree was not concerned with specifics. Instead, it ordered the district to comply with time-consuming procedural requirements, such as extensive documentation and record keeping regarding bilingual and ESL programs, as well as annual tests and reports of pupil progress. The compilation of these data for the court was not intended as a means of evaluation, but as an end in itself. Rather than enlarging educational opportunities in response to pupil needs, the abstract demands of the *Lau* decree diverted resources, distracted leadership, and reinforced bureaucratic tendencies.

In contrast, the opinion of the Human Rights Commission spoke to policy outcomes.

> Although the district's efforts have been far from perfect, they nevertheless aim at (1) reducing the disparities in learning achievement and (2) eliminating minority isolation and inter-ethnic group tensions.[62]

Finally, from the standpoint of the court's potential as a public forum for the representation and articulation of policy issues, the experience of the schools in court was especially disappointing. In *Johnson,* the few hearings that were held concealed rather than highlighted the real differences and controversies at stake. Third parties were limited, but are in any case no panacea, because they too present unresolved problems of representativeness. A host of

---

[61] Alan S. Maremont, in the *San Francisco Examiner*, December 14, 1971.

[62] San Francisco Human Rights Commission, "Bilingual Education in the SFUSD," 1977.

amici curiae were allowed to enter the *Lau* case before the court of appeals and the Supreme Court. They included the solicitor general, whose concern was the government's responsibilities under Title VI; the Center for Law and Education, an advocacy agency; the Mexican-American Legal Defense and Education Fund, the Puerto-Rican Legal Defense and Education Fund, and California Rural Legal Assistance—all concerned with the educational needs of Spanish-American children; the Anti-Defamation League of B'Nai B'Rith and other civil rights groups; and several other committees and organizations concerned with affirmative action. All spoke in support of the plaintiffs, and their expert and extensive participation may have influenced the unanimous Supreme Court ruling. None, however, contributed to enlarging the scope of the court's inquiry. The mobilization of multiple interests did not of itself produce a clear and persuasive ruling, one that might serve as a sound guide to policy and action.

The experience of the San Francisco schools in court has an important lesson: when courts confront cases from institutions with deep and multiple problems, the responsible course may not be judicial action, but rather judicially sanctioned mediation among the parties with interests at stake. This approach offers opportunities for identifying and clarifying values, setting priorities based both on principles and facts, and mobilizing the energies of all concerned in formulating and implementing policy. The limits of command in accomplishing institutional change—change that requires concerted action and includes the participation of all whose efforts are necessary for organizational performance—are realities that courts, when they serve as vehicles for the formulation of social policy, must understand and take into account.

PART III: OUTCOMES

8

Restoration of Order

Where there is no vision,
the people perish.[1]

The courts could not arrest the demoralization that, by the early seventies, had overtaken the San Francisco schools. Indeed, judicial intervention exacerbated the erosion of authority. The Horseshoe Plan did not speak to the substantive (educational) ends at stake precisely because means and ends were never joined in court. Nothing the courts did changed the basic conditions responsible for the district's difficulties: the school board's political weakness and lack of leadership; the rigidity and unwieldincss of the school administration; the social climate of opportunism and drift. Civic energies aroused by visions of more "just" schools dissipated amidst conflicts among various school constituencies. A plurality of special interests was no substitute for a community of purpose.

Part II explored these dynamics in the San Francisco schools and described the erosion of institutional integrity. The next two chapters (Part III) are concerned with some outcomes of the schools' demoralization.

The Schools Under Commission Inquiry

By the mid-seventies, consequences of shortsightedness on the part of school leadership were too numerous to pass unnoticed. Declining achievement scores were notorious. Violence and apathy, testifying to the depleted capacities of school staff to motivate and provide meaningful activities for students, were mounting.[2] In

---

[1] Proverbs 29:18.
[2] A striking indication of the extent of student apathy was the rate of student absenteeism during a brief municipal bus strike in 1976. In many schools, only 25 percent of the students made the effort to attend, according to a poll taken by the *San Francisco Progress*, April 29, 1976.

addition, the advent of tax-saving state school finance legislation was placing the fiscal future of the schools in jeopardy. Political and civic officials reacted with dismay to these symptoms of neglect. The San Francisco Planning and Urban Renewal Association (SPUR) complained that the deterioration of the schools was hastening the flight of middle-class families from the city.[3] The board of supervisors passed a resolution calling the school board to task for the school district's declining test scores and the mounting vandalism that was turning respectable school buildings into public eyesores.[4] In 1975, State Senator George Moscone made school reform a key issue in his mayoral campaign to succeed Joseph Alioto.

Mobilizing and concerting public opinion was a problem, however, because various groups within the school community, preoccupied with their own agendas, could not be relied upon to act responsibly. As for the board, it was clearly not responsive to long-range concerns. The situation resembled a period early in the century, prior to the professionalization of the city's school system, when business and city leaders similarly had wanted to improve the governance of the schools. To do so, they had to go outside the system. To obtain the necessary leverage, they sought assistance from the U.S. Office of Education. A survey of the San Francisco schools, conducted by the U.S. Commission of Education in 1917, supported their cause, and recommended severing the ties connecting the schools to local politics and placing them under professional management.[5]

Comparable aims, especially the curtailment of school board "meddling" and the restoration of administrative order, stimulated a comparable strategy in the mid-seventies. A casual remark by State Superintendent of Instruction Wilson Riles to the effect that the San Francisco schools were "so bad, they were embarrassing," encouraged local citizens and civic groups to solicit his help in establishing an outside commission of inquiry. The commission, it was hoped, would recommend changes in school management and promote the restoration of administrative efficiency. These changes, it was assumed, would resolve the district's problems.

---

[3] Letter from SPUR President Robert Kirkwood to School Board President Hopp, quoted in the *San Francisco Chronicle*, October 1, 1974.

[4] *San Francisco Chronicle*, October 8, 1974.

[5] "The Public School System of San Francisco, California, A Report of a Survey," *Bulletin #46* (Washington, D.C.: Bureau of Education, 1917).

While the office of the state superintendent, like that of the early U.S. commissioner of education, had virtually no authority over the affairs of local school districts, Superintendent Riles, after some informal consultations, agreed to lend his support and appoint a study group that, under his auspices, would "take a comprehensive look at the entire [school] system . . . assess the needs and then *effect the reforms*."[6] The editor of a local paper, speaking for the city's establishment, was highly enthusiastic:

> The schools, the teachers, the parents and their children are most fortunate to have the interest and attention of such a prominent (study) group . . . . We have *high hopes* . . . that their collective experience and judgment (will) be the salvation of a deteriorating system.[7]

To return the schools to professional management, to rescue them from the governance of board members representing special interests, and to regain broad-based public support, a commission of inquiry—the San Francisco Public Schools Commission (SFPSC), sponsored by the state superintendent—was thus created. "High hopes" were expressed that the commission would generate public discussion of school affairs, air and resolve conflicts over such issues as desegregation and community control, and restore public confidence in the schools.

The SFPSC was appointed quite soon after a period in which activists had turned to the courts to resolve their grievances with the school district. Despite the legal system's capacity for sober and dispassionate scrutiny of the issues that come before it, we have noted the limitations of judicial inquiry for the formulation of educational policy, and of judicial command for the rehabilitation of ailing schools. More could conceivably be expected from an impartial commission, unhampered by restrictions of legal doctrine and unencumbered by the adversary process. Under commission inquiry, no restrictions or distortions would be imposed by the transformation of policy issues into legal questions. Nor was the commission confined to the particular concerns of an individual or a special group. In contrast to the narrow focus of the courts, the commission's mandate was broad and open-ended.

Grants from several local foundations, as well as modest in-kind support from the school district, enabled the SFPSC to raise sufficient operating funds to hire its own staff and to retain

---

[6] Quoted in the *San Francisco Chronicle*, March 20, 1974 (emphasis added).
[7] Editorial, *San Francisco Chronicle*, October 10, 1974 (emphasis added).

independent consultants. In addition, individual members contributed considerable talent and experience. The chairman was William Matson Roth, a prominent local business and civic leader and former Democratic Party gubernatorial candidate. The 24 members, chosen by a committee of local university presidents, included officers of major corporations, a judge, a former undersecretary of HEW, a former member of the federal Equal Employment Opportunities Commission, and the like.[8] A timeline of 18 months, subsequently extended to two years, was agreed upon for completion of the inquiry.

Because of its broad mandate, the SFPSC was unlike conventional school survey teams, called upon to resolve specific or technical problems, and more like a British Royal Commission.[9] Such commissions are formed to remedy the performance of public agencies that lack capacities for self-evaluation and renewal. Because of their important mission, they are used infrequently and only on highly sensitive social policy problems. Ideally, by following open and equitable procedures of inquiry, a Royal Commission is able to overcome distrust and inspire public confidence. Facts are determined impartially by bringing in able outsiders, holding hearings,

---

[8] In addition to the chairman, William Matson Roth, president of Roth Properties and a former regent of the University of California, commission members included Bernice Brown, dean of students at Lone Mountain College; Lewis Butler, professor of health policy at U.C. San Francisco; Ruth Chance, retired executive director of the Rosenberg Foundation; John Crowley, secretary-treasurer of the San Francisco Labor Council; Dr. Roberta Fenlon, former president of the S.F. Medical Society; R. Gwin Follis, retired chairman of the board of Standard Oil Company; James B. Frankel, attorney and former chairman of the S.F. Citizens' Charter Revision Committee; Herman Gallegos, secretary of SPUR; Louis Garcia, former chairman of the S.F. Neighborhood Legal Assistance Foundation; James Hermann, president of Local 34, Ship Clerks Association of the I.L.W.U.; Aileen Hernandez, former president of NOW and member of the U.S. Equal Employment Opportunities Commission; Asa Hilliard, dean of the School of Education, San Francisco State University; Jerome W. Hull, chairman of the board of Pacific Telephone; G. F. Jewett, vice-president of Potlatch Corporation; Robert C. Kirkwood, president of SPUR; Reverend Donald L. Kuhn, former chairman of the Citizens Advisory Committee on Desegregation; Judge Harry Low, superior court, president of the Chinese-American Citizens Alliance; Leslie Luttgens, chairman of the United Bay Area Crusade; Thomas J. Mellon, Jr., attorney and president of U.S.F. Alumni Association; Einer Mohn, retired director of the Western Conference of Teamsters; Father Antonio Rey, Archdiocese of San Francisco; and Yori Wada, executive director of the YMCA and regent of the University of California.

[9] Hollis Caswell, *City School Surveys: An Interpretation and Appraisal* (N.Y.: Little Ives & Co., 1929); Charles J. Hanser, *Guide to Decision: The Royal Commission* (New Jersey: Bedminister Press, 1965).

and airing multiple points of view. High standards of selection and operation enhance a Royal Commission's capacity to establish authoritative guidelines for corrective social action that the agency in question can then follow.[10]

Despite its resemblance to commissions of this type, the SFPSC, or Riles Commission, as it was commonly referred to, fulfilled none of these expectations.[11] In its "Summary Report," a review of all its activities and major recommendations, the most striking feature was the absence of attention to the schools' salient problems. No mention was made of student violence; declining standards of performance were ignored; vandalism and staff demoralization were neglected; and while passing mention was made of the exodus of parents and students, and the resultant fiscal crunch, no serious study of these matters was undertaken.

On the topics the SFPSC did address, the report concluded with vague or innocuous statements that reflected inadequate and superficial inquiry. For example, on school management:

> The school board should revise its policies to make clear that in fact the principal is the chief executive officer for each school. . . . It should be district policy to give principals the authority to make all critical decisions at the school site and to hold them accountable for effective performance through a system of regular evaluation.[12]

On parent participation:

> The school board should adopt a policy that there be a School Site Advisory Council for each school.[13]

On student participation:

> There should be a student forum at each high school each year, attended by the school board and the Superintendent, as well as a city-wide forum organized by a Student Advisory Council.[14]

---

[10] Hanser, *Guide to Decision*. Also, Daniel Bell, "Government by Commission," 3 *Public Interest* (Spring 1966). For a contrary view on the potential of commissions of inquiry, see Anthony Platt, *The Politics of Riot Commissions, 1917-1970* (N.Y.: Macmillan Co., 1971.)

[11] Analysis of the SFPSC is based on personal observations, interviews, and review of commission documents. From 1974 to 1976, the author attended the commission's public meetings and its open committee hearings. Commission staff assisted in compiling a complete record of official memos and reports.

[12] SFPSC, "Summary Report," June 1976, pp. 6-8.

[13] Ibid., p. 7.

On relations with city government:

> The district should make increased use of joint task forces and staff committees to improve cooperation and communication with city departments . . . . Our findings can best be used to stimulate further discussions among those responsible for improving these relationships.[15]

On balancing the budget:

> The school board must anticipate the fiscal future of the district in order to make reasoned choices about reducing expenditures.[16]

The SFPSC did produce a few more substantial studies. However, these were strictly technical reports concerning accounting and budgetary procedures, the procurement of supplies, and the implementation of collective bargaining legislation. These reports were almost identical to reports the school district had recently obtained from accountants and management consultants. In some cases, for example with regard to purchasing and the cash flow between school and city treasuries, the commission's conclusions followed directly from the suggestions of previous studies.[17]

Considering the breadth of its mandate, and the resources of its prominent membership, the poverty of the commission's accomplishments was disappointing and also rather surprising. Why did this promising review agency fail to address the substantive policy issues at stake? Did it lack authority? Was it deliberately involved in a conspiracy of silence—a "cover-up"—to divert public scrutiny? Was its lack of candor and daring the result of inadequate conceptualization and ineffective organization, or was the commission's impoverished vision of the public schools itself an outcome of the schools' weakened and demoralized condition?

Management and Politics

Despite its broad mandate ("to take a comprehensive look at the entire system . . . assess the needs and effect reforms"),[18] the

[14] Ibid., p. 10.

[15] Ibid., p. 13.

[16] Ibid., p. 11.

[17] The SFPSC's reports built on the following studies: SFUSD, "Study of the Organization and Administration of Selected Business Services," prepared by consultants Booz-Allen and Hamilton, 1970; and "A Study of the Cash Flow Between School and City Treasuries," Chamber of Commerce, 1968.

[18] Superintendent Riles, quoted in the *San Francisco Chronicle*, March 23, 1974.

commission from the outset was determined that its chief contribution should be to separate the schools from local politics. According to the SFPSC, this required strengthening the authority of the school administration while simultaneously minimizing the influence of the board. Instead of providing a critical diagnosis of the condition of the public schools (as suggested by its official mandate), the commission instead defined its task and central mission as the restoration of orderly management. Commission doctrine presumed that if the schools' administrative operations were put in proper order, then all other problems would eventually solve themselves. This meant the resumption of control by professionals and a corresponding relegation of the board to its former posture of deference to the administration. The fact that the most substantial of the commission's final recommendations were its technical reports is largely traceable to this basic assumption.

Early and deliberate decisions based on the understanding that the commission would "restructure and reorganize, making the kinds of decisions business and industry operate under,"[19] shaped the commission's character and outlook. An important criterion in the selection of commission members had been their administrative background and experience; they in turn chose as their director Dr. Luvern L. Cunningham, an educator with a national reputation for his "problem-solving" approach to school management. Commission consultants similarly were hired for their technical expertise in various aspects of management.

In the spring of 1975, soon after the SFPSC was established, it began holding a series of public hearings to solicit testimony from school officials on the district's management problems. Backed by earlier consultant reports, Superintendent Morena testified that on the whole administrative operations were running smoothly, but that in any case further improvements would not have much effect on the district's basic problems, which he defined as high costs, low pupil performance, and the difficulties of eliminating nonproductive staff.[20] But the SFPSC, not satisfied with this "insider" information, commissioned its own report on the state of the school administration. The commission's report, prepared by a management consultant, presented a rather different view, one highly critical of the administrative structure of the schools. It found lines of

---

[19] Graham Sullivan, a consultant to Superintendent Riles, whose perspective on the commission is quoted in the *San Francisco Chronicle*, October 10, 1974.
[20] SFPSC, "Minutes," February 12, 1975, p. 3.

authority poorly delineated, executive powers fragmented, and direction confused and incoherent. The report recommended strengthening the administration's authority over budget and personnel, improving the management information system, involving principals in budget planning, and delegating to each school more powers over promotion and transfer of staff.[21]

Only the first of these recommendations was taken seriously by the commission. On the basis of its consultant's report, the SFPSC resolved to persuade the board to delegate more authority to the superintendent. The chairman of the commission, at his first public appearance before the school board, condemned its "meddling in administration" as the chief obstacle to school reform. "A business or government agency that managed its affairs in this cumbersome and redundant manner would soon grind to a halt," Chairman Roth charged.[22] His statement was echoed in the local press. As one editorial put it, "The School Chief needs Authority . . . . San Francisco school system is not working the way it should because the Superintendent has no authority."[23]

Members of the board were not exactly pleased by this public criticism. From the beginning, a three-member minority had been opposed to the idea of creating an outside commission. Considerable public pressure had to be exerted before this reluctant faction would consent to the inquiry. Board members feared that the SFPSC might turn the public against them, and they regarded State Superintendent Riles' intrusion into local affairs as unwarranted. While a majority of the board was open to some assistance, the commission's public assault on the entire board effectively ruled out the possibility that the two bodies might work out a cooperative relationship.

Meanwhile, many parents and the grass-roots organizations that had initially pressed for the creation of the SFPSC were also offended. They had felt slighted when they were not offered membership on the commission. And they became resentful of the commission's "imperial stance," a reference to difficulties of communication with commission members. The disaffection of the local school community did not especially alarm the commission, however, because its self-conception entailed an implicit decision to

---

[21] SFPSC, "Report to the San Francisco Public Schools Commission," prepared by Griffenhagen-Kroeger, Inc., April 1975.

[22] SFPSC, "Statement of William M. Roth, Chairman," May 5, 1975.

[23] *San Francisco Chronicle*, May 15, 1975.

rest its authority not upon any local political base, but rather upon its members' prestige and their business credentials. Indeed the commission feared its authority would be weakened if it appeared to be "entangled" with any special interest group involved with the schools, even the PTA.

Thus a pattern was established whereby the school board was identified as an impediment, the school community was largely ignored, and the school administration was regarded as the chief source of support for commission efforts. In effect, the administration became the SFPSC's first and favored client. Indeed, one of the duties assumed by SFPSC Director Luvern Cunningham was "to serve as a staff resource to the superintendent."[24]

Superintendent Alioto, who took office shortly after the SFPSC's inquiry began, welcomed this powerful alliance. There developed a close collaboration between commission and district staff on all kinds of managerial concerns such as accounting, procurement, data-processing, staff decision making, and the like. With the support of the SFPSC, an Office of Budget and Planning was finally established and a budget director hired. The commission's assistance was also enlisted in developing a reorganization plan for the senior administrative staff.[25]

When the school board balked at part of the plan that called for the creation of new staff positions, another confrontation with the SFPSC took place. According to the commission chairman, "The fact that . . . the board, using specious reasoning, would refuse to allow the superintendent to choose his own team, seems to me an act of profound irresponsibility."[26] To which a board member replied, "With the district facing a fiscal crunch, I don't see why we should be hiring any more high priced administrators."[27] The SFPSC, persisting in its efforts to hold the board to "basic principles of sound management," retorted, somewhat threateningly, "From the very first, we have made the point that unless some *basic principles of sound management* were accepted by the board, nothing we did would be of value . . . . As the months go on, however, and we see our work continually frustrated by unwillingness on the part of a majority of the board to accept any limitation

---

[24] SFPSC, "Minutes," July 1975, p. 2.
[25] SFPSC, "Proposed Administrative and Organizational Structure for the SFUSD," n.d.
[26] William Roth, quoted in the *San Francisco Examiner*, October 15, 1975.
[27] Lee Dolson, quoted in the *San Francisco Chronicle*, October 17, 1975.

whatsoever on the right to *meddle in the administrative processes of the district,* our concern with our ability to help you deepens."[28]

Retreat from Controversy

The commission regarded its posture of neutrality as necessary to assure the legitimacy of its inquiry. Expected to offer the school district the benefits of an independent review, the commission was disposed to remain "above politics" and untainted by any appearance of partisanship. Its preoccupation with management problems was one way of avoiding involvement in controversy. Such involvement could expose the commission to loss of credibility as a neutral third party. By confining itself to matters of administrative procedure, the SFPSC was able at once to affirm its objectivity and to invoke the authority of a special expertise. Moreover, on technical issues its own ranks were unlikely to divide and it could "speak with one voice."

Even matters of management procedure, however, can cause controversy. When they did, the commission retreated. For example, as mentioned previously, commission staff worked closely with Alioto in designing a major administrative reorganization. The plan called for firing the fiscal officer and demoting more than two dozen senior administrators, including several blacks. Members of the black community and administrator groups reacted strongly, threatening legal action.[29] To avoid being caught in the crossfire, the commission excused its staff from further participation in the controversial reorganization, and informed the superintendent not to expect commission support for such matters.[30]

Similarly, in the course of investigating the requirements of collective bargaining, a highly sensitive subject, the SFPSC deliberately limited its inquiries in order to avoid any risk of antagonizing powerful local unions. The commission's recommendation to the district on this matter—to hire a full-time employee relations officer—was strictly noncontroversial.[31] So, too, was the recommendation regarding improved communications between the district and various city government agencies. The commission was

---

[28] Letter from William M. Roth to the school board, December 10, 1975 (emphasis added).

[29] *San Francisco Chronicle,* July 30, 1975 and August 6, 1975.

[30] The controversy had repercussions within the commission. Memoranda were exchanged between Aileen Hernandez and William Roth, July 18, 1975 and July 23, 1975. See also, SFPSC, "Minutes," July 9, 1975.

[31] SFPSC, "Appointment of a Principal Negotiator," July 17, 1975.

unwilling to offend the Civil Service Commission, which had control over hiring and other matters involving the schools' nonteaching staff.[32] The SFPSC's timidity on such matters left it impotent when it came to addressing substantive issues of personnel.

Administrative decentralization, especially the delegation to school principals of greater authority on matters of budget and personnel, as recommended by the commission's own management consultant, was initially an area of some interest. But because of disagreements within the SFPSC on the merits and feasibility of "site-budgeting," it was decided to let the matter rest. "It would be a mistake to present a report now," noted the chairman.[33] By "mistake," the commission meant that proceeding with site-budgeting might undermine central administrative control over such matters as relations with unions, minority groups, and city agencies. And so, "speaking with one voice," the commission was only willing to say that principals be designated as "chief executive officers," that each school establish an advisory council, and that decentralization remain "a fundamental objective which will require time and detailed study to implement."[34]

It was almost a foregone conclusion that a body so ready to retreat from controversy would ignore the difficult and politically charged problems of race relations, student achievement, and teacher morale. When Alioto presented his proposal for "Educational Redesign," which effectively ended the Horseshoe Plan, a matter certainly deserving analysis and discussion, the commission decided it ought not to comment.

Not "Just Another Report"

From the beginning, the SFPSC took seriously State Superintendent Riles' charge "to effect reforms." The SFPSC wanted to get things done, not to produce "just another report" fated to be shelved and forgotten.[35] In defining its agenda, the commission thus gave priority to tasks that could be expected to produce

---

[32] SFPSC, "Minutes," April 28, 1975. Also, SFPSC, "Inter-Relationships Between the SFUSD and the City and County of San Francisco," May 1976.

[33] SFPSC, "Minutes of the Finance Committee," October 1, 1975.

[34] SFPSC, "Rewrite of the Site Management Paper," February 13, 1976; Letter from William M. Roth to Lee Dolson, February 18, 1976.

[35] SFPSC, "Summary Report," June 1976, p. 15. A spokesman for the state superintendent was quoted as saying, "There won't be a final report that can be stuck on somebody's shelf." *Saturday Review*, May 3, 1975, p. 39.

tangible outcomes. From this perspective, problems that particularly recommended themselves were those amenable to relatively quick study and/or remediable by actions the administration was willing to take. Such criteria effectively eliminated the more thorny issues plaguing the schools and reinforced the commission's emphasis on management.

When the commission began, it understood that one of its most important tasks was to arrest the declining performance of San Francisco pupils. A committee of the commission was formed to identify what was short-circuiting the schools' operation and to recommend means of improvement. It soon became apparent, however, that commission members had little confidence in their ability to perform such tasks. Judgments about the educational merits of school practices affecting pupil performance, such as principal selection and teacher evaluation, the use of standardized tests, and the relevance of curriculum materials, were not among the managerial concerns on which commission members could speak with authority.

The committee decided that the evaluation of the schools was a job for educational experts, not management generalists, and sought the advice of specialists in evaluation research. The committee also redefined the evaluation task. Instead of seeking an independent appraisal of the schools' performance, the committee began exploring various evaluation mechanisms that the district could utilize for administrative purposes. Several consultants were asked to devise a comprehensive information system that would enable the central administration to record, assess, and compare school performance.[36] Finally, an educational consulting firm was invited to submit a proposal. It came up with a complicated and expensive system that would have required five to seven years to install; the first phase alone, an assessment of "information needs," would take at least six months and cost over $55,000.[37] The idea was promptly abandoned. The plan was too ambitious, and the school administration found it faulty because it failed to address fiscal issues.[38]

---

[36] Consultant groups interviewed by the appraisal committee included the Research and Evaluation Consortium, Stanford University; the Far West Lab in San Francisco; and the Northwest Regional Laboratory in Portland, Oregon. SFPSC, "Minutes of the Appraisal Committee," September 2 and September 19, 1975.

[37] SFPSC, "Minutes of the Appraisal Committee," October 9, 1975; SFPSC, "Purposes and Objectives of the Information/Appraisal System," October 7, 1975.

[38] SFPSC, "Minutes of the Appraisal Committee," November 4, 1975.

Several months later, the commission learned of another method of school evaluation, one developed by Michael Scriven, a professor at the University of California, Berkeley. His method included an elaborate questionnaire designed to help school administrators, teachers, parents, and students periodically, say every third year, conduct a joint assessment of their school's performance, pinpointing problems requiring corrective action.[39] The materials comprised, in effect, a carefully thought-out "do-it-yourself" package that would enable a school community to examine itself without hiring expensive consultants or engaging in massive testing and/or computerized data analysis.[40] When Scriven presented his idea to the commission in June 1976, the SFPSC found it attractive, and Alioto agreed to authorize a field test when school opened in the fall. By then, however, the SFPSC was running out of time. Scriven's preliminary recommendations did not reach the commission until after its summary report had been published.

At one of its very last meetings, the commission hastily concluded that the evaluation instrument was "manageable and acceptable."[41] An administratively feasible plan had been found, or so it seemed. In fact, the school administration had no investment in the Scriven procedure, and the SFPSC had not seriously tried to obtain a commitment to self-evaluation. Needless to say, such a method of evaluation, one likely to elicit sensitive issues, threaten powerful interests, and trigger conflicts among various school groups, could not have been put into practice without considerable administrative and political work. This was not the kind of work the commission was prepared to undertake.

The Price of "Getting Things Done"

Shortly after the SFPSC was created, there was a serious disagreement between the chairman and the vice-chairman as to what the commission should do with regard to collective bargaining. The vice-chairman believed that the introduction of collective bargaining could have critical implications for school governance and finance. In his view, there was a need for the commission to determine what mechanisms of negotiation were compatible with

---

[39] SFPSC, "School Evaluation Profile," February 1976; also, "Minutes," February 4, 1976, p. 3.
[40] SFPSC, "A Procedure for Assessing the Performance of a Particular School," December 1976, p. 2.
[41] SFPSC, "Minutes," December 1, 1976.

proper maintenance of administrative and political authority, and to explore how collective bargaining would affect the direction and allocation of funds. In the chairman's opinion, however, to undertake such a study seemed a waste of commission resources. It would take a long time, raise all kinds of difficult questions, and potentially reach conclusions beyond the commission's limited powers. The SFPSC would be more helpful, he argued, if it confined its inquiry to a review of what was required under new state legislation (the Rodda Act), and then persuaded the board to hire a full-time labor relations specialist. This opinion reflected commission doctrine that under good management, substantive problems take care of themselves.

The chairman prevailed, and the result was that the commission produced a useful, if superficial, legal analysis of the statutory requirements.[42] To this, no one would object; moreover, the school board readily agreed to hire the recommended employee relations officer.

On its face, the chairman's argument seemed reasonable enough. The SFPSC had to husband its resources and be selective in determining the problems to which it would devote its energies. Success in tackling those problems would require it to accept compromises, to skirt some issues, and to avoid needlessly alienating powerful interests. The problem was not that the SFPSC should have disdained a concern for effectiveness, but rather that it pursued "getting things done" at the price of impoverishing its vision of what might have been accomplished. The criterion of effectiveness, detached from substantive ends, made short-run feasibility the touchstone by which the commission chose its tasks. Anything "do-able" within its short lifetime, no matter how trivial, had a claim on commission resources; whatever failed to meet this test was dismissed.

By this measure, minor matters of management were especially suitable. A quick cost-benefit analysis, based on earlier consultant reports, indicated that it would save time and money if the district would assume direct control of purchasing, transporting, and storing its supplies;[43] the school board agreed,[44] and the SFPSC immediately set about helping to implement the proposed changes. On less straightforward matters, the commission facilitated what

---

[42] SFPSC, "Collective Bargaining: The Impact of the Rodda Act," April 12, 1976.

[43] SFPSC, "Purchasing Report," October 9, 1975.

[44] SFUSD, Board Resolution #510-28, November 11, 1975.

was, in effect, administrative patchwork. For instance, the central administration had been hampered in its staff reorganization by the longstanding practice of granting tenure to school principals. Although a 1971 amendment to the city charter had formally abolished principal tenure as such, requiring that principals be appointed under four-year contracts, the administration had not been able to enforce this change in practice. In a special report, a commission consultant suggested that the SFPSC take the school district to court to compel compliance with the law.[45] This would have brought about a serious confrontation with the administrators. But the commission found a way to avoid such an outcome: the problem, it concluded, was not principal tenure; it was, rather, inadequate training. On this basis, the commission recommended that the district simply revise the principal's job description and introduce in-service training to upgrade performance.[46]

A preoccupation with "getting things done" was embodied in the commission's own organization. Following initial public hearings, the SFPSC divided its membership into three committees—finance, governance, and appraisal—each of which was assigned a relatively broad set of issues. Representatives of parents and teachers found the committees quite accessible, and disagreements among commission members, stifled at the public meetings of the whole body, were aired in committee. But the chairman became impatient with this system: it took too long to gather information and reach agreement and it was too unwieldy to get things done. At his suggestion, therefore, halfway through its inquiry, the commission was divided into eleven discrete task forces, each with a clearly defined responsibility, and all operating under a tightly controlled work schedule.[47] The practice of public notice and participation in the commission's inquiry thus came to an end. The task forces met irregularly and worked informally with commission staff. No minutes were kept of their activities. They operated in virtual isolation both from one another and from the public.

This reorganization enabled the SFPSC to produce more timely reports. But it did so at the price of fragmentation and loss of a shared sense of purpose. With the demise of the larger committees, the SFPSC dissolved the mechanism by which its members might

---

[45] SFPSC, "Minutes," March 17, 1976.
[46] SFPSC, "The Role of Principals," May 1976.
[47] SFPSC, "Memorandum from William M. Roth to Members of the Commission," November 15, 1975.

have formed a more comprehensive view of the schools' problems. Instead of pursuing an inquiry in keeping with its broad mandate, there remained only an agenda of unrelated items.

Without guidance from the commission, the task forces were reluctant to deal with any topic of substance. Those charged with more sensitive issues decided it was best just to "tip-toe around the edges."[48] The task force on students, for example, rather than dealing with apathy and alienation, ended up recommending that the commission sponsor an essay contest and conduct a few forums in the high schools.[49] And the task force on integration concluded its inquiry with well-intentioned commonplaces, such as "eliminate hidden patterns of inequity . . . correct racial isolation . . . use curriculum materials reflecting different cultures . . . ."[50] By trying to "get things done," the SFPSC managed to avoid contact with the tough issues and real problems of the schools.

The Benefits of Fact Finding

The most striking manifestation of the SFPSC's preoccupation with results was the lack of emphasis on fact finding. Inquiries in depth without tangible outcomes were not worth undertaking; furthermore, time had to be allowed for implementation. Major reports on collective bargaining or decentralization were thereby ruled out. No priority was given to sustained study. Serious issues, such as vandalism and truancy, the withdrawal of parent participation, the increasing alienation of teacher organizations and the power of administrator groups, the effects of federal legislation and judicial interventions—none of these, despite the commission's broad and open-ended mandate, were ever seriously analyzed. Determined to avoid reinventing the wheel, convinced that further investigations would be futile, the commission was satisfied to "tip-toe around the edges," suggest some "manageable and acceptable" remedies, and quietly go out of business.

More might have been accomplished by an authoritative, comprehensive factual report on the condition of the San Francisco schools. Even when findings do not generate specific policy conclusions, they can help disentangle complex problems, bring objectivity

---

[48] Personal notes of remarks by a commission member at the meeting of April 17, 1976.

[49] SFPSC, "Student Essays," December 1, 1976.

[50] SFPSC, "The Educational Components of an Integrated School System," November 17, 1976, p. 8.

to public debate, recall officials to their responsibilities, and set new directions for policy. Preferring quick and immediate results, impatient with politics, and fearful of controversy, the commission chose to avoid confronting troublesome facts and saw no value in producing a document that could establish the premises for further, more sober thinking about educational policy. A consequence of this strategy was the fostering of complacency. Unlike a Royal Commission, the SFPSC neither aroused public interest in the schools nor restored public confidence in their performance.

The "Last Hurrah"

By the late seventies a somber mood settled over the San Francisco school community, the residue of frustrations and disappointments generated by a rapid succession of changes and reforms, none of which were improving school conditions. The Riles Commission was the community's "last hurrah," a final burst of civic interest. The poverty of accomplishment of this prestigious and resourceful body conveyed a sense that the school situation was beyond repair.

The SFPSC's final report did not renew energies, nor did it stimulate a new vision of the future. On the contrary, it left the impression that, aside from the restoration of order, nothing much could be done to improve the schools. In the commission's aftermath, instead of working toward renewal of the schools, district leaders viewed their contribution in terms of the disheartening task of keeping the schools afloat—"bailing out the sinking ship," as the president of the school board described his work in 1980.

The Demise of Political Leadership

Just after the court-ordered desegregation plan went into effect in November 1971, the voters reelected Joseph Alioto and also chose a new member of the board of supervisors, Quentin Kopp, the attorney who had represented the Chinese intervenors in their efforts to stop the busing plan. The electorate, further expressing displeasure with school leadership, voted to make the school board elective, and at the same time confirmed three new mayoral nominees to the board, all of them opposed to forced busing. They were George Chinn, the first Chinese-American to serve on the school board (replacing Laurel Glass); Dr. Eugene Hopp, a former chairman of the local Commonwealth Club's Educational Committee (replacing Alan Nichols); and a new labor representative, John Kidder. All three were elected the following year in the first school board election since 1897. The board the commission confronted (from 1974 to 1976) consisted of four members appointed by the mayor[51] and three elected members.[52] Regardless of how they came to hold office, however, members of the school board were attached to special constituencies. They had no common platform or consensus except that a majority generally did *not* support school busing.

The majority faction also initially opposed the commission and contributed to the hostile relations that characterized the two years of the SFPSC's inquiry.[53] For its part, the commission viewed the board majority's involvement in school affairs as "negative and destructive," inhibiting the exercise of sound management.[54] But while a new mayor, George Moscone, and the local newspapers sided with the commission, many supporters of the board majority resented the time wasted over exchanges between the board and the commission and urged the SFPSC to put all its efforts into "determining why our children are failing to read and write."[55] People citizens remained unconvinced that the commission's preoccupation with restraining the board and strengthening the school administration was the best way to approach the schools' problems.[56]

Belatedly the commission agreed. "The board somehow has to measure what management does against the achievement of kids."[57] From this revised perspective and recognition that the school board had a necessary and important role to play in

---

[51] Two of Mayor Alioto's earlier appointments, Dr. Hopp and John Kidder, were reelected in 1974, and two conservatives, Father Reed and Samuel Martinez, were appointed as replacements for George Chinn and David Sanchez who resigned shortly after their election in 1972.

[52] The three elected members were Lucille Abrahamson, a representative of the liberal community, Dr. Lee Dolson, a local college administrator, and Charlie May Haynes, wife of a black minister. Dr. Dolson subsequently served his conservative constituency as their representative on the board of supervisors.

[53] Originally only three board members, Dr. Hopp, Lee Dolson, and Father Reed, opposed the commission, but they were later joined by Mr. Martinez.

[54] Letter from Chairman Roth to the school board, December 10, 1975.

[55] Letter from a local parent to the editor of the *San Francisco Chronicle*, January 15, 1976. Other parents made similar charges over local radio and TV programs. See "The Little City," Vol. 1, #9 (March 1976).

[56] The Center for Public Education, a school-community interest group, published a number of articles critical of the commission. *Nexus*, Vol.1 #3, #4, #5, #7 (April, May, June, and August 1975). As director of this agency, the author was involved in monitoring the commission and reporting on its impact.

[57] Commission member Lewis Butler, personal notes of the commission meeting, May 5, 1976.

monitoring the administration, the elected board's "meddling" became the subject of criticism because it went beyond monitoring.

To assist in identifying and supporting a new and more desirable kind of leadership, the commission decided that it should play a role in the upcoming board election. At the last minute, therefore, instead of terminating in June 1976 (when its initial 18-month timeline expired), the commission extended its activities for another six months, devoting the extra time primarily to a publicity effort aimed at scoring "deficiencies in the attitude and competence of the board."[58] As the election campaign began, the chairman of the commission called a press conference and announced that the SFPSC would remain "on duty," in order to influence the composition and character of board leadership.[59] "If our district is not being as well run as others in the state, and we believe it is not," the chairman reported to the state superintendent, "the fault lies ultimately with the board."[60]

However, when it came to selecting specific candidates and supporting their campaign for office, the commission held back, reluctant to become involved in local school politics. Just as it had earlier refrained from exerting pressure on the administration, the SFPSC again proceeded with utmost caution and restraint, unwilling to undertake the necessary political work. Thus no candidates were sponsored by the SFPSC, nor did any receive the commission's endorsement, not even one of the commission's own members. Indeed when he announced his candidacy, the commission reacted with surprise and embarrassment, insisted on his resignation, and went out of its way *not* to support him.[61]

Nevertheless, only one of the four incumbents was re-elected.[62] This evidence of public disaffection with the board was not new, however, nor could it be attributed to the influence of the SFPSC. Two years earlier, before the commission's inquiry, the incumbents had been similarly rejected by the voters, or chose not to run.

---

[58] William M. Roth, in a public letter to Dr. Riles, June 30, 1976.

[59] SFPSC, "Minutes," June 30, 1976, p. 3; also, the *San Francisco Chronicle*, July 2, 1976.

[60] Roth's letter to Dr. Riles, June, 30, 1976.

[61] Notes, commission meeting, September 22, 1976. The candidate, Thomas Mellon, Jr., son of the former chief administrative officer of the city of San Francisco, had a familiar local name. Nevertheless, he was not elected.

[62] Dr. Hopp was the incumbent reelected. Of the three new school trustees chosen, one, Peter Mezey, had previously been active in the civil rights movement (serving as chairman of the Richmond Complex parents council).

Successive changes in the membership of the school board during the seventies brought new, but not more effective leadership. Newly elected members were neither more qualified nor better equipped for leadership than their predecessors. Given these limitations, the more restrained role of "monitor" was not realistic. Members of the board could not cease "meddling" in an administration that was dealing with issues board members and their constituencies cared about. The staff reorganization plan, for example, placed affirmative action in jeopardy and threatened seniority rights of administrators. These were not matters elected school trustees could ignore.

In the decade since 1972, 18 individuals served on the school board (compared to 12 during the previous decade). Average tenure was less than the four-year term of office because a number of people resigned before their terms expired, their energies consumed by the excessive burdens and minimal satisfactions of their work. The critical condition of the schools required more from board members than limited oversight of the administration, but the erosion of public confidence, fragmentation of effort, and loss of energy—symptoms of the schools' demoralization—precluded an effective leadership role.

The SFPSC's criticisms undermined the board's political authority, but did not serve as a corrective for weaknesses of leadership. Moreover, its own counterexample of political caution and retreat from controversy provided little guidance. Had the commission concentrated on fact finding, emphasizing the areas requiring board attention, it might have set a critical agenda for leadership. Basing its recommendations on a diagnosis of school conditions, taking into account what schools can and must do, the commission could have set long-range policy goals. The establishment of reasoned priorities might have forced the school community and its political leaders to resolve their differences and focus on issues of common interest, such as the quality and fairness of school programs. Instead, reasserting the obvious, and failing to deal with real problems, the commission put its stamp of approval on the restoration of official authority and encouraged an attitude of complacency toward the public schools.

9

Disenchantment and Retrenchment

It is not the effort nor the failure tires,
the waste remains,
the waste remains and kills.[1]

The commission's managerial preoccupation and its retreat from controversy, the impotence of the board and its decline into opportunism—these were some of the outcomes of the school system's weakened and demoralized condition. Additionally, as demoralization deepened, capacities for cooperation were diminished, enfeebling organizational action. Ideals and objectives that once stirred energies and motivated behavior no longer had appeal, and in their absence, there was apathy and cynicism. A mood best characterized as disenchantment began to permeate the institution, calling attention to the changes that occurred and pointing to the erosion of integrity.

The stages of demoralization, I have suggested, were characterized by withdrawal of energies, loss of institutional coherence, and erosion of purpose. During the advance of these stages, their presence was not conspicuous, nor were their effects obvious. In its full state, however, demoralization produced such pronounced outcomes that, all at once, institutional lapses became highly visible. Disillusion festered and spread, and a sense of urgency to restore order emerged. But since energies and resources for reconstruction were weakened and in short supply, the prospects of restoration were bleak. Instead, the resultant order had to be imposed, and was experienced as oppressive. To minimize and conceal the full extent of institutional incompetence and malaise, school authorities, returning to "business as usual," fostered attitudes of complacency and cynicism.

---

[1] William Empson, "Missing Dates," in Oscar Williams, ed., *A Little Treasury of Modern Poetry* (N.Y.: Scribners, 1950), p. 440.

For those who had to remain, school life went on. But without aspiration, work became tedious and studies seemed meaningless. Staff and students continued performing their prescribed tasks and executing the familiar motions, but with little enthusiasm and minimal care. The outward forms persisted, but the content of school experience was eroded of its human and social values. Only "the waste" remained.

Civil Rights in Retreat

A corollary to the restoration of administrative order and authority and the chief outcome of the Riles' Commission was the weakening of support for the issues of racial justice raised by the civil rights movement. Instead, problems of school finance and collective bargaining dominated the agenda of the late seventies and, because none of the choices confronting the school district allowed for much advance of the values of equal educational opportunity, observing their fate was painful for those concerned with civil rights. By 1977, in the aftermath of the commission, the administration was insisting that the school community face up to the steady decline of pupils, the rising costs of salaries and operations, and the inevitable fiscal crunch these trends were creating. Recent state legislation aimed at bringing school finance into line with the equity requirements of the *Serrano* decision threatened basic education as well as opportunities for disadvantaged and minority school children.

Redesign and the Redefinition of Racial Balance

To shrink the school district's operations (i.e. close schools and dismiss staff), Superintendent Alioto proposed a new school reorganization. His plan involved abandoning Horseshoe and replacing it with a pupil assignment scheme that would substantially reduce busing. (This was the controversial "Educational Redesign" on which the SFPSC had chosen not to comment.) The local NAACP tried to stop the plan, but failed to convince the court that the school district should be held in contempt for violating the 1971 court order. On the contrary, Judge Wiegal at this time, the reader may recall, dismissed the *Johnson* case without prejudice. Although the NAACP promptly filed a new lawsuit, this action did not delay implementation of the new assignment scheme.

Alioto's plan (Redesign) entailed regrouping all the schools, reconverting primary and intermediate facilities into elementary schools (grades K-5), absorbing junior highs into middle schools (grades 6-8), and creating four-year high schools (grades 9-12). Pupil assignments were redrawn to accommodate the closing of small (and inefficient) schools, and maximize the use of larger school buildings. The plan called for including as many pupils as possible in neighborhood schools, provided each school contained at least four racial groups. The only other condition to prohibit resegregation was that no racial group was to exceed 45 percent of a given school's total population. Busing was not excluded, but its use was reduced to transporting pupils to those elementary and middle schools not filled to capacity according to the guidelines, which meant that it was used primarily to bring nonwhite pupils into middle-class districts. The total number of bused pupils was thus substantially reduced, and very few white pupils had to leave their neighborhoods.

Besides these major changes in grade structure and pupil assignment, Redesign also affected the administration and coordination of the schools. Four area offices replaced Horseshoe's seven zones, strengthening the arm of the central administration and terminating all prospect for community-based schools. The Office of Integration was closed, and with its demise commitment to enforcement of racial balance, albeit consistently frustrated, dissolved altogether. A new division of pupil assignment was given responsibility for distributing pupils according to the new guidelines and issuing OERs (optional enrollment requests). Such requests continued to be granted in special cases, in particular to pupils electing to attend one of the district's alternative schools. The number of such schools increased to 15 at this time, partly to encourage diverse school programs and partly to satisfy parent and staff objections to the closing of particular schools. If a school could guarantee a sufficient enrollment to warrant its operation, the administration was willing to designate it an alternative school.

In spring of 1978, at public hearings held throughout the city, there were anguished cries of protest both over Redesign and the proposed closing of 17 schools. Many parents were upset and fearful of the disruptive effects of yet another massive reorganization of schools and programs. In particular, the black and white parents affected by a proposed pairing of the schools in Hunters Point with those on Treasure Island objected that they were carrying an excessive busing burden. Moreover, neither community wanted to be integrated with the other. Other minority spokesmen objected that it was primarily poor children living in overcrowded public housing projects who would be bused to various schools outside their neighborhoods, while middle-class children would walk to school. Teachers described the plan as a potential disaster for educational programs and urged that it be phased in gradually, allowing for due process in the transfer of teachers. Because combining the ninth grade with the three-year high school population was expected to produce overcrowding in many facilities, parents and staff urged that at least this component of the plan be phased in according to available space.

But Superintendent Alioto staunchly defended his proposal and insisted that the district could not afford to wait any longer to institute the necessary reductions in schools and staff. He acknowledged certain weaknesses in the plan, especially that it could not guarantee that the 45 percent racial limit would be maintained for every school. The schools in Hunters Point, for example, given the community's refusal to participate in the proposed pairing, would not even come close to this guideline. Nevertheless, the superintendent was determined to press for adoption, and he was supported by the business community and the local press on grounds of fiscal necessity, and in lieu of any alternative proposal for reducing the school budget. "The plan is imperfect . . . but it will certainly be worse if subjected to another year of debate and compromise." [2]

By a four to three vote, the school board agreed. Dr. Zuretti Goosby, a black liberal who had rejoined the board in 1974, promptly submitted his resignation. Another black community leader complained that despite the hearings, not enough in-depth information concerning the justifications for the Redesign Plan was presented, inhibiting community attempts to analyze the plan or to offer serious alternatives.[3] A disheartened black community, mustering all its reserves, organized a successful one-day boycott of the schools (26 percent of the students, almost the entire black school population, stayed home or attended special programs sponsored by a consortium of black churches), but under the circumstances, this action had virtually no impact.[4]

---

[2] "Alioto's School Redesign Plan," Editorial in the *San Francisco Examiner*, February 14, 1978.

[3] Bernice Brown, interviewed in the *San Francisco Examiner*, May 3, 1978. Ms. Brown was a former member of the SFPSC.

[4] *San Francisco Chronicle*, May 25, 1978.

Cutbacks

Redesign was implemented in the fall of 1978, shortly after the passage of Proposition 13, the statewide property tax reduction initiative that decimated state support for schools and other public services. A few small schools were kept open as alternative schools, but Alioto warned that increasingly stringent fiscal constraints would soon necessitate additional school closings and staff reductions. Recently hired minorities would be the most affected by such cutbacks. Over half the black staff had been hired during the previous five years, and would, under the rule of seniority, be among the first fired.[5]

Also seriously affected by the proposed reductions were special programs and support services. A 50 percent reduction in the central office administrative staff and the demotion of 40 principals meant that classroom teachers would be "bumped" and reassigned to grades and subjects outside their fields of specialization, and that some special projects, such as the recently introduced minimum standards program, would be cut back and others eliminated. New board member, Peter Mezey, who had hoped to help the district sustain a concern for educational values while it coped with its fiscal problems, felt whipsawed. As the former chairman of the Richmond Complex Parents Council, he appreciated the adverse effects on students and teachers of inadequate supplies and supervision. In his opinion, life in schools had become a mockery of the schools' historic commitment to serve the diverse educational needs of the community.[6] But the public, disenchanted with such liberal notions, was more concerned with high costs and poor performance than with social ideals. Blaming the board for the schools' shortcomings, especially in light of the SFPSC's charges against board "meddling," was increasingly common. A punitive attitude was also discernible behind the state's tax-cutting legislation, as though starving the schools of resources would somehow force them to shape up and improve.[7]

---

[5] Of a total of 63,500 students, there were then 18,200 blacks in the schools (28.4%); but among school administrators (283), there were only 40 blacks (14.1%), and among teachers *and* administrators (4,186), there were only 438 blacks (10%). SFUSD figures, quoted in the *San Francisco Examiner*, May 17, 1978.

[6] Peter Mezey, "What 13 Has Done to San Francisco Schools," *San Francisco Examiner*, August 22, 1978.

[7] Then Governor Jerry Brown said, referring to the San Francisco schools, "It's time they got some efficiency and reform . . . because of the geniuses they've had running the schools, they've designed a way to spend more with minimum results. Do we all have to pay for that?" *San Francisco Examiner*, April 24, 1977.

Tough Superintendent

In Robert Alioto, fiscal conservatives and taxpayers found a ready and able ally. Alioto had no qualms about "biting the bullet," particularly when he perceived that his actions were welcomed by the local business community. Appointed shortly after the commission began its inquiry, Alioto reaped the benefits of the SFPSC's emphasis on restoring administrative authority. Further, he had the personal qualifications for the role of "hatchet-man" —"he is decisive and tough, but also abrasive and remote, manipulative and unfeeling"[8]—and he took pride in the efficiency with which he managed the job of reducing school operations. A "profile" of the superintendent, based on close observations of his daily activities and behavior over a period of three months, cast a positive light on these accomplishments and revealed the dedication with which Alioto worked and his striking ability to extract equally hard work from his staff.[9] His attention to the personalities and interests of individual board members, and his relentless behind-the-scenes efforts to obtain their support for his plans spoke to his skills and conviction.

What the "profile" failed to illuminate, except by omission, were the consequences of Alioto's actions on an ailing institution. For example, consolidation of teachers, necessitated by declining enrollments and school closings, was carried out with little concern for effects on learning. Even before the drastic personnel changes entailed by the plan, some 272 teachers in 1976 and another 250 in 1977 received notices in August, just before the opening of school, informing them that they would not be returning to their former positions. Many were not reassigned for months, but were kept on hold in a day-to-day substitute pool. Alioto was willing to ignore what such treatment did to teachers, and the message it conveyed to students regarding their worth. A number of teachers took leaves of absence, or resigned, not because they wanted to stop teaching but because of the way they were treated. "After serving 20 years in this district, I've been put through a year of humiliation . . . . I can't take it . . . . Those of us consolidated feel second-rate . . . and there is tension and insecurity for everyone."[10]

---

[8] Joe Flower and Judith Berger, "Are San Francisco's Schools the Worst in California?" *San Francisco* (February 1980): 57.

[9] John F. Feilders, *Profile: The Role of the Chief Superintendent of Schools* (Belmont, Calif.: Signature Books, 1981).

[10] *San Francisco Examiner*, August 28, 1977.

Alioto also had no qualms about demoting and firing administrators. A prominent black educator had been hired to fill the vacant position of associate superintendent of instruction, but Alioto was disappointed with his inability to placate the black community and obtain its support for the Redesign Plan. At the first opportunity he was fired.[11] The administrator complained that he was denied due process—that it was not his job performance that was unsatisfactory, but his unwillingness to "run interference" in the black community. He challenged Alioto publicly, but to no avail.[12]

A preoccupation with problems of reorganization, including the political support needed to implement plans and decisions devised by the administration, characterized Alioto's activities. Given the district's management problems, this preoccupation was understandable, but it was not without costs. It meant that educational and student problems consumed very little of Alioto's daily time and attention. And when such issues did arise, they dealt mainly with the district's testing program or the latest test results, not with the requisites of learning.[13] Administrators and principals, regardless of their other merits, were demoted if they failed to produce results compatible with the superintendent's plans, or if measures of pupil performance showed no improvement.

Many dedicated staff tried their best to moderate Alioto's actions. Within the administration there remained a number of advocates of the values and programs associated with the civil rights movement. Since the sixties, they had fought to broaden access and upgrade opportunities for minorities, to increase parent and teacher participation in decision making, and to develop a curriculum that met the needs of blacks and non-English-speaking minority pupils. Some had helped recruit minorities, and had involved teachers and parents in the planning of the two school complexes. Others had worked on the Horseshoe Plan and on secondary school desegregation, and had tried to make the zone concept work as a viable means of decentralization. Still others had sponsored and directed teacher-learning centers, bilingual programs, multicultural curriculum projects, and alternative schools. Their experience and knowledge of the school system was widely respected, and they were invaluable, at least initially, to the new superintendent. As time passed, however, their responsibilities

---

[11] Feilders, *Profile*, p. 73.
[12] *San Francisco Examiner*, May 18, 1978.
[13] Feilders, ibid., p. 54.

were shifted and downgraded. One by one, this former "van-guard," worn out by years of patient and often obscure work, took leave or resigned. Several left because of physical exhaustion.

Teacher "Burnout"

The loss of the "vanguard of civil rights" was serious. It meant that within the administration there would no longer be vigorous support for programs to enhance educational opportunities for minorities and ensure their full participation. But disenchantment and physical exhaustion went beyond former civil rights leaders. The district's teachers (those who remained) were also "burned out" and demoralized.

The teachers' union, one might suppose, was a likely source of organized internal resistance not only to Redesign, but also to the administration's attitude regarding the use of human resources, and its general disdain for the values of education. Indeed, the union bitterly castigated Alioto's proposed reorganization as a retreat to "order, stratification, inequality and segregation." [14] Teachers had a strong interest in opposing the erosion of supportive services, and good reasons to fight for recognition and maintenance of the requisites of learning. Why didn't they? What was happening to the teacher organizations during this period?

Teachers and Collective Bargaining

Since the mid-sixties, San Francisco teachers, like their counter-parts nationally, had become increasingly aware of their interests, but these had been perceived largely as job-related benefits, i.e. better wages and fringe benefits. Many teachers, however, also wanted a voice in decisions affecting working conditions, such as assignment and transfer policies, regulation of the workday, and specific job responsibilities. Better wages and control over working conditions were means of enhancing an otherwise low-paying and low-status occupation. Some teachers wanted even more than these basic improvements. They wanted a role in developing classroom curriculum and a voice in such school-site decisions as selecting the principal and allocating the budget. The teachers' task force, organ-ized to plan and implement the two experimental school complexes, had set an example of teacher involvement in decisions affecting the fate of pupils, school, and the community. Later, some teachers

---

[14] *San Francisco Progress*, January 25, 1978.

formed alternative schools, such as Rooftop, where, together with parents, they created a cooperative community of talents and resources.

Meanwhile, state legislation in the mid-seventies (the Rodda Act) authorized collective bargaining, strengthening the power of organized school employees at the local level. However, the presence of competitive teacher organizations in San Francisco—(1) a local branch of the California Teachers Association (CTA), a professional group, and (2) the local American Federation of Teachers (AFT), AFL-CIO, the teachers' union—diluted the thrust of the legislation and exacerbated differences among teachers. San Francisco teachers were fairly equally divided between the two organizations (with a few unaffiliated). but under the new legislation, they had to choose one of the rival contenders as their bargaining agent. In the spring of 1977, after extensive campaigning, the more militant AFT won the election by a substantial margin.[15]

The union, now representing all the district's teachers, immediately adopted a defiant stance toward the administration; the teachers demanded an 11 percent raise, as well as guarantees of orderly assignment and transfer. The AFT's posture can best be understood as a statement to the district and the community to the effect that teachers were no longer willing to accept low wages and second-class treatment. (In 1977 the salary of a beginning teacher in San Francisco was $9,375, the second lowest in the state, and the maximum earnings for teachers employed 20 years or more was $20,080.)[16]

In response, the administration presented its own demands, which included a 200-day work year (an increase of 20 days), differentiation of teacher positions (creating five levels with associated wage differences), and an evaluation scheme to be used as the basis for pay increases.[17] The AFT immediately labeled the administration's response "blatantly contemptuous," and refused to consider it seriously.

The district was in a bind. Until the administration knew what funds the state would make available for the next school year, it could not bargain in good faith. However, the union, fearful of

---

[15] The AFT received 2,469 votes, and the CTA 1,871, with 48 abstentions. Eighty-eight percent of the teachers voted in the election. *San Francisco Chronicle*, February 9, 1977.

[16] *San Francisco Examiner*, August 3, 1977.

[17] *San Francisco Examiner*, April 27, 1977.

losing the support of teachers who had voted their resentments into a call for action, could not afford to be reasonable and wait. AFT President James Ballard, to prove that his organization deserved confidence and support, scheduled a strike vote, and, together with a group of union teachers, conducted a sit-in in the offices of the administration. Only then did the legislature complete its school finance bill. The amount of state aid to San Francisco was substantially reduced, but by less than the administration's worst projections. The stage was now set for a confrontation between the teachers and the district.

Hard bargaining began in earnest. The administration postponed the opening of school, inconveniencing parents and attenuating public support for the teachers. Despite this pressure, a first offer was rejected by the teachers. But then both sides quickly compromised, and a two-year contract was signed. The teachers won an eight percent raise, but had to accept more stringent working conditions, including a longer school year, a seven-hour work day, and unrestricted class size.[18]

Teachers Test Their Collective Power

City officials and the local papers had not been sympathetic to the teachers' demands. On the contrary, they endorsed Alioto's efforts to cut costs by trimming staff and supported his attempt to tie salaries to teacher performance as measured by pupil test scores.[19] Earlier, in support of Redesign, they had agreed with the educational argument the superintendent made on its behalf. He claimed that because the plan would enable children to remain in the same elementary school for two more years (through grade 5), pupil performance and the quality of instruction would improve. Third-grade pupils were already being tested for minimum competence, and plans were under way to test fifth and eighth graders as well, in keeping with Alioto's promise to put an end to "social promotions." A homework policy had also been adopted. Given the district's embarrassing test scores, these policies appealed to the public, and a majority of the board, despite some misgivings, had voted for Redesign. Alioto's school reforms, plus his success in averting a strike and achieving a hard bargain with the union, won him a raise and a two-year extension of his contract.

---

[18] *San Francisco Examiner*, September 12, 1977.
[19] Editorial in the *San Francisco Examiner*, August 25, 1977.

We have already noted the uncertain effects of the third-grade testing program, and the misleading expectations fostered by the concept of "minimum competence." Moreover, while Redesign recognized the value of setting standards, and from the point of view of the learner, providing repeated opportunities for success, it failed to take into account the effects of yet another massive relocation and reassignment of pupils and staff. The immediate result was not more effective learning opportunities; it was more confusion. Redesign entailed a rejuggling of bus routes, staggered school schedules, revised curriculum, major cutbacks in services as well as school closings, and, in addition, the largest shift of teachers and students ever attempted by the San Francisco schools. Classes were larger. In the secondary schools, there were not enough books and in some schools not enough chairs to accommodate the influx of ninth graders. Physical education teachers were assigned classes in math and biology. And instead of more, there were fewer janitors to keep the overcrowded buildings clean, and fewer hall aides to insure safety. Substitute teachers were not available. Truancy and disorder, including several shootings, rose sharply, and teachers felt harassed, resentful, and embittered. "I have never seen the opening of school where morale is so low," commented an exasperated teacher.[20]

Layoffs

The worst was yet to come. That spring (1979), faced with the impact of Proposition 13, the administration issued layoff notices to the entire school staff. Every person's job was threatened by political tensions and the uncertain state of school finance. This was the bitter reward teachers received for their extraordinary efforts in carrying out Redesign. The teachers could not have been expected to respond passively, and indeed they did not. They insisted on their due process rights, but without foreseeing the consequences of invoking the legal process as their means of redress.

Under state law teachers receiving termination notices were entitled to a hearing to determine if the administration had acted reasonably in light of its fiscal constraints. An administrative law judge was appointed to review the district's layoff guidelines and procedures and determine how many teachers could be fired. Each case was then reviewed individually, but final pronouncements were

---

[20] Rebecca Cherney, an AFT official, quoted in the *San Francisco Examiner*, September 6, 1978.

dependent on budgetary decisions at the state level. Despite the uncertainty of the outcome, San Francisco teachers nevertheless chose to proceed.

From early April until late June, teachers together with their families and friends jammed into the gymnasium where the hearings were held. The administration submitted a list of over 1,200 teachers hired since 1970, largely minority and younger teachers. The AFT insisted that it was willing to fight for every teacher's job, and, as proof, provided union attorneys to represent individual teachers. However, under the rule of seniority supported by the union, attorneys had few good arguments. Under this rule, it did not matter how effective a teacher was, or what the impact of a particular loss would be in a given school setting, or what would happen to specific programs, including affirmative action. Given the irrelevance of the seniority rule to these issues, some teachers, declining the union's offer, chose to represent themselves. Others were more persuaded than the union that, due to fiscal constraints, staff would inevitably have to be fired. Thus, in addition to antagonisms between those on the layoff list and the more senior staff who would be retained, there were serious divisions even among the terminated teachers.

That tumultuous spring, while agitated teachers were occupied with the hearings, only 81 percent of the third graders passed the minimum competence test, down from 95 percent the previous year. Among fifth graders, only 71 percent passed the math test. This high failure rate exceeded the administration's expectations, and so, despite the budget crunch, some 2,600 youngsters who would otherwise have been retained were asked to enroll in special summer classes.[21] Hundreds of teachers, afraid of losing their jobs, also began making plans to take summer courses or to find new opportunities outside teaching.

As summer began, a sad and depressed school staff said their good-byes, many teachers and pupils uncertain whether or not they would be back, and everyone wondering what school would be like with so many gone. Even among those not fired, there were teachers who decided it was time to change occupations. Those in technical fields, such as math and science, could afford to leave teaching. But others had fewer employment options, and some wanted to stay. Despite their harsh treatment, many dedicated teachers still remained committed to their work and to the welfare of their

---

[21] *San Francisco Examiner*, July 20, 1979 and October 5, 1979.

pupils. They knew who would suffer if the better teachers left the profession.

Meanwhile, the administrative judge concluded that, given the district's much reduced and still uncertain budget, the layoff plan was necessary, and that it was reasonable to terminate a total of 1,200 teachers and administrators, just as Alioto had proposed.[22] This amounted to one-fourth of the certificated staff, and entailed reducing the minority component by 40 percent and eliminating one-third of the pupil services staff (counselors and psychologists). The board began to grapple with such painful decisions as whether to shrink the number of high school classes from six to five per day (reducing the number of units required for graduation); whether to eliminate such programs as after-school childcare, libraries, and music in the elementary schools; or whether to discontinue transportation to alternative schools.

Teachers Strike . . . Out

The AFT mobilized for action. Departing from its earlier emphasis on substantial wage and benefit increases, the union's basic demand in renegotiating its contract was that the district not fire *any* teachers. In response, Alioto offered to rehire 700 of those laid off, including a large proportion of minority teachers, as long-term substitutes, and to give everyone a five percent raise.[23] But the AFT was not satisfied, and demanded an independent audit of school finances. Anticipating an encouraging financial report, union leaders began preparations for a strike to force the district to rehire all the remaining teachers. However, the audit failed to reveal discrepancies in the district's budget figures, and instead confirmed the necessity both for the firings and the modest wage increase.[24]

Nevertheless, San Francisco teachers voted overwhelmingly (1,466-572) to strike.[25] Alioto postponed the opening of school, and both parties, with the assistance of the mayor, began hard bargaining. This time, however, the administration had very little leeway: given the reduced budget, the district could not afford to rehire all the teachers, nor could it pay higher wages. City officials and the press pleaded with the teachers to be reasonable. When the

---

[22] *San Francisco Examiner*, June 4, 1979.
[23] *San Francisco Examiner*, August 29, 1979. Long-term substitutes earn a regular salary but receive fewer benefits. Moreover, their appointment can be easily terminated.
[24] *San Francisco Examiner*, September 1, 1979.
[25] *San Francisco Examiner*, September 11, 1979.

teachers paid them no heed and instead carried out their strike, the pleas became strident attacks. Compounding the assault on the teachers, Alioto ordered the elementary schools to open and recruited substitute teachers to staff them. Shortly thereafter, he opened the middle schools, and after three more weeks of fruitless talks, the high schools. Only 10 percent of the teachers crossed the picket lines, but 70 percent of the students thus belatedly began the school year.[26] In a dramatic act of solidarity, a number of high school students joined the strikers, entreating the board and the mayor to seek more funds for programs and services as well as staff, but to no avail. Finally, after almost six weeks, the impasse was broken and a tentative agreement was reached that involved retaining 120 of the 700 rehired teachers on a contract basis, rather than as long-term substitutes, and increasing the 5 percent raise to 5.3 percent the following year. Ironically, these modest concessions were made possible by the extra funds the district realized from salary savings accrued during the course of the strike.[27] Despite their unhappiness with this outcome, the teachers reluctantly accepted it and returned to work.

The strike exacted a bitter toll. The teachers felt their efforts had been not only misunderstood and misrepresented, but also futile. They were embarrassed by the high price parents and students, not to mention the school district, had to pay for such meager gains. By the end of the strike, enrollments were down an additional 1,500 students and the district suffered a proportional reduction in state aid. Thus only 600 teachers could actually be rehired. Only Alioto apparently benefited from the strike; for his perseverance, the board rewarded him by again extending his contract, this time for four more years.

Some hard lessons were learned from this experience. The teachers now understood that taxpayers were not willing to continue spending more money for schools and, therefore, given declining enrollments, that teachers were going to be fired, schools closed, and programs terminated. Teachers realized they could not alter these harsh political and economic realities and that militant protests and strikes were exercises in futility. Alioto's regime of retrenchment had the strong backing of the board and city officials, and, regardless of the educational costs, the schools were now going to operate on the administration's terms and conditions. Those

---

[26] *San Francisco Chronicle*, October 3, 1979.
[27] *San Francisco Examiner*, October 23, 1979.

who remained in the school system had to accept this restoration of administrative power, as well as the prospect of a prolonged period of austerity.

In the spring of 1980, the administration announced another round of layoffs for the 1981-82 school year. An additional 600 positions had to be eliminated. This time, however, there were no outcries and no demonstrations. The administrative hearings proceeded quietly and without fuss. Approximately 500 teachers received final termination notices, but the AFT did not protest and there was no mention of a strike. The teachers' militant impetus— their brief burst of collective power—had dissipated.

Schools in Decline

Rising Costs and Declining Enrollments

According to Alioto, the central problem facing the San Francisco schools was "to reduce operating expenditures to match both declining enrollments and the imposition of Proposition 13 and the *Serrano* decision." [28] The steepest enrollment decline occurred in 1971, when the Horseshoc Plan was implemented, but between 1977 and 1979, the years of Redesign and the teachers' strike, the district again suffered substantial losses. These were also the years that the state legislature, in response to the *Serrano* decision, was engaged in school finance reform aimed at equalizing per pupil

---

[28] Alioto, quoted in *San Francisco Business,* September, 1980, p. 7. The declining enrollment trend is shown in the following table:

SFUSD Grade K-12 Enrollments, 1965-1980	
Year	Enrollment
1965	93,269
1970	88,749
1971	80,902
1972	79,923
1973	74,723
1974	72,443
1975	70,045
1976	67,778
1977	63,872
1978	60,113
1979	56,862
1980	57,432

Source: SFUSD, "Grade K-12 Enrollments, 1965-1980."

expenditures so as to benefit pupils in property-poor school districts. At the same time, legislators were also belatedly responding to a major property tax rebellion.

State legislation in 1977 to equalize expenditures proposed taking tax revenues away from San Francisco, which was then spending over $1,900 per pupil (compared to a statewide average of $1,500),[29] and diverting the funds to other districts. It was in anticipation of this substantial loss that Superintendent Alioto proposed the extensive staff reductions, school closings, and the dismantling of court-ordered desegregation that comprised the Redesign Plan. Redesign was a blueprint for operating the schools on a greatly reduced scale. In conjunction with this plan, also to reduce expenses, the school reconstruction program was hastily concluded, forcing the closure of buildings scheduled for repairs. In addition, incentives for early retirement were put into effect to hasten staff attrition.

Meanwhile newspaper editors, speaking for disgruntled taxpayers and supportive of the superintendent, kept pointing out that the cost of educating pupils in San Francisco was still too high. "At $1,915 per student, the results have been disheartening." [30] Other public spokesmen agreed. "How can citizens be expected to keep pouring money into the system?" [31] There was little sympathy for the complaints of minority community representatives that the unsafe schools they had been promised were to be closed permanently. Their people had voted in good faith for the school reconstruction bonds, spokesmen said, and now they felt betrayed. "We Chinese still suffer second-class treatment," complained Lawrence Jue. "We too pay taxes, but receive only the crumbs of public benefits." [32]

A last-minute reprieve from the state, delaying full implementation of statewide revenue redistribution for one year, enabled the

---

[29] *San Francisco Progress*, January 7, 1977. However, *Serrano* lawyers complained that wealth-related disparities in pupil expenditures were not adequately reduced, and threatened further legal challenges. *San Francisco Chronicle*, August 25, 1977 and October 26, 1977. Finance experts began predicting that San Francisco schools would lose 60 percent of their state aid, forcing a radical curtailment of the school system. Subsequently, the legislature added resources to the least well financed districts, but as funding became more closely tied to sales and income taxes, total state resources available for schools began to shrink. *San Francisco Chronicle*, June 13, 1978.

[30] "Evaluating the Teacher," Editorial, *San Francisco Chronicle*, April 14, 1977.

[31] Kevin Starr in the *San Francisco Examiner*, May 7, 1977.

[32] *East/West*, June 8, 1977.

administration to satisfy some grievances, and also to negotiate the first two-year teacher contract. Also, several small schools designated for closure were kept open as alternative schools, and the district agreed to seek federal funds to complete reconstruction of three schools in minority neighborhoods.[33] A fourth school in Chinatown was also authorized.[34]

Such compromises became impossible, however, after the passage in 1978 of Proposition 13, the Jarvis-Gann property tax limitation initiative,[35] although, due to a bountiful surplus of funds in the state treasury, this did not happen right away. In 1978, San Francisco schools lost only 15 percent of their expected state allocation. Nevertheless, Redesign was implemented in a context of financial constraints, including a 50 percent reduction in administration, heavy cutbacks in staffing and school maintenance, curtailment of extracurriculum activities, and decimation of the curriculum. It was an "austerity" program, but to teachers and students it was experienced as an imposition of unnecessary hardships. The embattled school system, still suffering from years of disruption and fragmentation, needed relief and support, not further depletion of resources. But given declining enrollments and the harsh economic climate, such support was not forthcoming. (The futile teachers' strike the following year can perhaps thus be understood as the reaction of harassed and frustrated workers, who, perceiving Proposition 13 as "the last straw," exploded with rage, but then, defeated and exhausted, numbly resigned themselves to a state of acquiescence.)

State Assumption of School Finances

Serrano and the impact of Proposition 13 went beyond the emasculation of organized teacher efforts in San Francisco. The fiscal power of the school district—its economic basis—was also drastically curtailed. With *Serrano*, substantial responsibility over local school finance was transferred to the state. Only the state could carry out the responsibility for equity mandated by that decision. However, it was not clear how much control over revenues and their allocation the state would need for this purpose. In any case,

---

[33] *San Francisco Chronicle*, July 1, 1977.

[34] *East/West*, December 5, 1979.

[35] Proposition 13 limited local property tax rates to one percent of property value. In San Francisco, the school district's tax rate was cut from $3.74 to $1.21. *San Francisco Examiner*, September 13, 1978.

Proposition 13 placed limits on the state's ability to raise school revenues through the property tax.

Various solutions to this predicament were proposed. On the one hand, it was suggested that the state substantially reduce its portion of local school aid, offering assistance mainly to the more needy districts (in keeping with *Serrano)*, but leaving basic fund raising to local communities.[36] This would reduce the current dependence of local districts on the state and restore local control over the school budget. Districts would have more flexibility to conduct their affairs in accordance with changing local needs, hiring or laying off staff in a more orderly fashion, setting local curriculum priorities, etc. The policy of collective bargaining at the local level would certainly function better if the district had control over its revenues.

On the other hand, given the preponderance of state funding for schools (approximately 72 percent of San Francisco's school budget had come from the state), and the unlikelihood of finding sufficient local revenues, another alternative was to strengthen state authority. The retrenchment forced upon local school districts de facto eroded local control and increased the powers of the state. Many local officials, including Alioto, supported the transfer of collective bargaining to the state level, so as to avoid the tensions and bitterness that accompanied contract negotiations.

But to assume the authority commensurate with its fiscal powers, the state would have to expand its policy role and develop plans for long-range school finance. In a context of political and economic uncertainty (since 1977 the legislature has approved the annual state school budget at the last possible moment), this was not likely. Moreover, state legislators were not used to grappling with the kinds of thorny issues that plague local school boards: e.g. should there be special funds for inner-city schools, should parent councils be mandated at school sites, should funds be tied to students' test performance, should teacher evaluation practices be standardized, and so on. Finally, it was not clear that local schools would be well served by statewide solutions of such issues. As matters stood, however, with no clear demarcation of the division between state and local authority, one critic observed, "the schools [seem] . . . out of control [like] some remorseless engine functioning for its own purposes."[37]

---

[36] This was the proposal of the State Commission on Government Reform. *San Francisco Chronicle*, January 16, 1979.

[37] Kevin Starr in the *San Francisco Examiner*, October 29, 1979.

Private Initiative and the Voucher Plan

By the end of the decade, the economic recession was placing California public schools, as well as other social services, increasingly at risk. The state surplus was exhausted and there were warnings that federal aid for schools would also be curtailed. Two ways of responding were becoming evident. One was for the schools to seek alliances with the private sector, working out cooperative arrangements whereby local business and corporate benefactors would add private support to the financing of public schools. The other approach was to accept as inevitable the trend of decreasing public support for schools and introduce a voucher system that would provide families with state aid in the form of a voucher, and also give them choices, including that of adding private resources to supplement publicly funded schooling. Conditions of supply and demand would replace school governance and policy issues would be settled by a "free market" in education.

In San Francisco, the first approach was a natural sequel to the work of the SFPSC. Members of the commission had strong local business, university, and foundation contacts. During their tenure they succeeded in establishing several school-community enterprises. Local corporations, for example, in an effort to improve relations between schools and industry, undertook an Adopt-a-School program in which employees served as occasional tutors or special guests. Other companies provided skilled executives "on loan" to the school administration to assist with data processing systems, accounting, and similar business functions. Finally, a Business Advisory Council was formed to oversee the development and operation of a pilot high school program for advanced business and commercial arts students, utilizing computers and modern office equipment obtained from the private sector.[38]

In addition to these public relations and technical contributions, the private sector initiated a special Community Education Fund devoted to obtaining substantial grants from corporations and foundations to support local school programs. In 1980, 12 projects were funded with $39,000 raised by the fund's board of directors, who, not surprisingly, consisted primarily of former members of the SFPSC.[39] In addition, several local foundations contacted by the fund provided major grants for substantial school improvement

---

[38] *San Francisco Examiner*, August 8, 1978.

[39] In 1981, the fund raised $133,000 for 35 projects. See SFUSD, "Summary of Grant Funds," 1981-1982.

projects. The San Francisco Foundation, for example, allocated $360,000 over three years to the schools in Hunters Point.[40] This support made it possible for the school district to sustain activities and services that would otherwise not exist. Moreover, in a school system where every teacher had been employed since at least 1970 (the average teacher age in 1980 was 45), the availability of these private resources was a much needed source of stimulus. However, although these resources were significant, especially in the context of retrenchment, they were not solutions to the problem of diminishing public support for education.[41]

A second response, also involving the private sector, but in a quite different way, was the voucher plan. This was a scheme long advocated by economist Milton Friedman. The basic idea was to bypass state and local school systems and, through the distribution of resources in the form of tuition-vouchers, give the control of education directly to families of school children. The vouchers would be redeemed both by public and nonpublic schools, thereby creating a marketplace for educational consumers. This scheme, it was claimed, not only would encourage diversity, but would also remove the schools from the sphere of public policy and government.

> Parents could express their views about schools directly, by withdrawing their children from one school, and sending them to another, to a much greater extent than is now possible.[42]

A proposal to initiate a statewide voucher system, drawn up by University of California law professors John Coons and Stephen Sugarman, now began to arouse considerable interest. Especially after the 1979 teachers' strike, many San Franciscans agreed that it was time to try the voucher plan. However, there was not sufficient statewide political organization to qualify the proposal for the ballot in 1980, and its proponents lost interest. Subsequently, national legislation regarding federal tax credits for families whose children

---

[40] Also the Cowell Foundation gave $76,000 to Woodrow Wilson High School for programs to improve student attendance and motivation. SFUSD, "Summary of Grant Funds," 1979-80 and 1981-82.

[41] A similar corporate-benefactor program has since begun at the state level, spearheaded by the Bank of America and Chevron. Between 1979 and 1983, the California Educational Initiatives Fund awarded $3 million to 281 programs statewide. *San Francisco Chronicle*, February 3, 1983.

[42] Milton Friedman, *Capitalism and Freedom* (Chicago: University of Chicago Press, 1962), p. 91.

attend nonpublic schools received strong support from the Reagan administration. The beneficiaries of this proposal would be limited to those who withdraw from the public schools, however. It thus offers little incentive to parents for whom this option is not possible or desirable, and therefore is not a comprehensive alternative.[43]

Insofar as these reform strategies—corporate aid and vouchers— emerged out of a context of disenchantment and retrenchment, they did not come to grips with the underlying causes of demoralization, but merely served to shore up or bypass the ailing San Francisco schools. Such patchwork and evasion are best understood as symptoms, not cures of the serious condition of public education.

Apathy and Cynicism

By 1980, the various coalitions that were once actively involved in San Francisco school affairs had unraveled. Fewer people had a personal stake in the condition of the schools. The groups organized around issues of civil rights had long since dissolved, and after the 1976 school board election, the SFPSC quietly expired. Since the strike, teachers have had less confidence in organized action; in 1983, they opted for the less militant CTA as their local bargaining agent. Working mothers and the poor have little time and energy to give to PTAs, let alone to spend on active involvement in school affairs. A declining population, the presence of nonpublic school alternatives, and competing social issues raised by the city's more politically active elderly and homosexual populations have all contributed to a marked lack of interest in the public schools. Finally, a growing scarcity of public resources has served to highlight the failure of school leadership to appeal with any conviction and urgency to educational values worth supporting.

Under these conditions, it was not surprising that a self-regarding administration, eager to dissipate public disenchantment, began making strenuous efforts to show evidence of success. Alioto used every opportunity to stress the positive accomplishments of the public schools. Test scores were especially useful for this purpose. In interviews and public meetings, the superintendent never failed to mention that since 1977 the test scores of San Francisco third

---

[43] To counter this objection, the Reagan administration has proposed that states or local school authorities convert their federal aid for disadvantaged pupils into vouchers that families can use toward private school tuition, thus providing the same options to "the less fortunate that have traditionally been available to the affluent." Gary Jones, former undersecretary of education, quoted in the *New York Times*, April 13, 1983.

graders had begun to rise.[44] He pointed to these results as indications that San Francisco now had a "quality school system."

Since 1977, however, gains in basic skills, especially among pupils in the lowest quartile, are a national trend, the result of federal aid targeted to the disadvantaged.[45] In any case, test experts consistently find that standardized achievement scores tend to be closely related to income levels and parents' educational backgrounds, not to specific school programs. (The state's top scores, for example, regularly occur in wealthy, predominantly white districts, while the lowest scores appear in low-income and minority districts.)[46] In 1979, a school-by-school comparison of San Francisco's scores confirmed that what really mattered was school composition: the three predominantly black schools in Hunters Point were all below the district average, whereas schools in more affluent neighborhoods had above-average test results.[47]

Despite the administration's public relations efforts, the impoverished condition of the schools was apparent to parents who were concerned about their children's education and could afford alternatives. Nonpublic schools continued to attract and maintain a substantial clientele—fewer than 50 percent of the 116,752 children under age 18 (17.2 percent of the total population) were enrolled in public schools. San Francisco schools were in danger of becoming a welfare agency for minorities and the poor.[48]

---

[44] *San Francisco Examiner*, November 11, 1977 and November 8, 1979. Also SFUSD, "California Assessment Program Year-to-Year Comparisons of Mean Scores, 1976-1979," November 1979.

[45] *New York Times*, April 10, 1983.

[46] *San Francisco Chronicle*, October 30, 1982.

[47] SFUSD, "California Assessment Program," 1979.

[48] Following is a racial breakdown of the 1980 school and city population.

Racial Percentages and Total Numbers: 1980		
	San Francisco	Public Schools
% White	58.2	20.4
% Black	12.7	27.6
% Asian	21.7	30.2
% Hispanic	12.3	15.3
% Other	7.3	6.4
Totals	678,794	60,113

Source: SFUSD Enrollment Reports and 1980 Census printout, Bureau of the Census. Hispanics are not counted as a racial group. San Francisco's elderly population was approximately 15 percent of the total (compared to the national average of 11.3 percent).

10

Conclusion: Education's Place in the National Tapestry

One thing is clear. The builders of a new pro-school coalition must be artisans—perhaps artists—who see *education's place in the national tapestry*, and who can weave local and parochial interests as well as the nation's golden (if tattered) thread of noblesse oblige, into an original and compelling grand design.[1]

Since the early sixties, public schools have served as symbols of a crisis of conscience on questions of racial and social justice. Because American education historically has sought justification in promises of democratic equality, social betterment, and civic participation, the schools were ultimately powerless to disclaim such responsibilities. In the end, moral awareness penetrated barriers of self-protection and overcame the resistance of vested interests. However, response to the civil rights movement also lent legitimacy to demands that distracted the schools from their instructional tasks. Further, tensions between social accountability and the schools' formal mission tended to be resolved at the expense of education. The resultant loss of distinctive mission and competence eroded the schools' integrity and led to institutional demoralization.

In San Francisco, even after the days of activism and social reform had come to an end, these dynamics persisted. Well into the seventies, the school district's agenda was set by the exigencies of social and political issues, such as declining enrollments and annual financial crises. Except for the diffuse protests of unorganized parents, disparaged teachers, and beleaguered administrators, there was no voice—certainly no forceful or persistent voice—to speak for the schools' educational values. Changing economic

---

[1] Stephen K. Bailey, "Political Coalitions for Public Education," *Daedalus* (Summer 1981): 42 (emphasis added).

193

conditions called for retrenchment, staff reductions, and curtailment of programs. Under conditions of demoralization, these hardships were not easy to accept.

Demoralization constrained adaptation to an economy of limited resources. When there is a common cause uniting people, periods of austerity, such as wartime, can be tolerated. Personal sacrifice in such a context has meaning, and there is an end in view to lift spirits and sustain energies.[2] In the past, school leaders used hard times to strengthen the schools. During the panic of 1837, Horace Mann argued that support for public education would restore economic growth. In the depression of the 1930s, public education did not merely survive, it expanded. Despite economic hardships, there was no comparable erosion of the integrity of the public schools.[3] But mobilization of morale and restoration of public confidence requires leadership, and, as we have seen, such leadership was lacking in the San Francisco school system. Furthermore, neither the courts nor the commission could arrest the erosion of confidence and the attenuation of purpose in the public schools.

As the "vanguard" of civil rights retreated, it was replaced by a reaction of voices urging a return to order, discipline, and efficient management. The reluctance of the SFPSC to issue a set of critical findings that might have set an agenda for purposive action enabled Alioto to use its report as an endorsement for the reassertion of centralized, professional authority. By restoring the powers of the school superintendent and administration, the SFPSC unwittingly served to deflect the pursuit of lasting reforms, offering instead a quick fix for the more obvious problems. This gave the district's standing with local business and city officials an immediate boost and permitted the administration to once again pat itself on the back for abiding by "basic principles of sound management."

Subsequently, the board seldom challenged the superintendent's professional judgment. Indeed, following his "victory" over the teachers' union, Alioto has faced virtually no major problems with the board, teachers, or minority groups. Those who care have presumably been silenced by the effects of demoralization and the exigencies of retrenchment.

---

[2] The Vietnam War, an exceptional case, underlines the crucial importance of wartime morale. See Herbert Blumer, "Morale," in William F. Ogburn, ed., *American Society in Wartime* (Chicago, Ill.: University of Chicago Press, 1943), pp. 207-31.

[3] David Tyack, "Education and Social Unrest," 31 *Harvard Educational Review* (Summer 1981): 194-212.

Six Failures of Leadership

Following the school board, the administration, the courts, and the blue-ribbon commission, as they responded to the challenge of the civil rights movement, has been like watching helpless rescue teams cope with a disaster area. Their failures of leadership compose a catalogue of the types of pitfalls that can beset even well-intentioned efforts.

Failure of Perspective

Superintendent Spears failed to recognize the aims and scope of the movement for racial equality in the public schools. Yet the great currents of change in America's attitudes toward racial problems had long been visible. Every city superintendent should have been aware of the developments, taken stock of the local situation, and prepared contingency plans. Spears, instead of analyzing the problems and acting decisively at the outset to address the needs of racial minorities (e.g. by bringing black and white children together, hiring and upgrading opportunities for minority staff, and strengthening educational programs), stubbornly refused to acknowledge and face these challenges.

A perspective of "color-blindness" obstructed Spears' view of the issues at stake. From this perspective, facing a situation in which inequalities resulting from a long history of slavery and discrimination served to handicap many black children, Spears was unable to perceive the educational values of desegregation. Instead of seeking creative and educational uses for racial balance, Spears resisted moving the schools beyond entry-level justice. Instead of leading, he held the schools back and tried to stifle the forces for change.

Failure of Nerve

Unlike Spears, members of the school board during the sixties understood the moral and social significance of the civil rights movement. However, their heightened awareness and desire to respond to ideals of justice were frustrated by political inexperience and lack of nerve.

Fearful of the consequences, board members were reluctant to step outside the prescribed role of deference to the administration. Instead of taking the initiative, they elected to defer to the judgments of the professionals, and thus incited the community to organize a strategy of resistance. Unwilling to set and hold a steady course of action, the board found itself caught in a maelstrom of conflicting pressures. Opposing forces, unmediated by leadership, escalated the conflict, and passions prevailed. The board's failure of nerve brought the schools to an impasse, created the conditions for circumventing political channels, and precipitated the intervention of the court.

Failure of Judicial Authority

Courts can analyze differences, resolve disputes, and order remedies for aggrieved parties. However, they cannot put their prescriptions into practice. Courts are not equipped to run institutions.

Reconstructing the mission and goals of the schools so as to build into their organization the values underlying the remedy of desegregation was beyond the capacity of the federal district court in the *Johnson* case. Instead, the judge expected the schools to cooperate and carry out his commands. Like a physician who hands his patient a prescription, the judge was relying on the cooperation and willingness of the schools to accept and put into practice the prescribed remedy. But just as the doctor cannot take the patient in hand to encourage the adoption of a new regimen of care, neither could the court conduct the parties through the complex ramifications of the desegregation order. The court was not equipped to provide ongoing instruction and guidance to administrators, school principals, teachers, parents, and pupils. The conduct of the schools remained the responsibility of its officials and members.

Yet courts expect compliance and issue orders regardless of institutional capacities and commitments. Even when auxiliary mechanisms, such as court monitors, are invoked to facilitate implementation, they are no guarantee of institutional reform. Limitations such as these support prudence in the exercise of judicial command.

Failure of Responsibility

It was the responsibility of school officials to set the goals for desegregation, while protecting educational values and competence. At stake was the integrity of the public schools.

Weakened by earlier failures of understanding and nerve, however, school officials defaulted on their basic responsibilities. Neither a succession of superintendents (Jenkins, Shaheen, Morena) nor members of the school board were able to secure the smooth implementation of desegregation while upholding educational standards. Distracted by daily pressures and by many vocal and conflicting publics, school leaders failed to focus on the schools' educational mission and were unable to set priorities. Consequently, they failed to engage participants and to secure their loyalty and cooperation.

The challenge for official leadership was to mobilize resources, to arouse and motivate followers, to inspire confidence, engender excitement and in myriad ways to reshape organizational commitments in keeping with the values of desegregated education. Instead, the basic educational mission of the school was neglected, and "racial balance," a statistical, not an educational measure, was identified as the outcome. This lack of responsible leadership exacerbated the withdrawal of energies and led to the erosion of public support.[4]

Failure of Vision

Embarrassed by the district's incompetent leadership and by the declining performance of the public schools, members of the community sought to restore stability and to rebuild the schools' reputation. Experienced civic and business leaders were appointed to the San Francisco Public Schools Commission to investigate the problems and propose remedies for the schools' deficiencies. But this effort was an exercise in short-run thinking, and the consequence of a doctrine of managerial efficiency.

The SFPSC's stress on quick solutions and an excessive focus on technological change inhibited the emergence of a deeper understanding of the social and institutional issues at stake. The commission confused the symptoms of organizational success, such as stability, smooth-running management, reputation, and public image, with the requisites of institutional achievement based on the embodiment of values that uphold the legitimacy of public education. Concentrating on the immediate and the technical, the SFPSC failed to address the more elusive ends that convey shared values and give meaning to action. The commission failed to achieve a vision that would link a commitment to equality with

---

[4] Irving Janis and Leon Mann use this example of the default of official leadership to take responsibility for the desegregation plan to illustrate their theory of "defensive avoidance," which, they argue, arises under conditions of "high conflict . . . pessimism about the prospects of finding a satisfactory solution . . . awareness of the consequences of serious losses . . . and availability of another group to which responsibility can be shifted (i.e. the Citizen's Advisory Committee)." Irving Janis and Leon Mann, *Decision-Making* (N.Y.: Free Press, 1977), p. 112; also pp. 109-20.

educational excellence. The results of their study left the practices and programs of the schools without the benefit of clear guidance toward the achievement of these values.

Failure of Commitment

The restoration of administrative order and the return of professional control demonstrates the skills of what James MacGregor Burns calls "transactional" leadership. "Transactional leadership . . . occurs for the purpose of an exchange . . . not to bind leader and follower in mutual pursuit of a higher purpose."[5] This type of leadership, ably executed by Superintendent Alioto, included installing management systems, setting clear agendas, building a loyal team, establishing visibility, creating coalitions, being tough, reinforcing words with actions, and the like.

But there is another level of executive leadership, one that is essential in transforming an efficient organization into a competent one. Burns calls this level "transforming" leadership; it calls for commitment to values beyond those dictated by the "bottom line," values that touch on social needs and human aspirations. The public schools have historically served as vehicles for social mobility, individual achievement and economic betterment. They have aimed to instill sentiments of patriotism and loyalty, and to embody the principles of democracy, renewing the political and social ideals of the community for successive generations. Schools without "transforming" moral leadership, without ethical aspirations, cannot begin to raise the level of human conduct; nor can they engage participants in an enterprise of shared meaning, motivating performance that is fulfilling. Lacking commitment to larger ends, Alioto's routine leadership neither engendered excitement nor inspired confidence.

The Problem of Local Control

San Francisco school leadership has been dynamic. As social and political conditions changed, and institutional arrangements shifted, leadership relocated. The reins of command, its obligations and privileges, became variously attached to elected and appointed school officials, and at times they fell into the hands of judges and prominent citizens. Minority groups, parents, teachers, and students seeking to influence decisions affecting their rights and

---

5 James M. Burns, *Leadership* (N.Y.: Harper & Row, 1978), pp. 19-20.

opportunities have at different times had to appeal to these various sources of school leadership.

Loss of Autonomy

These appeals, particularly the claims of minorities and the interventions of lawyers, judges, and citizens, were experienced by the school administration as assaults on its autonomy. From the administration's perspective, they undermined the institution's right to set its own agenda and challenged its expertise to determine what was or was not "educationally sound." Professional sovereignty, threatened by demands for new practices, sought refuge in the separation between education and politics. But this foundation of the system's autonomy no longer served to safeguard its vested interests.

The loss of professional autonomy was accompanied by a loss of institutional integrity. Leadership failed to identify and protect the schools' distinctive identity and mission. The result was disarray and demoralization. Resources became strained, organization disrupted, and participation weakened, while the schools' basic instructional tasks were neglected. Public confidence, a vital source of morale, waned, and teachers and pupils became victims of apathy and neglect.

Loss of autonomy and the onset of demoralization and disarray were outcomes of failed leadership. School leaders proved incapable of responding to changing social needs while sustaining "educational soundness." Their failure thrust the schools into a new era. Judicial verdicts, issued on behalf of minorities asserting claims to rights, began modifying school programs. Business principles and technologies, such as those advanced by the SFPSC, although not a new influence, exerted a strong hold on administrative practices. The growing presence of federal- and state-mandated programs on behalf of disadvantaged, handicapped, and bilingual pupils generated new mechanisms for parent and public participation in school-site decisions.

The Principle of Plurality

These developments had the potential to replace autonomy with plurality as the underlying principle of school governance. Plurality assures openness to multiple sources of influence, and affirms the interdependence of education and politics. Under conditions of plurality, "educational soundness" is no longer exclusively defined and upheld by a professional elite; it emerges as the outcome of the school community's shared understandings. The realization of plurality was handicapped, however, by vestiges of a long-standing but outmoded argument that linked the preservation of professional autonomy with local control. Although the primacy of local control in public education is no longer common practice, it has become enshrined in doctrine and myth, shielding its disappearance from view. Yet we have only to look closely to notice that "the emperor is wearing no clothes."

In California, key policy decisions in education—collective bargaining, teacher certification, standards, and curriculum—have shifted to the state level. Legal action, with regard to school finance and intelligence testing, has also been targeted at the state level.[6] Major commercial providers of educational hardware and materials, such as textbook publishers and computer manufacturers, have become a major source of influence over school programs and curriculum. Testing agencies that serve university entrance requirements, such as Educational Testing Service (ETS), by selecting and testing knowledge, also affect curriculum and teaching practices. In addition, federal policies continue to afford important protection for populations and programs lacking local support.

Thus many different groups and agencies have a growing stake in public education. Contrary to the doctrine of local control, education is no longer a uniquely local interest. This does not mean that teachers and parents are or should be excluded from assuming key roles in local schools. It does mean that schools need not feel tied to the values and resources of local districts, but rather can expand their horizons and attach their programs to larger ends and a public purpose. Moreover, a federal presence, particularly in the older cities where there is keen competition for dwindling resources, is necessary to offset countervailing local pressure groups. The explosion of knowledge and the crucial role formal education plays in social and economic development also justify strong federal interest in the nation's schools. Like commerce, defense, health, energy, and the other vital centers of public purpose, education serves the national interest.

The demise of local control thus need not be cause for grief. Rather, it is a loss that calls for reconstruction of a viable education community, bringing to bear the contributions of its multiple members and emphasizing the responsibilities of teachers and

---

6 Donald Jensen, "New Plaintiffs, Changing Issues and Challenges to the State," *IFG Policy Perspectives* (Summer 1982).

students for learning outcomes. The principle of plurality takes account of local involvement and local interests, but is not limited by it. Leadership likewise needs to transcend local perspectives and relate educational goals and reforms to public purpose.

Civil Rights: A National Concern

Local leadership of the San Francisco schools failed to forge a viable response to the challenge of the civil rights movement. The schools' political isolation and their defensive posture toward the intrusion of social issues inhibited leadership. Further, the ideology of local control served to restrain a concerted search for assistance and guidance. The experience of other communities was not perceived as a resource, nor were attempts made to organize efforts at the state or federal levels to secure and share information with local districts. Although by 1960 school desegregation was a national problem, its fate remained almost exclusively in the hands of local authorities.

Millions of black children both in the South and in northern cities were living in poverty, heirs to a legacy of slavery, discrimination, and humiliation. Hispanic children from low-income families also were coming into the schools in increasing numbers, proud of their culture, but with limited aspirations. The expectation that these children, as well as other non-English-speaking children, would be able to compete on an equal basis with middle-class children was no longer tenable.[7] Moreover, by 1960, the time had long since passed when a high-school education was a luxury, and when immigrants with little education could enter the labor force and work their way up. Additional efforts, on a large scale, including pupil reassignment and special kinds of instruction, were needed to equalize opportunities. The principle of entry-level justice, justifying equality of access to the schools, was no longer sufficient; this principle required revision in the light of the special needs of minority groups. To overcome institutional deficiencies and inertia, desegregation policy warranted national attention and study, and extensive and systematic experimentation.

The realization of racial justice was and remains a national concern. The expectation that public education provide all children equally with mastery of basic skills and a sense of public-

---

[7] These problems were further aggravated by the fact that increasingly the nation's students come from homes where there is no adult during the day, and a significant proportion are being raised by one parent. *Time*, March, 16, 1980.

spiritedness constitutes a fitting national democratic purpose. But how to accomplish this purpose raises difficult and complex problems, including the formulation of racially aware assignment policies, as well as the design of instructional programs sensitive to the needs of particular student populations. While such policies and programs need tailoring to local conditions and circumstances, their formulation, and an assessment of trials and errors resulting from controlled experiments warrant not just state and local involvement, but national leadership.

Desegregation, carried out with care and understanding, was a potential vehicle for local schools to impart common values as well as common skills to all children, and thus to contribute to the establishment of common citizenship and full participation. But limited by the inadequate resources of local leadership, the quest for racial justice overwhelmed capacities for resolving the tension between democracy and integrity, and left the public schools demoralized and in disarray, and not only in San Francisco.

Across America: Outcomes of Failed Leadership

San Francisco was not unique. In its response to desegregation, local leadership, given the constraints and limitations of its institutional capacities, was bound to fail. Across America, since the sixties, public education has undergone a period of disarray, as evidenced by such symptoms as student apathy and violence, teacher incompetence, and declining standards of discipline and achievement.[8] Besides the civil rights movement, the schools had other major problems, such as rising costs, reduced enrollments, shortages of qualified teachers, and an erosion of public support. All of these difficulties had local variations—some districts gained pupils; those with few minority children had no civil rights crisis; many communities continued to provide adequate financial support for their schools. Despite these local and regional differences, however, three major features of the period illustrate the critical role lack of leadership played in the widespread, if not pervasive decline of the public schools: "white flight," "community control," and a "crisis of authority."

---

[8] "Big City Schools—Can They Be Saved?" *Newsweek*, September 12, 1977; "Help! Teacher Can't Teach," *Time*, June 16, 1980; "Is Anyone Out There Learning?," a week-long CBS news special, September 1978.

"White Flight"

By 1980, the public schools in most large cities had black and/or Hispanic majorities, an outcome of the exodus to the suburbs of the white middle-class that followed World War II. By 1968, whites were already a minority in 13 large city school districts (those with pupil populations exceeding 50,000), such as Washington, D.C. with only 5.6 percent white, Chicago 37.7 percent, Detroit 39.3 percent, and New York 43.9 percent white. By 1976, eight other large cities had become majority nonwhite, including cities outside the North, such as Los Angeles with 37.1 percent white, Miami 41 percent, and Houston 34.2 percent, leaving only a handful of cities with white pupil majorities.[9]

This phenomenon—the transformation of urban schools into enclaves for lower-class, minority pupils—did not attract much attention until the late seventies. At that time, a controversy erupted over the role of court-ordered desegregation in hastening the exit of the middle class. James Coleman published a study of population trends in which he claimed that the courts were responsible for the "white flight."[10] His findings and methods were challenged, and Professor Coleman later admitted that his views went "somewhat beyond the data."[11] While rates of white population decline in cities such as Boston did accelerate at the time of a mandated busing plan,[12] school districts that did not desegregate also suffered large losses of white pupils. New York, for example, lost 139,000 white pupils between 1968 and 1976; whites went from 43.9 percent to 30.5 percent of the school population.[13]

Research is inconclusive as to whether the middle class was leaving because of actual or anticipated desegregation, or whether life in cities generally had become undesirable for other reasons. Nor is it clear to what extent the flight is purely "white." Some have argued that it is a class, as much as a race phenomenon.[14] Regardless of

---

[9] Diane Ravitch, "The White Flight Controversy," in Nicolaus Mills, ed., *Busing U.S.A.* (N.Y.: Teachers College Press, 1979), pp. 250-51.

[10] James Coleman, "Recent Trends in School Integration," 4 *Educational Researcher* (July/August, 1975): pp. 3-12.

[11] *New York Times,* July 11, 1975.

[12] Boston's rate of white decline went from 6.6 percent for the school year 1973 to 16.2 and 19.3 percent, respectively, in 1974 and 1975, after desegregation. Emmett H. Buell, Jr., *School Desegregation and Defended Neighborhoods: The Boston Controversy* (Lexington, Mass.: Lexington Books, 1982), p. 152.

[13] Ravitch, "The White Flight Controversy," pp. 250-51.

[14] Lillian Rubin, *Busing and Backlash* (Berkeley, Calif.: University of California Press, 1972).

the causes, however, substantial sections of the nation's major cities are racially segregated, and city schools have become enclaves for black and other minority groups.

The withdrawal of middle-class participation has lowered academic standards and weakened confidence in the public schools. In most city schools, high school achievement levels are three years or more below the national average.[15] One-quarter to one-half of the students attending city schools graduate without the skills necessary for productive adult life. According to the recent findings of the National Assessment of Educational Progress, 12.5 percent of American 17-year-olds enrolled in school in 1975 were functionally illiterate (unable to comprehend and respond correctly to very simple written instructions); of these youngsters, 21 percent were from urban areas and 41.6 percent were black.[16]

Desegregation, where it occurred, may have accelerated the forces contributing to the decline of city schools. Because school leaders failed to acknowledge and address the needs of black and other minorities in a timely fashion, in city after city, they were unable to avoid the disruptive consequences of court orders. Exceptions to this pattern, however, illustrate the impact leadership might have had in avoiding such outcomes. In Atlanta and Dallas, for example, a broad coalition of school officials, parents, and ministers intervened in school desegregation litigation. Through a process of strenuous and time-consuming negotiation, a broader solution than racial balance was obtained and desegregation plans were formulated that aimed at improving "educational quality" and eliminating "the disparity in academic achievement" between minorities and whites.[17] A "magnet schools" program in Buffalo, New York (54 percent nonwhite), in conjunction with mandatory desegregation, the closing of segregated schools, and a "massive job of persuasion" appears to be achieving both desegregation and

---

[15] Robert J. Havighurst and Daniel Levine, eds., *The Future of Big-City Schools* (Berkeley, Calif.: McCutchan Publishing Co., 1977), pp. 4-5.

[16] These figures do not encompass the full extent of illiteracy because they do not include the 17-year-olds who had already dropped out of school, an estimated 10 percent of the age group. Barbara Lerner, "American Education: How Are We Doing?" 69 *The Public Interest* (Fall 1982): 58-81.

[17] *Tasby* v *Wright*, U.S. District Court (N.D. Texas, 1981), p. 8. The Atlanta outcome is described by Joel Fleishman, "The Real Against the Ideal—Making the Solution Fit the Problem: The Atlanta Public School Agreement of 1973," in Robert Goldmann, ed., *Roundtable Justice: Case Studies in Conflict Resolution* (Boulder, Colorado: Westview Press, 1980), pp. 129-81.

better education.[18]

But when local leadership failed, racial and social class exodus accelerated. A withdrawal of resources and political energies from the nation's urban schools left parents with little assurance that their children would attend safe and effective schools. This was especially true in financially hard-pressed cities, such as Chicago, Detroit, and St. Louis. These cities lack the tax base to maintain attractive school facilities, provide remedial instruction, and offer the social services that their school population needs, let alone to service existing buildings and pay decent salaries and other costs of operation. Further, as a proportion of the total population, school-age children in the older cities are at an all-time low. Increasingly, citizen demands on public funds involve adult needs and wants, and state legislatures, many dominated by suburban and rural constituencies by and large unwilling to subsidize urban schools, can muster little support for schools. By 1981, 17 states had passed measures like Proposition 13, setting limits on taxation and school spending. A state senator from Michigan where public school support dropped from 19 percent of the state budget to 15 percent observed, "Public perceptions of schools now center on crime and violence, teacher strikes and declining test scores. These perceptions have shaken the security blanket that once encapsulated education."[19]

"Community Control"

Across America, poverty of leadership has accelerated the withdrawal of energies from city schools, depleting their resources and weakening their structure and performance. This was the case even in New York City where events took a somewhat different turn. There "community control" became a central thrust of civil rights activists, but because school officials failed to formulate a timely and politically feasible response, the outcome was again systemwide disarray and demoralization. However, just as desegregation per se did not cause demoralization, neither did "community control" as such disrupt schooling. Both, however, presented challenges to leadership that called for creative reconstruction of the conditions of schooling, taking into account the conditions of social

---

[18] James Traub, "Magnet Schools: Busing Without Tears?" *The New Republic,* November 7, 1983, pp. 18-20.

[19] "Hard Times Threaten Public Schools in Michigan," *Education Week,* March, 17, 1982.

organization that schools must satisfy if they are to accomplish their educational tasks.

Schools have been described as "loosely coupled" organizations, bound by weak linkages, their units readily spun off, and the whole easily dissoluble.[20] While suggestive, this image of schools adds little to our understanding of the conditions that variously strengthen or weaken their organization and performance. Can a handful of schools be spun off as "alternatives" within the system without affecting other schools? Clearly not. Such schools, for example magnet schools, draw disproportionate reserves of staff and pupils from the same universe of talent and energy, thereby depriving ordinary schools of special resources. Can schools be grouped into contiguous attendance zones, with pupils distributed to sites within each zone, to produce racial balance at the sites, as in the Horseshoe Plan, without reinforcing the low socioeconomic concentration of the inner city? Again, we note the interdependencies that affect resource allocation. Schools that serve poor and unstable populations confront more severe educational problems and need more resources. In short, as long as schools aim to realize norms of equity, decisions affecting components of an educational system need to take into account their effects on other components. This entails centralized decision making, and indeed that is the system the public schools have evolved, up to a point.

Nevertheless, despite centralization, schools are cumbersome and not as susceptible to manipulation as reformers might like. Schools are unwieldy because their administration must take into account many different considerations. In addition to matters of equity, school activities are governed by state and federal regulations and by collective bargaining agreements, constraints that produce conflicts and necessitate compromises. And there are the exigencies of schooling itself, the implicit regularities that circumscribe school conduct, such as the school calendar, the rhythms of daily life, and the personal and social networks that support the tasks of teaching and give meaning to school life. For example, because most teachers are still basically solo practitioners, their incentives and rewards are highly personal and derive from daily interactions with pupils. Likewise, principals are used to planning and conducting programs that suit their particular community's needs. They tend to be inept facilitators of top-down curriculum planning and are not responsive

---

[20] Karl Wieck, "Educational Organizations as Loosely Coupled Systems," 21 *Administrative Science Quarterly* (March 1976): 1-19.

to central supervision; they are also unused to acting as entrepreneurs, hustling for resources.[21]

Schools thus present an organizational paradox: on the one hand, for purposes of planning and coordination, they require centralization and bureaucratic organization, and therefore one might expect schools to respond easily, like loosely coupled trains, to changes in direction; on the other hand, unlike baggage cars, schools have natural inclinations of their own and, more like donkeys, they do not respond well either to prodding or exhortations. The tasks of teachers and principals, and the dynamics of student life have an inner logic that is highly resistant to new directions.[22] When changes are enforced, they are easily subverted in practice, or they engender disarray such that both the desired change and the normal program of instruction are disrupted.

Reformers in New York, frustrated by the slow pace of compensatory education strategies and the alleged "sabotage" of pilot desegregation projects, decided to try a more direct political approach, which they called "community control." In 1966, antipoverty program organizers aroused the community to demand control over Intermediate School 201, a new facility in the heart of the Harlem ghetto, and similar all-black schools. They argued that if the minority community obtained direct political control over the ghetto schools, it would be able to overcome the organizational obstacles to change.[23]

As a political strategy, "community control" was a version of the black power movement of the late sixties. "What they wanted, in effect, was to get rid of the central school administration, with its complacent bureaus, its record of failure, and its insularity, and to take charge of the ghetto schools themselves."[24] In urging that the

---

[21] Mary H. Metz, *Classrooms and Corridors* (Berkeley, Calif.: U.C. Press, 1978), pp. 188-211.

[22] According to John Goodlad's study of over 1,000 public school classrooms in 13 communities, as long as teachers remain isolated from one another and largely excluded from curriculum planning, improved teaching methods are impossible. John Goodlad, *A Place Called School: Prospects for the Future* (N.Y.: McGraw-Hill, 1983). See the *New York Times,* July 19, 1983.

[23] Mario D. Fantini, "Community Control and Quality Education in Urban School Systems," in Henry M. Levin, ed., *Community Control of Schools* (N.Y.: Clarion Books, 1970), pp. 40-76; and Marilyn Gittell, "Community Control of Education," in Marilyn Gittell, ed., *The Politics of Urban Education* (N.Y.: Praeger Publishers, 1969).

[24] Jason Epstein, "The Politics of School Decentralization," in the *New York Review of Books,* June 6, 1968, pp. 26-31. For a discussion of why desegregation was not chosen as the strategy of reform, see David Rogers, "Obstacles to School Desegrega-

ghetto communities be given the power to run their own schools, reformers seemed to believe that changes in the distribution of power and jobs would affect learning, that children would let down their defenses and, embraced by a more familiar culture within the school, rapidly develop reading and other necessary skills.

After months of demonstrations and boycotts, the New York City Board of Education yielded and agreed to create three local districts. However, these local boards became increasingly radical in their demands, and in May 1968 ousted a group of teachers in the Ocean Hill-Brownsville district in Brooklyn. The predominantly Jewish teachers' union (UFT) protested, and a teachers' strike in the fall of 1968 effectively shut down the entire school system for two months. According to Martin Mayer, "it was the worst disaster my native city has experienced in my lifetime . . . reducing to the condition of a Boston . . . a school system wretchedly ill-organized and weakly led, but by no means . . . completely ineffective."[25]

The schools' effectiveness was indeed far from satisfactory for the 50,000 children in the third grade "who read so poorly that their success in higher grades is highly unlikely."[26] But the strike made matters even worse. Principals, overwhelmed by the forces that polarized the system, found themselves caught in a hopeless bind for which nothing in their background prepared them. Observers during that period noted that, as the principals' educator role became increasingly irrelevant, their capacities for leadership diminished.[27] Particularly in the experimental programs, the schools experienced high absenteeism and little academic progress.[28] The three demonstration districts were subsequently coopted into a statewide decentralization plan, placating the union and in effect foreclosing the kind of control envisaged by community activists.[29]

---

tion in New York City," in Gittell, *The Politics of Urban Education*, pp. 122-42.

[25] Martin Mayer, *The Teachers' Strike* (N.Y.: Harper & Row, 1968), p. 15.

[26] Epstein, "The Politics of School Decentralization." Epstein also mentions a statistic issued by the Urban League to the effect that of nearly 30,000 diplomas awarded in New York in 1967, only 700 went to black graduates.

[27] Arthur J. Vidich and Charles McReynolds' study of 23 principals during the 1967-68 school year, cited in David Tyack and Elizabeth Hansot, *Managers of Virtue* (Cambridge, Mass.: Harvard University Press, 1982), p. 238.

[28] Diane Ravitch, "Community Control Revisited," *Commentary* (February 1972).

[29] In 1980 only 8 percent of those eligible participated in elections for district board members. "Apathy is crushing," and $32 million to staff and maintain the community board offices is "a waste," according to Hattie-Jo Mullins, "The Community Bored," *New York Times*, April 30, 1983.

In New York and elsewhere, community control thus failed to achieve its objectives, and instead led to disarray and the decline of educational standards. These outcomes were in part the consequences of school leadership's inability and unwillingness to recognize and respond to the grievances of the black community. But the strategy developed by the reformers also failed because it neglected to take into account the needs of the system they wanted to adapt to their needs. Depriving principals and teachers of prestige and respect not only denigrated them personally, but also incapacitated the institution. However justified the grievances of the ghetto community, seizing "control" over the schools could not command good teaching.

In addition, the premise of *community* control was unsound. Wherever blacks live in poverty and despair, theirs is not a viable community, but rather an anguished and impoverished version of the larger community from which they are excluded. Removing the bonds of slavery did not destroy barriers to participation, nor does striking down the laws enforcing segregation erase all of their effects. America has yet to make a wholehearted commitment to include black people as full and equal members.

"Community control," since it could not redress underlying social and economic inequalities, can best be understood as an act of desperation. Black school boards, black principals, and black teachers "control" the schools in Washington, D.C. and other cities, but they have not yet succeeded in overcoming the brutal effects of segregation and ghetto life. Nor have attempts, such as Jesse Jackson's program, PUSH, which aims to instill pride among black pupils, regardless of who runs the schools, had more than a modest impact.[30] These experiences reinforce the obvious but painful lesson that the ghetto lacks the resources and power to change itself. The future of black children is tied to their status as Americans, and depends on the commitment of the polity to provide equal opportunity to all children.

A similar analysis applies to the struggles of other ethnic groups who have sought "control" as a means of improving their life chances, such as the Citizen's Task Force on Bilingual Education, which, the reader will recall, recommended that the San Francisco

---

[30] PUSH (People United to Save Humanity) seeks a "renewal of spirit" and supports the development of individual motivation. Eugene Eubanks and Daniel Levine, "Jesse Jackson's PUSH Program for Excellence in Big-City Schools," in Havighurst and Levine, eds., *The Future of Big-City Schools*, pp. 218-35.

school system be subdivided into four language-based systems, each controlled by one of the city's major ethnic groups. Had such a division taken place, it would have negated the desegregation program, divided the school community, and jeopardized what remained of its precarious commitment to public education.

During this same period the federal government, through compensatory education programs, had begun to institutionalize a commitment to minorities and the poor. "Legislated learning," however, suffered from some of the same misconceptions as "community control." It assumed that alterations in the balance of power would improve learning, regardless of local capacities and commitments.[31] Ironically, while the burden of regulation made sound management essential and reinforced centralization, the ideology of local control encouraged resistance and downgraded federal interventions as unwarranted and lacking in authority.

"Crisis of Authority"

There is a continuing "crisis of authority" in public education. Political consensus regarding educational values, once taken for granted, has disintegrated. Conservatives blame the schools for declining standards, poor discipline, and neglect of talented students, while radicals regard the schools as instruments reproducing the repressive social order of capitalism.[32] There are no longer collectively shared aims to engender meaning and inspire action. The purpose of the schools—why we should educate—is in question.[33]

Ideological differences dominate, the result of leadership's failure to create a commanding vision of the central purpose of education in a racially just society. The conservative position, now in ascendancy, emphasizes such tasks as providing basic skills for the masses and academic preparation for the talented, in conventional settings that rely for efficiency on strict discipline and tracking systems. In this view, even if all that the schools accomplish is the reinforcement of effects of family and social background, that is all that should be expected of them. From this minimalist position, it

---

[31] Arthur E. Wise, *Legislated Learning: The Bureaucratization of the American Classroom* (Berkeley, Calif.: U.C. Press, 1979).

[32] The conservative viewpoint is expressed by Joseph Adelson, "What Happened to the Schools," *Commentary* (March 1981): 36-41. For a radical critique, see Michael Apple and Lois Weis, eds., *Ideology and Practice in Schooling* (Philadelphia: Temple University Press, 1983).

[33] Torsten Husen, *The School in Question: A Comparative Study of the School and Its Future in Western Society* (London: Oxford University Press, 1979), pp. 11-19.

follows that to attempt anything more ambitious, given public education's limited role and low priority, is a waste of resources. Rather, schools should be left alone or returned to "local control" where they can be held accountable by setting minimum competency levels, strengthening professional norms, and following sound principles of management. Adherents of this position would restore local authority, emphasize professional expertise, and preserve the separation between schools and politics.[34]

But there is a a contrasting view that takes issue with this conservative position. Schools are not expected to be socially neutral, according to this perspective, but neither are they subservient to the interests of a dominant class. Rather, they are integral with and derive their authority from a public mandate that enhances their power to shape a national community dedicated to democratic principles. Accordingly, schools should afford opportunities not provided by families and compensate for differences in family background by stimulating and developing children's curiosity, knowledge, and skills. Schools thus can reshape the structure of opportunity by breaking through social barriers of poverty, ignorance, and despair. Grouping black and white children together, according to this point of view, mitigates the effects of slavery and segregation and encourages individual growth. Teaching immigrant children in Spanish or whatever language they speak at home preserves their dignity and self-respect, and aids in establishing full participation in school and in the community. Important gains are thus realized well worth the additional resources spent on ensuring equal opportunity. The purpose of education is enhanced, and its members share a sense of mission. Tying education to public purpose broadens participation and is a source of empowerment both for the individuals affected and the institution. The schools, by acting responsively to the needs of their members and taking seriously the challenge to teach everyone equally the basic knowledge necessary for an educated citizenry, make a distinctive contribution to the social good.[35]

Given these contrasting ideologies, schools today, according to Stephen Bailey, require an "original and compelling grand

---

[34] This perspective guides Diane Ravitch's recent critique of American education, *The Troubled Crusade: American Education, 1945-1980* (N.Y.: Basic Books, 1983), esp. pp. 267-321.

[35] This view is explicated by Michael Walzer in *Spheres of Justice: A Defense of Pluralism and Equality* (N.Y.: Basic Books, 1983), pp. 197-226.

design."[36] Although leadership has failed to produce such a vision, there is an agenda for reform upon which renewal can proceed. The experiences of the San Francisco schools during the past 20 years offer some important lessons in addressing that agenda.

An Agenda for Renewal

Pupils

Insofar as they fail the poor and discriminate against minorities, schools perpetuate an underclass without economic and social opportunity. This failure reduces the self-esteem of teachers and principals, and perpetuates institutional demoralization. But limiting school enrollments to successful students and tightening the curriculum (dropping or curtailing athletics and arts programs), as some have suggested, does not address the needs of an educated citizenry.[37] Nor will the Reagan administration's proposal to convert compensatory education, which has recently demonstrated important gains in the achievement of low-income children, to vouchers.[38] Rather, the direction renewal must follow is to reach out to all children, but especially to those most at risk, namely, those who live in near-poverty households (over one-fourth of the total pupil population).

That this can be done is indicated by the results of the Ford Foundation's City High School Recognition Program. A number of high schools in cities across the country, with enrollments of 30 percent or more low-income pupils, were cited and awarded grants for reducing drop-outs, motivating all students to learn, upholding academic standards, and placing graduates in jobs or college. One school, Morris High School in the South Bronx, with a primarily black and Hispanic population, recently sent 86 percent of its seniors on to college. The ingredients of these schools' success were identified as "superior leadership" by a principal or district superintendent, "unmistakable commitment to social and racial harmony," and "ingenuity" in coping with alienation and despair. The principal of Morris High School insisted that his school's success also depended on federal assistance for remedial programs.[39]

---

[36] See quote at the beginning of this chapter.

[37] This was the recommendation of the National Association of Secondary School Principals and the National Association of Independent Schools. *New York Times*, February 12, 1984.

[38] David Tatel, "Depriving Deprived Children," *New York Times*, March 23, 1983.

[39] Edward J. Meade, Jr., Ford Foundation program officer, quoted in the *New York*

A commitment to improve the life chances of all pupils, regardless of such constraints as poverty and deprivation, is the first priority for renewal.

Teachers

In 1981, only 22 percent of American teachers said they would "certainly" choose the same career, and 36 percent indicated they would not teach again.[40] A common response to the schools' troubles has been to blame the teachers, and to urge changes such as teacher competency tests. But teachers are not the cause, they are the casualties of lack of leadership. To meet their daily challenge—balancing the tension between order and learning—teachers no longer have the moral and institutional support needed to tip the scales, and therefore, along with students, they have become victims of circumstances that frustrate their aims and damage their well-being.[41]

Yet, despite deplorable conditions, there are still thousands of teachers who are effective and dedicated. And there continue to be idealistic young people, concerned with social justice, who would like to teach. Turning the teaching profession around will not just happen, however. It does not depend on economic recovery alone.[42] Salaries in 1982 for the nation's largest profession, with over two million members, of whom two-thirds are women, averaged only $17,360.[43] Considerable political and organizational work is needed to stimulate action at federal and state levels to raise salaries, challenge entrenched practices of teacher colleges, and confront the resistance of professional associations to reforms such as

---

Times, April 12, 1983. Also Sydney H. Schanberg, "Voodoo Education," *New York Times,* May 21, 1983.

[40] *Phi Delta Kappan,* May 1982. This figure confirms the survey taken by the *New York Times,* September 19, 1982.

[41] "Help! Teacher Can't Teach," *Time,* June 16, 1980; and "Teaching as an Imperiled Profession," unpublished paper issued by the Boston Women Teacher's Group, 1981.

[42] President Reagan would have us believe that as the health and spirits of the nation recover from the recession, public education will again be recognized as important. This justifies a passive approach at the federal level. *New York Times,* March 13, 1983.

[43] This is for 10 months; if teachers worked a full year, they would receive $20,530—among the lowest wages for college graduates, and representing a decline since 1972 of 12.2 percent in purchasing power. National Education Association, "Status of the American Public School Teacher," 1982. *New York Times,* August 24, 1983.

merit pay.

The Education Commission of the States, describing current salary levels for teachers as "symbolic of the low value our society places upon public school teachers" has called for substantial raises to attract more qualified personnel, and also proposed "extraordinary rewards for extraordinary teachers," a less costly reform.[44] Others have suggested that inner-city teaching be treated as "combat duty," involving the use of highly trained and experienced staff, replaced as frequently as necessary (to prevent burnout), and rewarded accordingly. Finally, a "team teaching" approach has proven successful in fashioning support systems to alleviate stress and frustration.[45] Meanwhile until the social value of public education recovers its worth, schools may have to constitute their own supportive communities to satisfy personal and professional needs for validation.

The potential for renewal thus depends on acknowledging and rewarding teachers, and supporting them in developing ways to revive the ésprit de corps of the profession. Such work requires imagination and political daring, and constitutes one of the central tasks of educational leadership.

Leadership

The schools need strong national leadership to affirm the mission and goals of public education, to put an end to mindless drift, and to institute actions and programs dedicated to renewal.

Resources for educational leadership used to reside in universities, where persons were trained for school administration. But political incapacities of educational leaders and school officials coincided with the emergence of new types of leaders—union spokesmen and minority representatives, as well as noneducators, such as lawyers, judges, and social scientists—who identified a set of social goals for the schools at variance with education practice. This "shadow" government has not displaced conventional school leadership, however, and from its status outside education, has difficulty infusing its values into the lifestream of the schools.

---

[44] "Action for Excellence," Report by the National Task Force on Education for Economic Growth, Education Commission of the States, 1983. *New York Times,* May 5, 1983.

[45] John Goodlad recommends that teaching at all levels be conducted by teams. "It would open up a whole new career category for able teachers who are frustrated by the limitations of the present system." "A Study of Schooling," *New York Times,* July 19, 1983.

Politicians, lawyers, and judges, although their actions and decisions aim to alter the school system's internal commitments, are not in charge of organizational capacities.

Nevertheless, the infusion of politics, together with changes in the schools' clientele, programs, and resources, has expanded the composition of the school community and made specific leadership needs highly visible. These include the need for the education community to reach agreement on its core values and to formulate a compelling program for public education, including a clear statement of mission, public purpose, and civic goals. To restore morale and achieve a renewal of public confidence, leadership has to direct attention to the schools' civic function and its unfinished civil rights agenda—the communal provision of basic skills and common values. Legislators and judges, educators, and citizens concerned about the future of public education need to combine their competencies so as to restore the organizational and political integrity of the schools. Leadership can then attend to its key responsibility, the shaping of education policy.

The recent outpouring of reports criticizing various aspects of public education does not meet these requirements of leadership. These reports dramatize deficiencies of the schools and call for more rigorous approaches, but they have neglected issues of equity and, in particular, the needs of inner-city youngsters.[46] Whereas overall spending for public education dropped 12 percent from 1980 to 1982, the amount received by inner-city schools was reduced 21 percent.[47] The exhortations and recommendations of educational commissions and task forces, by failing to focus on the unfinished civil rights agenda, cannot lead the schools to renewal. They have given little attention to the tasks of citizenship and the schools' responsibility to provide "the common values we ought to have as a people."[48] Not only command of grammar and mathematics, but also respect, courtesy, and moral sensitivity are appropriate educational outcomes. And these should be available to all children equally, preparing everyone, regardless of race and family background, for full participation in the community.

---

[46] "None of the reports proposes what might be done for youngsters from low-income homes where adult determination is lacking." Andrew Hacker, "The Schools Flunk Out," *New York Review of Books*, April 12, 1984, p. 39.

[47] Figures from the Council of Great City Schools, quoted in the *New York Times*, December 27, 1983.

[48] Lawrence Cremin, quoted in the *New York Times*, June 5, 1984.

Policy

In the absence of a controlling set of aims, educational decisions tend to be reached in reaction to external or internal pressures, and the force of circumstances. Thus the policy of desegregation in San Francisco was never firmly joined to institutional purpose, but rather, imposed by the court and only loosely attached to the schools, desegregation quickly became subject to competing agendas, such as internal transfer policies (to save certain constituencies), bilingual and special education programs (to satisfy and placate other minorities' needs and demands), and school reconstruction (to ensure safety). Because the policy aims of desegregation were incompatible with pressing institutional imperatives, they were readily susceptible to compromise. In addition, insofar as the values to be achieved were vague and abstract, programs specifying clear objectives remained elusive and actions lacked authority.

In San Francisco, the transformation of entry-level justice to affirmative action was constrained by difficulties in specifying the terms of racial justice. The principle of equal respect was not sufficiently elaborated, and therefore did not serve as a guideline in the formulation of desegregation policy. Treating children with equal respect called for affirming, not ignoring the racial and ethnic particularities that define individual children, but because there was a lack of clarity regarding the meaning of respect, this was not understood. The requirement of equal respect that all children reach universal standards of excellence (and its implications for curriculum and teaching—that schools take account of their population, and adjust the curriculum to the pace of the learner, ensuring that most succeed) was similarly not perceived. Where leadership did recognize these principles, however, and mobilize resources to meet them, desegregation policy was enacted and became integral with institutional practice. In Louisville, Kentucky, for example, Superintendent Owen Carmichael's personal commitment and astute political actions were effective in replacing a dual system with districtwide desegregation in 1956, just two years after the *Brown* decision.[49]

Instances of such success were rare, however, because the policy of desegregation was not addressed at the national level, but rather left to local communities. The shibboleth of "local control"

---

[49] Omer Carmichael and Weldon James, *The Louisville Story* (N.Y.: Simon & Schuster, 1957).

prevented the attention that might have established national guidelines for desegregation, preserved the schools' mission, and saved local districts from disarray and demoralization.

Educational policy must recognize the national interest in public education and insist that "schooling provide the common currency of political and social life."[50] Public education should not be regarded as a consumer product, and it also must be more than a welfare program. As education consumers, people care primarily for the schoolin of their own children, as they should. They have no incentive to support a school system that assures every child, including those from poor, black, or other minority families, a good education. Left to local resources, inner-city schools thus face major obstacles in the struggle to avoid becoming way stations for poor and minority youngsters to unemployment lines, prisons, and welfare rolls. Without assistance for remedial programs, the high schools recognized by the Ford Foundation could not have coped with student alienation and despair.

An agenda for renewal calls for policies restoring the schools' public mission and common purpose. This is the only sure way to reverse the deterioration of morale among staff, improve the accomplishments of students, and rebuild public confidence and support.

Summary

Issues of civil rights have engaged the nation's public schools these past 20 years, and in the effort to improve the education of blacks, the schools have become more sensitive to the needs of other minorities as well. The opportunity to achieve communal provision for all school children is thus greater now than ever. While gains may seem slight, their impact is not. School reform can no longer avoid including the quest for social and racial justice in the mission and purpose of public education.

From the experience of desegregation in San Francisco, we have gained insight regarding the risks at stake in transforming the public schools, and learned that change, if it is to generate concerted action, must issue from internal capacities. Without sustained commitment, even a court order is impotent. Given the limitations of commands, whether issued by a court, a legislature, or a teacher, educational renewal can best occur when orders are constructed in

---

[50] Michael Walzer, *Spheres of Justice* (N.Y.: Basic Books, 1983), p. 203.

the light of social and moral imperatives that issue from and rein-force the institution's own commitments and purposes. Policy imposed from without, insofar as it fails to attend to inner needs and is not informed by a sense of institutional mission, will not generate such commitment. Nor can imposed order restore the vio-lation of integrity that has eroded the schools' competence. But public policy that identifies with and confirms a fundamental aim can bolster weak commitments and restore shattered capacities. Legislation that enables, policies that permit, and orders that clarify and direct action can renew institutional integrity. To overcome the effects of demoralization, renewal must harness education's potential to serve as a vehicle of public purpose.

Index